THE NECESSITY OF ATHEISM

BY

DR. D. M. BROOKS

British Library Cataloguing-in-Publication Data
A catalogue record for this book is available from the
British Library

CONTENTS

Atheism

'Atheism' is, in a broad sense, the rejection of belief in the existence of deities. In a narrower sense, atheism is specifically the position that there are no deities. Most inclusively, atheism is simply the absence of belief that any deities exist – this is contrasted with 'theism', which in its most general form is the belief that at least one deity exists. The term atheism originated from the Greek ἄθεος (atheos), meaning 'without god(s)', used as a pejorative term applied to those thought to reject the gods worshipped by the larger society. With the spread of freethought, sceptical inquiry, and subsequent increase in criticism of religion, application of the term narrowed in scope. The first individuals to actively identify themselves with the term 'atheist' lived in the eighteenth century.

The first known explicit atheist was the German critic of religion Matthias Knutzen, who set out his thinking in three texts, written in 1674. He was followed by two other explicit atheist writers, the Polish ex-Jesuit philosopher, Kazimierz Łyszczyński and in the 1720s by the French priest, Jean Meslier. In the course of the eighteenth century, other openly atheistic thinkers followed, such as Baron d'Holbach, Jacques-André Naigeon, and other French materialists. John Locke (the famous British empiricist) in contrast, though an advocate of tolerance, urged authorities not to tolerate atheism, believing that the denial of God's existence would undermine the social order and lead to chaos. The philosopher David Hume developed a sceptical epistemology grounded in empiricism, and Immanuel Kant's philosophy has strongly questioned the very possibility of a metaphysical knowledge. Both philosophers undermined the metaphysical basis of natural theology and criticized classical arguments for the existence of God. They were not atheists themselves however.

Arguments for atheism range from the philosophical, to social and historical approaches. Rationales for not believing in any supernatural deity include the lack of empirical evidence, the problem of evil (the question of how to reconcile the existence of evil with that of a deity who is, in either absolute or relative terms, omnipotent, omniscient, and omnibenevolent), the argument from inconsistent revelations (which asserts that it is unlikely that God exists because many theologians and faithful adherents have produced conflicting and mutually exclusive revelations), rejection of concepts which cannot be falsified, and the argument from non-belief (an argument that posits an inconsistency between the existence of God and a world in which people fail to recognize him). Although some atheists have adopted secular philosophies, there is no one ideology or set of behaviours to which all atheists adhere. Many atheists hold that atheism is a more parsimonious worldview than theism, and therefore the burden of proof lies not on the atheist to disprove the existence of God, but on the theist to provide a rationale for theism. This last view is perhaps better known as 'Ockham's Razor', propagated by William of Ockham (1287 – 1347); a principle of economy and succinctness used in logic and problem-solving. It states that among competing hypotheses, the hypothesis with the fewest assumptions should be selected.

Atheism in the twentieth century, particularly in the form of practical atheism, has advanced in many societies. Atheistic thought found recognition in a wide variety of other, broader philosophies, such as existentialism, objectivism, secular humanism, nihilism, anarchism, logical positivism, Marxism, feminism, and the general scientific and rationalist movement. A new development in mankind's history though has been 'State Atheism'; the official promotion of non-belief by a government. The twentieth century has seen the political advancement of atheism, spurred on by interpretation of the works of Marx and Engels and the patronage of one-party Communist states. Historian Geoffrey Blainey has noted however, that although Christian principles had influenced some socialist thinking, they did not strongly influence the

3

central figures in the revolution. Later leaders, especially the Soviet leaders Vladimir Lenin and Joseph Stalin energetically pursued a campaign against religion though, particularly Russian Orthodoxy. Several other communist states have also opposed religion and mandated state atheism, including the former governments of Albania, and currently, China, North Korea and Cuba.

Since conceptions of atheism vary, determining how many atheists exist in the world today is difficult. According to one 2007 estimate, atheists make up about 2.3% of the world's population, while a further 11.9% are nonreligious. According to a 2012 global poll conducted by the WIN/GIA, 13% of the participants say they are atheists. According to other studies, rates of self-reported atheism are among the highest in Western nations, again to varying degrees: United States (4%), Italy (7%), Spain (11%), Great Britain (17%), Germany (20%), and France (32%). It is a trend in human thinking which appears to be consistent, although most certainly controversial. Such movements have inspired the notorious 'Secularisation thesis', most famously postulated by Max Weber, Émile Durkheim and Sigmund Freud – who have attempted to chart the transformation of society, from close identification with religious values and institutions toward nonreligious values and secular institutions. This is understood as progress, particularly through modernisation and rationalisation where religion loses its authority in all aspects of social life and governance. Many have criticised this theory however, with some arguing that numbers of religious believers are not declining, and even for professed atheists, religious authority is merely replaced by other secular self-affirmations of culture. Finally, some claim that demographic forces offset the process of secularisation, and may do so to such an extent that individuals can consistently drift away from religion even as society becomes more religious. This is especially the case in societies like Israel (with ultra-Orthodox and religious Zionists) where committed religious groups have several times the birth rate of seculars. This is a complex area spawning a massive amount of discussion and debate; the concept of 'atheism' represents a fascinating modification of human society and thought. It is hoped that the current reader enjoys this book.

DEDICATED TO
JOSEPH LEWIS IN AMERICA
AND
CHAPMAN COHEN IN ENGLAND
OF WHOM
IT MAY BE SAID:

"How often it has happened that one man, standing at the right point of view, has descried the truth, and, after having been denounced and persecuted by all others, they have eventually been constrained to adopt his declarations!"—(DRAPER.)

For the old Gods came to an end long ago. And verily it was a good and joyful end of Gods!

They did not die lingering in the twilight—although that lie is told! On the contrary, they once upon a time laughed themselves to death!

That came to pass when, by a God himself, the most ungodly word was uttered, the word: "There is but one God! Thou shalt have no other Gods before me."

An old grim beard of a God, a jealous one, forgot himself thus.

And then all Gods laughed and shook on their chairs and cried: "Is Godliness not just that there are Gods, but no God?"

Whoever hath ears let him hear.

"Thus Spake Zarathrustra"—FRIEDRICH NIETZSCHE

THE NECESSITY OF ATHEISM

PREFACE

PLAIN speaking is necessary in any discussion of religion, for if the freethinker attacks the religious dogmas with hesitation, the orthodox believer assumes that it is with regret that the freethinker would remove the crutch that supports the orthodox. And all religious beliefs are "crutches" hindering the free locomotive efforts of an advancing humanity. There are no problems related to human progress and happiness in this age which any theology can solve, and which the teachings of freethought cannot do better and without the aid of encumbrances.

Havelock Ellis has stated that, "The man who has never wrestled with his early faith, the faith that he was brought up with and that yet is not truly his own—for no faith is our own that we have not arduously won—has missed not only a moral but an intellectual discipline. The absence of that discipline may mark a man for life and render all his work ineffective. He has missed a training in criticism, in analysis, in open-mindedness, in the resolutely impersonal treatment of personal problems, which no other training can compensate. He is, for the most part, condemned to live in a mental jungle where his arm will soon be too feeble to clear away the growths that enclose him, and his eyes too weak to find the light." The man who has allowed his mental capacities to clear his way through the dense underbrush of religious dogma finds that he has emerged into a purer and healthier atmosphere. In the bright light of this mental emancipation a man perceives the falsities of all religions in their historic, scientific, and metaphysical aspects. The healthier mental viewpoint holds up to scorn and discards the reactionary religious philosophy of morals, and the sum total of his conclusions must be that religion is doomed; and doomed in this modern day by its absolute irrelevance to the needs and interests of modern life. And this not only by the steadily increasing army of freethinkers, but by the indifference and neglect of those who still cling to the fast slipping folds of religious creeds—the future freethinkers.

It was Spinoza who remarked that, "The proper study of a wise man is not how to die but how to live." Religious creeds can but teach how man should live, so that when he dies, he may be assured of salvation; and the important thing is not what he does to help his fellow men while he is living, but how closely he lives in conformity to a reactionary code of dogmas. Religion has always aimed to smooth the sufferer's passage to the next world, not to save him for this world.

Freethought has dethroned the gods from the pedestal, and has replaced, not an empty idol, but an *ideal,* the ideal of a man who is his own god.

It has become increasingly apparent that what men have hitherto attributed to the gods are nothing but the ideals they value and grope for in themselves. The ideal of the freethinker, the conception that places the supreme worth of human life in the expanding horizon of man's usefulness to man, is forever menaced by the supernaturalism of the theist which manifests itself in the multifarious religious sects that are the most active and constant menace to civilization and to mankind today. That religion in the past has produced suffering incalculable and has been the greatest obstacle in the advance of secular knowledge is a fact too well attested to by history to be denied by any sincere and unbiased intelligent man. That today it constitutes a cultural lag, an active menace to the best interests of humanity and the last refuge of human savagery, is the contention of the freethinker.

The conception of the God-idea as held by society in general stands in the same position as the vermiform appendix does to the anatomy of man. It may have been useful in some way thousands of years ago, but today it constitutes a detriment to the well-being of the individual without offering any compensatory usefulness. Agree or disagree with this contention you may, but only when you are made aware of the facts that can be brought to the aid of this conviction. Just as the fundamental principle of justice is outraged when a man or an institution is condemned by jurist or popular opinion when an opportunity is not given to present the facts on both aspects of the case, just so is no man justified in making a decision between theism and atheism until, he becomes acquainted with both sides of the controversy. Freethought but asks a hearing and the exercise of the unbiased reason of the man who has not hitherto been made aware of its contentions.

In the religious revolution of this twentieth century, the battle ground is squarely seen to be between supernaturalism and secularism. Although the supernaturalists are well entrenched and fortified, it is well to remember that it is the man with vision who finally prevails. The time has passed when the freethinker could be held up to the community as an example of a base and degraded individual. No manner of pulpit drivel can delude even the unthinking masses to this misconception. The freethinker is today the one who beholds the vision, and this vision does not transcend the natural. It is a vision that is earth-bound; a vision it may be called, since it leaps the boundary of the present and infers for him what the future of a secular organization of the entire constituency of humanity will bring forth. This vision is but a product of his scientific armamentarium and is the means by which he is assured of victory over the well-entrenched and fortified position of the supernaturalists who are still creed-bound to use antiquated and useless weapons. The supernaturalist's armamentarium of God, Bible, Heaven, Hell, Soul, Immortality, Sin, The Fall and Redemption of Man, Prayer, Creed, and Dogma, leave as much impression on the mind of intelligent man as would an arrow against a battleship. And the comparison is apt, the supernaturalists have made full use of force, be it in physical warfare or in mental coercion. The freethinker has as much use for physical force and war as he has for mental coercion; both are abhorrent to him.

Supernaturalism vs. Secularism—that, and that alone is the field of argument. The supernaturalist, be he the fundamentalist of whatever denomination, or the more advanced modernist, is as tenaciously clinging to the transcendental, to revelation, to the infallibility of the Bible, if not in all respects at least in some (although this is a contradiction *per se*), to the interdisposition of a deity in the affairs of mankind, as were his ancestors of five hundred years ago. In these aspects as well as in the armamentarium enumerated above, the supernaturalists are agreed and are making their last stand.

The secularists, the opinion of the theists to the contrary, are also agreed. It matters not what a man calls his mental process; be he infidel, sceptic, rationalist, agnostic, or atheist; he is firm in the conviction that religions of all varieties are rapidly sinking into the limbo of all other ancient superstitions. To him it is but a matter of time for the inevitable crumbling and disappearance of these superstitions, and the time involved is directly proportional to the ease and rapidity with which scientific knowledge is disseminated to men who have the mental capacity to understand the value of this knowledge and its utter destruction of all forms of supernaturalism. When man becomes fully cognizant of the fact that all the knowledge acquired by the human race has been the result of human inquiry, the result of reasoning processes, and the exercise of mind alone, then secularism will have overcome the long night of supernaturalism. And it is this mental attitude of secularism that proceeds with an ever accelerated rapidity to overcome the problems that confront humanity by substituting human inquiry for divine revelation. Thus this attitude of man to proceed through life dependent only on his own resources will expand and strengthen his mentality by doing away with the inferiority complex of the God-idea. This vision of man, the master of his own destinies, the searcher for truth and the shaper of a better life for the only existence that he knows anything about, this reliance of *man upon man*, and without the supposed interference of any god, constitutes atheism in its broadest and true sense.

Science and reason, the constituents of secularism, are the mortal enemies of supernaturalism. Secularism, however, is at a disadvantage at this stage of our mental development, since it is approached only by the calm light of the intellect. And intellect can but make an appeal to reason. If the seeds of these appeals fall on the fertile minds of mentally advanced humanity, they will flourish; if they fall on the barren ground of creed-bound minds, they take no root. Recognition of facts and honest deductions are not natural to the human mind. As far as religious matters are concerned, the vast majority of men have not reached a mental maturity; they are still in the infantile state where they have not as yet learned that the sequences of events are not to be interrupted by their desires. The easier path lies in the giving way to the unstable emotions. The primitive instincts are for emotion and for loose imaginings, and these are the provinces of supernaturalism.

Supernaturalism arouses the stupid interests and the brutish passions, and from these are born the bitter fruits of ignorance and hatred. The secularist is one in whom the intellect is passionate, and the passions cold. The supernaturalist on the other hand reverses the order, and in him the passions are active and the intellect inert. In each man there dwells a tyrant who creates for him a deity materialized out of these factors of ignorance and fear. It is science and reason which must destroy for him this monstrous apparition. But, as yet, there is no indication that our mental development in relation to social progress has made the great strides that our purely material progress has made. The twentieth century man utilizes and enjoys the material benefits of his century, but his mental progress lies bound and drugged by the viewpoints of 2000 years ago.

Sir Leslie Stephen has declared, "How much intellect and zeal runs to waste in the spasmodic efforts of good men to cling to the last fragment of decaying systems, to galvanize dead formulæ into some dim semblance of life! Society will not improve as it might when those who should be leaders of progress are staggering backward and forward with their eyes passionately reverted to the past. Nay, we shall never be duly sensitive to the miseries and cruelties which make the world a place of torture for so many, so long as men are encouraged in the name of religion to look for a remedy, not in fighting against surrounding evils, but in cultivating aimless contemplations of an imaginary ideal. Much of our popular religion seems to be expressly directed to deaden our sympathies with our fellow men by encouraging an indolent optimism; our thoughts of the other world are used in many forms as an opiate to drug our minds with indifference to the evils of this; and the last word of half of our preachers is, 'dream rather than work.' "

There is always a great deal of discrepancy between that which is best for the gods and that which is best for the individual and for society in general. One cannot serve man perfectly and the traditional gods as well. It is, therefore, the contention of freethinkers that if man had given to the service of man all that he had given to the gods in the past, our present stage of civilization would be much in advance of where it is today.

If there is anything in the discussion to follow that may seem irreverent to the reader, the author wishes to call attention that he has but presented well substantiated facts. It is not only his opinion that he is voicing, but it is the facts as he has found them recorded in the researches of numerous sincere men. Finally, it is the conviction of all freethinkers that, as Professor James H. Leuba has stated, "It is, furthermore, essential to intellectual and moral advances that the beliefs that come into existence should have free play. Antagonistic beliefs must have the chance of proving their worth in open contest. It is this way scientific theories are tested, and in this way also, religious and ethical conceptions should be tried. But a fair struggle cannot take place when people are dissuaded from seeking knowledge, or when knowledge is hidden."

The cultivation of the intellect is a duty that is imposed on all men. Even those who still cling to the dying beliefs must admit the force of what Winwood Reade said, "To cultivate the intellect is therefore a religious duty; and when this truth is fairly recognized by men, the religion which teaches that the intellect should be distrusted and that it should be subservient to faith, will inevitably fall."

When the principles of freethought shall have dispelled the intellectual cloud of the God-idea and the vanishing dream of a heaven which has too long drawn men's eyes away from this earth, then, and then only, will these words of Cicero have widespread meaning:

"Men were born for the sake of men, that each should assist the others."

CHAPTER I

THE EVOLUTION OF RELIGIOUS BELIEFS

To early man, the gods were real in the same sense that the mountains, forests, or waterfalls which were thought to be their homes were real. For a long time the spirits that lived in drugs or wines and made them potent were believed to be of the same order of fact as the potency itself. But the human creature is curious and curiosity is bold. Hence, the discovery that a reported god may be a myth.

MAX CARL OTTO.

THE geologists estimate that the age of the earth is somewhere between 80 and 800 millions of years; that the Neanderthal race existed for more than 200,000 years; that between 40,000 and 25,000 years ago, as the Fourth Glacial Period softened towards more temperate conditions, a different human type came upon the scene and exterminated Homo Neanderthalensis. These first "true men" descended from some more ape-like progenitors and are classed by ethnologists with the same species as ourselves, and with all human races subsequent to them under one common, specific term, Homo Sapiens.

The age of cultivation began with the neolithic phase of human affairs about 10,000 or 12,000 years ago; about 6000 or 7000 years ago men began to gather into the first towns and to develop something more than the loose-knit tribes which had hitherto been their highest political organization. Altogether, there must have elapsed about 500,000 years from the earliest ape-like human stage of life on this planet to the present time.

It necessarily follows that the age of our present civilization is by no means that which the Bible stipulates, but is merely an atom in the vast space-time of this earth. The reason for this disparity is that with the development of the mind of man throughout the ages there was conceived also his self-made religious systems, based on a subjective interpretation of the universe, and not on an objective one, devoid of emotional bias.

"Primitive man did not understand the natural cause of shadows, echoes, the birth and death of vegetable and animal organisms. Of this ignorance religion was born, and theology was evolved as its art of expression." (*Draper.*)

Our story takes us back some twelve thousand years to neolithic man. Squatting in his rude hovel or gloomy cave, he listens to the sounds of a storm without. The howling of the wind, the flashes of lightning, and crashing of thunder give rise to that elemental emotion—fear. Fear was always with him, as he thought of the huge stones that fell and crushed him, and the beasts which were so eager to devour him. All things about him seemed to conspire for his death: the wind, lightning, thunder, rain and storm, as well as the beasts and falling trees; for in his mind he did not differentiate animate from inanimate objects. Slowly, through his groping mind there evolved the thought, due to past experience, that he could not contend with these things by physical force, but must subdue them with magic; his magic consisted of the beating of crude drum-like instruments, dances, and the mumbling of words.

Upon falling asleep he dreams, and awakening, he finds that he is still in the same place where he had lain the night before. Yet, he is certain that during the night he had traveled to his favorite wood and killed an animal whose tender flesh he was still savoring. Since the conception of a dream was as yet foreign to him, the logical conclusion he arrived at was that he had both a body and a spirit. If he possessed a body and a spirit, then all things about him, he reasoned, must likewise possess a similar spirit. Some spirits, he felt, were friendly; some, hostile to him. The hostile spirits were to be feared; but that powerful factor, "hope," had at last entered into his mind, and he hoped to be able to win them over to the camp of friendly spirits.

In this manner, man passed from the stage of contending against the spirits to one of placating them. It was believed that certain men carried more favor with the spirits than others, and these became the original priests, called the "Shamans."

Another expedient for warding off evil spirits was by means of the fetish. The primitive fetish was an object containing an active friendly spirit, which, if worn by the individual, protected him from the evil spirits. In a short while the manufacture of fetishes became a sacred profession, and the men who were thought to fashion the best ones became the professional holy men of the period, the priests.

At first, idols were used to drive away the evil spirits, and then, the conception changed to one of attracting the good spirits to man. From the individual fetish man passed to tribal ones, which in their first form were huge boulders and trees.

As the primitive mind gained cunning, it slyly smeared the surface of the idol with oily substances, hoping that the spirit, like some wild beast, would come and lick, be gratified, and remain in the idol. When some favorable signs denoted that a good spirit had entered into the idol, it was regularly smeared with oils and then blood, in the hope that the spirit would be pleased sufficiently to remain there permanently. As time went on, it became a custom, a rite, and the spirit having performed to the satisfaction of the tribe, ways were invented to manifest their gratitude. Instead of smearing the idol with blood, it was thought more fitting that an animal be killed and offered to the good spirit contained within the idol. In this manner arose the beginning of "sacrifice." It was at this time, when man began to persuade the idols or spirits to do things for his benefit that religion began.

Slowly, slowly, down through the ages, as the mind of man progressed, his self-made religious conceptions advanced. He now worshiped idols, and these idols were his gods. The Celts, the Babylonians, the Greeks, the Romans, all had their idols. All were certain that their gods were the true ones, and that the others were all inferior and even false gods. But, is the modern worshiper who is contemptuous of the ancients very different from them?

The centuries pass by, and in their wake is man's self-conceived religion. Now, some men take the prerogative in the manufacture of religion, and there evolve Brahmanism, Jainism, Buddhism, Hinduism, Confucianism, Taoism, and Zoroastrianism, all inspired, all supernatural, and with their myriads of followers who believed and still believe that theirs is the only true creed.

Very recently, in the time-scale of our development, man adopted the methods of "Big Business," and the religion of many gods and idols, polytheism, has given way to one Supreme God, monotheism. Man found that it made for simplicity and saved his valuable time if he worshiped one god, instead of obeying the hitherto many. The "Chosen People" took it upon themselves to bring the next divinely concocted conception of a Supreme God, and they manufactured the creed of Judaism.

After many years, a rift arose among the Jews, and the sectarians were defeated and expelled. Foiled in their first object, they cast aside the laws of Moses and offered the Hebrew religion without the Hebrew ceremonies to the Greek and Roman world. Jesus was the man who prepared the way for this remarkable event.

When Mohammed conceived the divine conception that he would follow in the footsteps of his brother-prophets, Moses and Jesus, the latest of the major religions was revealed.

At the present time, the Hebrews and Christians, although worshiping the same Jehovah, are disputing with each other, and indeed, amongst themselves, with regard to the various attributes, amorous pursuits, and lineal descendants of the Godhead. Jehovah himself appears to be on the decline and his unity is steadily disintegrating into a paradoxical trinity. But we are progressing, for in 1300 years no new prophet has arisen, and no new divine revelation is perturbing our race; the old ones, however, are causing quite enough disturbance.

It would be of value for the modern religionist who believes that the worship of a deity in our own age is far removed from the worship of an idol by our savage ancestors, to retrace his steps and compare the savage mind worshiping his particular idol and a so-called civilized mind of today worshiping his deity.

The savage prayed to his idol, that is, he *begged*. He begged the idol to watch over his flock or his fields. The modern prays, that is he begs of his idol, his deity, to prosper his business, to guard his life, and, as one of my "super-devout" acquaintances recently informed me, on the eve of an important golf match, for the Deity to give him endurance; in other words, "to cut down his golf score."

The savage voiced his incantations; the modern sings hymns, that is he flatters. There is still a great deal of the charlatanry of the magician in the construction of the houses of prayer, with the sunlight shut out and only filtering through the leaded and multi-colored panes, the semidarkness, the solemnity, the rise and swell of the organ; all things combined to overcome the senses, to play upon the emotions, and to subdue the reason.

The savage made sacrifices to his idols, that is, he paid tribute, chiefly out of fear, but partly in the hope of getting something better in return. The modern does not offer human or animal sacrifice, it is true; but it must be borne in mind that the wealth of the savage consisted of his sheep, oxen, oils, and wines, not money. Today, the devout offer a sacrifice of money to the Deity. We are all familiar with the requests of religious institutions for gifts, which nearly always finish with the phrase, "And the Lord will repay you many fold." In other words, sacrifice part of your worldly goods to the idol, and he will repay with high interest. He will give in return long life and much riches. The savage was afraid to utter the real name of his god, it was taboo. The modern says, "Take not the name of the Lord in vain." Even today, the followers of Moses consider it taboo to utter the name of Jehovah except in prayer.

The present-day methods of worship are no different from those of the savage; the method of supplication has changed with the advance of the years, but the fundamental ideas at the base of all worship are just as crude today as they were 4000 years ago. Primitive man was no more a fetishist than is the modern Catholic. The latter still wears medals and images suspended from the neck and pinned to the inner clothing.

Moreover, a survey of the various religions extant indicates that the religious factor is no less prevalent today than it was in primitive societies.

In Greenland, one finds, that through nearly all of its vast area religion has no place, but that is chiefly the result of its being largely uninhabited. In Alaska, the population is for the most part Catholic, although the natives are animists. In Canada, 33 per cent are Catholic, the rest are mainly Protestant. In the United States, 20 per cent are Catholic, 3.5

per cent are Jewish, and the remainder are Protestants. Mexico, Central and South America, are almost entirely Roman Catholic. In Europe, Russia was until recently dominantly Greek Orthodox; the Scandinavian peninsula, the English Isles, and Central Europe are dominantly Protestant, while France, Portugal, Spain, Italy, and the rest of the countries bordering the Mediterranean Sea are Catholic. The rest of the continent is divided between Jews and Mohammedans. In Asia, the entire vast area of Siberia is only sparsely settled and its religions include Animism, Taoism, and Christianity. In China, we find the land of three truths, Confucianism, Taoism, and Buddhism. India, Tibet, and Burma are dominated by Hinduism and Buddhism; Arabia, Persia, and the rest of the continent are Mohammedan. In Japan, there are the Shintoists. The East Indies, where the population is native, are Animistic. In Australia, the dominant religion is Protestantism. In North Africa, the west coast inhabitants are Mohammedans, while the Abyssinians are Christians. There are some Coptic Christians, in Egypt, while in the Congo and South African countries down to the Cape Settlements, the natives are Animists. The Cape Settlements themselves are Protestants.

More concretely, it is estimated that 10.7% of the inhabitants of the globe are Protestants; 16.2% are Catholics; 7.1% are Greek Orthodox; 10% are Animists; 1.4% are Shintoists; 18.2% are Confucians and Taoists; 12.8% are

Hindus; 8.4% are Buddhists; 13.4% are Moslems; and 1.8% are Hebrews and unclassified sects. Truly, a religious babel! and 10% of all the inhabitants of the globe, about the same number of people who profess to Protestantism, are Animists. This is the lowest stage of primitive religion, and millions of humans are still quagmired in the sloth of a primitive faith which once must have been the faith of all human beings.

The Mohammedan, the Jew, the Christian, will readily agree that the animism, the fetishism, and idolatry of the savage were man-made foolish beliefs. They can readily perceive that there was nothing supernatural, nothing revealed, in such beliefs; but they do not realize that to him, in his infantile development, the fetish and the idol were just as supernatural and superior as the modern conception of a Supreme Being. In each age man creates his god, in his own image, and within the confines of his own mental development. The mind of man has expanded so that it has conquered more and more of his environment; it has grown and wrested from nature those secrets which constitute his civilization. Along with this has progressed the conception of a deity, but only to a certain extent. The mind has embellished the outward appearance of its gods, consolidated them, and built upon them intricate systems of theology, upon which feed vast hordes of clergy; but the basic conception, the fundamental principle, that there must be something supernatural to explain something which we cannot explain at the present moment, that conception still drugs the mind of man. Primitive man did not understand the meaning of lightning, thunder, shadows, echoes, etc., and he placed these among the supernatural phenomena. The modern mind explains these phenomena, understands the laws governing their production. Yet, it is this same modern mind which persists in going back to our savage ancestors and their mental sloth, by attributing the myriads of phenomena which still elude its present stage of mental development, to a particular idol, this time, a Supreme Being. Brahmanism, Jainism, Buddhism, Hinduism, Confucianism, Taoism, Zoroastrianism, Hebrewism, Mohammedanism, Christianity—which is the true religion?

Let us suppose for a moment that an inhabitant of Mars, if there be such, were by a "miracle" to be transported to this earth and endowed with the mental capacity of the average inhabitant of the earth (a thing which perhaps would not be so flattering to our guest), were to be approached by a zealot of each one of these faiths, who hoped to convert this stranger to its ranks. Since the factor of coercion by force of environment to which each of these earthlings was subject would naturally be absent, the Martian would be in a position to make a fair choice. How much would the visitor be impressed by the statements of the Christian, Mohammedan, or Jew, when advised that unless he embraced their particular creed, he would be damned to eternal torture in their particular Hell?

If a Christian were to accost him and endeavor to put the fear of God into him, and if our visitor, being from Mars, already knew that of the world's population, only about 27 per cent are Christians, and the other 73 per cent are Non-Christians, is it logical to suppose that he would ever be convinced that an omniscient, omnipotent, benevolent, Supreme Being would select only one quarter of his children whom he had created for redemption, with the infallible knowledge that nearly three-quarters of them would be confined to Hell for not believing what He could have made them believe if He were truly omnipotent, omniscient, and benevolent? Would he not rather reply that on his planet such a "Father" who would select some of his children for rewards, and maliciously torture his other children, would not be designated as a God but a Devil? Were the Martian to be further informed that each one of God's children was represented in actual figures by hundreds of millions and that these have been living on the planet Earth for hundreds of thousands of years, and were the visitor to contemplate the vast incomprehensible number of souls that have been confined to Hell by such a father, might he not cut his visit short? He would be apt to repeat with James Mill, "Think of a being who would make a Hell, who would create the human race with the infallible foreknowledge and therefore with the intention that the great majority of them should be consigned to horrible and everlasting torment." I believe that our guest would assert that if such a Being actually existed and demanded worship, he would certainly have revealed his true belief to the first man Adam, and therefore saved his children an inestimable amount of suffering.

Were the visitor to be further pressed by the zealot with the vision of eternal hell, I believe he would retort that there is no reason for God to punish those who doubt or deny faith in His existence, since it is His own doing; and if He desired each one of His children to worship Him according to the precepts of a certain creed, He surely would have instilled that creed into man's make-up together with the rest of his characteristics. Undoubtedly, He would not esteem any creed which damned the human intellect by cursing the doubts which are the necessary consequence of its exercise, or the creed which cursed the moral faculty by asserting the guilt of honest error.

If our visitor would but glance at the history, the evolution, of religious beliefs, he would realize and soundly assert that all religions are human in their origins, erroneous in their theories, and ridiculous in their threats and rewards.

CHAPTER II

THE KORAN AND THE OLD AND NEW TESTAMENTS

The Jews emerge into history, not a nation of keen spiritual aspirations and altruistic ethics, but that pagan people, worshipping rocks, sheep and cattle, and spirits of caves and wells, of whom the Old Testament, tending towards its higher ideal, gives fragmentary but convincing evidence.

JAMES T. SHOTWELL.

Consider Jahveh. Cruel god of a horde of nomadic invaders settling in a land of farmers, he had his images, ranging in elaboration from an uncut mazzebah or asherah, to a golden bull. He was plural by place and tribe and function. What did the prophetic movement do with his Sacred powers? It identified his taboos with a written constitution.

HORACE M. KALLEN.

36

The mental attitude of these priest-dominated ancestors of ours is amazing. They were like children in the hands of unscrupulous teachers. In reading these old chronicles it is impossible not to be shocked by the incongruity ever arising out of the juxtaposition of theory and practice.

LLEWELYN POWYS.

OUR Martian visitor, having withstood the blasts of the Zealot, is approached by a Mohammedan who places in his hands the Koran and tells him that it is a divinely inspired revelation, as revealed by Allah through his prophet, Mohammed. Having already had some experience with earthly religionists, the Martian is disposed to avail himself of the historical evidence regarding the life of Mohammed.

He finds that Mohammed, from all accounts, was a demagogue, a charlatan, and a victim of mental disease. It strikes him strangely that such an individual should be chosen by Allah as his disciple on earth to make known his commands. He notes Mohammed's appearance on earth in 600 A.D. and wonders why the Creator should have procrastinated for such a long time; but decides to read the revelations anyhow.

He discovers that "from the literary point of view, the Koran has little merit. Declamation, repetition, puerility, a lack of logic, and incoherence strike him at every turn. He finds it humiliating to the human intellect to think that this mediocre literature has been the subject of innumerable commentaries and that millions of men are still wasting time in absorbing it."

A Hebrew next takes his turn at this obstinate guest and sets before him the Old Testament. Again, the Martian is informed that it is an inspired book actuated by God.

In his attempt to find the historical evidence corroborating this book, the Martian finds that authentic history begins for the Israelites with the constitution of Saul's monarchy about 1100 B.C. All that precedes this—the deluge, the dispersal of mankind, Abraham, Jacob, Joseph, the captivity in Egypt, Moses, Joshua, and the conquest of Canaan, is more or less mythical.

In the Old Testament, our Martian reads the first chapter, glances at the chronology, and is immediately bewildered since he has a fair knowledge of our scientific advances. As he reads on, he becomes aware of a host of errors, contradictions, and manifest absurdities. When he questions the zealous Hebrew, he comes in contact with what he is informed is Concordism, which he perceives is a false science that consists in determining, at any cost, a perfect harmony between modern science and the knowledge possessed by God's people. He is thus told that the days of creation were not days at all, but periods; although the Bible mentions the morning and evening of each day. Delving further in this most holy of revelations, he learns that

God is represented in a manner most unworthy of what such a being should be represented. He finds the Lord walking in the cool of the evening, showing his hind quarters to Moses, ordering abominable massacres, and punishing chiefs who had not killed enough people. On further perusal, there is revealed, "A great deal of Oriental bombast, incoherence and absurdity, that the marvels recounted are often ludicrous or grotesque."

In a chance moment, when the Hebrew had relaxed his hold for a second, a vile heretic points out to the visitor (*Exodus XXII, 18*): "Thou shalt not suffer a witch to live!" and explains the witchcraft delusion to him.

From a comparison between Exodus XXXIV and Exodus XX, he is at a loss to decipher which are the true commandments that the Lord gave to Moses. The first five books of the Pentateuch, he finds, are attributed to Moses, although they contain the account of the latter's death. On inquiry, he learns that this is still maintained by the synagogue. His Martian intellect is unable to comprehend the logic of a God who would demand human and animal sacrifice, and the story of Abraham about to sacrifice his son Isaac fills him with disgust. His estimate of the mentality of Jehovah receives a severe jolt when he reads in Leviticus XVI, "Herewith shall Aaron come unto the holy place with a young bullock for a sin offering and a ram for a burnt offering. He shall put on

39

the holy linen coat, and he shall have the linen breeches upon his flesh, and he shall be girded with the linen girdle, and with the linen mitre shall he be attired; they are the holy garments; and he shall bathe his flesh in water and put them on. And he shall take of the congregation of the children of Israel two he-goats for a sin offering, and one ram for a burnt offering. And Aaron shall present the bullock of the sin offering, which is for himself, and he shall make atonement for himself and for his houses. And he shall take the two goats and set them before the Lord at the door of the tent of the meeting."

Our visitor reads on to Leviticus XVIII, after which he must stop to question the Hebrew, for here he finds, "None of you shall approach to any that is near of kin to him, to uncover their nakedness; I am the Lord. The nakedness of thy father, even the nakedness of thy mother, shalt thou not uncover; she is thy mother; thou shalt not uncover her nakedness. The nakedness of thy father's wife shalt thou not uncover; it is thy father's nakedness. The nakedness of thy sister, the daughter of thy father, or daughter of thy mother, whether she be born at home, or abroad, even their nakedness thou shalt not uncover. The nakedness of thy son's wife—the nakedness of the wife of thy father—the nakedness of thy father's sister, thy mother's sister, the nakedness of thy daughter-in-law, thy brother's wife, the nakedness of a woman and her daughter, thou shalt not uncover. And unto a woman separated by her uncleanliness thou shalt not approach to uncover her nakedness. Thou shalt not be carnally with thy neighbor's wife, to defile thyself with her. Thou shalt not be with mankind as with womankind. And thou shalt not be with any beast to defile thyself thereto; neither shall any woman stand before a beast to lie down thereto; it is confusion."

The Martian, totally aghast, is constrained to exclaim that he cannot believe that a Deity should find it necessary to place this in a divine revelation. The Hebrew Zealot relents somewhat to explain that perhaps this was not revealed, but found its way into the divine text as a moral lesson to the primitive tribes for which it was written. To this, our guest counters with the remark that if this be a parable of manners and morals, then, from what he observes on the earth, we, Earthlings, have certainly outgrown the need for such coarse and obscene statements made some 2000 years ago; and that on Mars, although the inhabitants are not blessed with such divine revelations, common sense and reason have taught their most primitive men the same lessons in morality while they were yet in their infancy.

Reflecting on this maze of contradictions, the Martian determines to analyze the Old Testament and the Hebrew religion in the same manner that he would investigate any other problem presented to him.

Thirty-five hundred years ago, the Hebrews were a pastoral, primitive people inhabiting the wilderness known today as the

Arabian Desert. Their religion was that of all other primitive peoples—Animism, an illusion which made primitive man recognize everywhere spirits similar to his own spirit. They worshiped the spirits of the sun and the moon, the mountains and rocks, as well as the spirits of the dead.

It appears certain that the barrenness of this desert land necessitated these wandering tribes to migrate to adjacent areas of greater fertility. To the north lay the fertile valleys of the Tigris and Euphrates and the coast of the Mediterranean Sea; to the west lay the land of the Egyptians. Time and time again, these Bedouin tribes hurled themselves against the inhabitants of the northern fertile valleys. Babylonia, to the northeast, was the first country to be invaded, and later Canaan to the northwest. Successful at times in establishing themselves in Babylonia and Canaan, they were at other times driven back into the desert when the native inhabitants in turn attacked the invaders. Migrating into Egypt in search of food, they were made a captive nation and escaped again into the desert when the Egyptians were engaged in fighting the savage invaders from Libya.

The leader of this flight from Egypt was the prophet Moses. The Martian decides to investigate the character and deeds of this influential figure at another time. It is probable that, the exodus gave the proper stimulus for the beginnings of a distinctive Hebrew religion, and was the reason for their finally establishing themselves in Canaan, with Jehovah as their chief deity. It has often been proclaimed that the value of Judaism has been in first establishing a religion of monotheism; but it must not be forgotten that centuries before the Hebrews escaped into the desert, the Egyptians were tending to monotheism. It is known that one god was exalted over all the rest in Egypt, and that as far back as 1375 B.C. King Ikhnaton made the religion of Egypt an absolute monotheism. The Hebrews, in proclaiming their Yahveh as the one and supreme deity, were but following what they had assimilated from the Egyptians. The faith of these desert marauders, at the time of their entrance into Canaan, was as crude and savage as the Hebrews themselves. Brought into contact with the gods of the Phœnicians and Babylonians, their Yahveh underwent a change, as have all other creeds since that time when brought into contact with another creed. The final idea of Yahveh accepted by the Hebrews was not the product of a sudden revelation but of a gradual evolution.

The Hebrews, about the twelfth century B.C., gained access into Canaan, and at first were successful in warfare, so that under King David they presented the aspect of a united nation. However, following the extravagant reign of King Solomon, the nation was embroiled in a revolution, and the land was divided into two kingdoms—Israel in the north, Judah in the south. These two tiny kingdoms were habitually at war with each other and, finally, in 722 B.C. Israel was conquered, while in 586 B.C., Judah was defeated and its population either scattered or taken into captivity.

In 538 B.C., Cyrus of Persia conquered Babylonia and set the exiles free. Returning to their own land, the exiles took back with them the law code which the priests had manufactured for them. Then began a period of priestly domination and corruption, a period of subjugation to Rome, of insurrection against Rome, and the capture and destruction of Jerusalem in 70 A.D. With the capture of Jerusalem, the Hebrew nation was finally dispersed.

Just as the Martian was able to trace the evolution of the Hebrews from the stage of the marauding tribes of the Arabian desert who wandered' into Egypt, Canaan, and Babylonia, and finally established a kingdom for themselves which was dispersed by Rome; just so could he trace the evolution of their religious beliefs from their incipient crudities to their not too great refinement at 70. A.D. This evolution of the Hebrew religion is best exemplified by an analysis of the Old Testament itself.

There are several canons, or official collection of books which comprise the Old Testament. The Jews and Protestants accept fewer books than the Roman Catholics. The Jewish Canon consists of those so-called sacred books of, which the Synagogue possessed Hebrew texts about a century before the Christian era. "About 150 B.C. the sacred books of the

Jews were translated into Greek for the use of those Egyptian Jews who could not read Hebrew. This translation is called the Septuagint, from a tradition that seventy or seventy-two translators had worked upon it." (*Salomon Reinach, "Orpheus."*) The earliest manuscripts of the Hebrew Bible date only from the tenth century A.D., but there are very much older manuscripts of the Greek and Latin translations in existence. At the time of Jesus Christ, three divisions of the Old Testament were recognized. These were, the Law, the Prophets, and the other Scriptures. The first five books, Genesis, Exodus, Numbers, Leviticus, and Deuteronomy, are known as the Pentateuch, and are attributed to Moses himself; although, as has been noted, they contain the account of his death. This conception of the Mosaic origin of the Pentateuch was accepted by the Israelites as early as the fifth century B.C. and has been maintained by the Synagogue since that time. Following the example of the Hebrews, the Christian Churches accepted this version as to origin, and the Roman Catholic Church still upholds this view. The Jewish Synagogue and the various Christian Churches further hold that the Old Testament is a collection of works inspired or dictated by God. Even as late as 1861, the famous Dean Burgon, in a sermon preached at Oxford University, declared, "The Bible is none other than the voice of Him that sitteth upon the throne. Every book of it, every chapter of it, every verse of it, every syllable of it, every letter of it, is the direct utterance of the Most High. The Bible is none other than the Word of God, not some part of it more, some part of it less, but all alike the utterance of Him who sitteth upon the throne, faultless, unerring, supreme." The Martian compared this statement with the words of the scholar Loisy, "If God himself wrote the Bible, we must believe Him to be either ignorant or untruthful."

As he delves further into the intricacies of the construction of the Bible, our visitor perceives that the Old Testament gradually evolved from the tenth century to the second century B.C., and in its present form is mainly a fifth century compilation, so distorting the facts that it has taken scholars one-hundred and fifty years to get them straight. "It may rightly be said that there is not a single book in the Bible which is original in the sense of having been written by one man, for all the books are made up of older documents or pre-existing sources which were combined with later materials, undergoing, in this way, several revisions and editions at the hands of different scribes or compilers. Deep traces have therefore been left upon the text of the Bible by these several stages of expansions, additions, modifications, revisions, and incorporations—they appear to the scholar of biblical literature much like the striations grooved in the rocks by large glaciers to the student of Geology." (*Trattner, "Unravelling the Book of Books."*)

The Martian ascertains that to most thinking men it has become very obvious that the Bible is the work of man, and not the inspiration of a god; that an increasing number of liberal theologians are discarding the theory of the divine inspiration of the Bible. He likewise clearly perceives that there are as yet many men that have given this matter but little thought; with the Divine inspiration looming up as a corner stone in the Hebrew faith he realizes that it behooves him to carry his investigations further.

The Christians, accepting the Old Testament as a book dictated by God, had fixed the age of the earth as 4004 B.C. The harm done by the Christian ecclesiastics in attempting to force science to conform to the ridiculous concept of the construction of the universe as contained in the Bible, and as interpreted by the Church, the Martian considers in a further chapter. Scientists incline to the view that the earth has existed as a separate planet for something like two thousand million years (2,000,000,000,000). The rocks give, a history of 16,000,000,000. Just as in the study of the origin of primitive beliefs, one finds that man made his gods and invented all that they are reported to have said, so a study of the Old Testament reveals that the ancient Hebrew invented his God, and manufactured the vast mass of myth and fable that are recorded as the words and deeds of God. Throughout the ages, the words of these ancient Hebrews have been taken as the words of a god.

"Everything goes to show that the Hebrew literature was produced like other literatures. Hebrews were not the first to tell tales. When they did come to write 'for our learning' they borrowed from other people. The only reason why anything more than a literary attention is paid to these old Jewish writings is that Jesus was a Jew. When Christianity was founded—a difficult date to fix—there was no such thing as a Bible. The old Brahmans and Buddhists had Holy Scriptures; the Egyptians had a Book of the Dead, and the Sayings of Khuenaten; the Persians had the Zend-Avesta; the Chinese had sacred books. They were all as sacred as the Jewish books. Priests made them sacred. Priests generally rewrote and edited them, even if they had not originally imagined them. There is nothing to guide the man of common sense save knowledge and reason. Every priest swears his religion and his scriptures are true. But they cannot all be true. If the first are true, then the Jews are past further consideration, for they were not the first in the field with sacred writings. . . . Holy scriptures are merely Jewish classics. We have had to accept these old writings of the Hebrews as holy and inspired because the priests said so, and for no other reason whatsoever. There is no other reason." Assuming the existence of a deity, a man exercising his common sense would be compelled to deny that the Old Testament is inspired of God, because it abounds in stupidities and errors such as no god could inspire. "But because the Jews accumulated these writings, the subsequent

48

adopters of Christianity, realizing that Jesus was a Jew, and had been a professing Jew, promptly annexed these tales of fancy and of fear, of muddled, sensual, silly things and said they must be accepted with the teachings of Jesus. And in the course of time, people had to believe these old Jewish writings were the Word of God." (*W. H. Williamson, "Thinker or Believer."*)

The Hebrews had as one of their gods, Yahveh, whom they endowed with their qualities; qualities inherent in a primitive people: jealousy and might, trickery and fickleness. They evolved a worship that contained in a modified form many of the ceremonials that they witnessed when they came into contact with the Babylonians and Phœnicians. Their Bible they maintained to be a collection of books which appeared at intervals, with divine inspiration, during a thousand years of Jewish history. Similarly, they insisted that Moses wrote the Pentateuch, that Judges, Kings, and Chronicles go back to the times they describe, that the prophecies were added from the ninth century onward, and so on.

The Martian found that not a single book of the Old Testament is older than the ninth century B.C. and that in the fifth century B.C. all the older books and fragments were combined together into the Old Testament as we have it, and were drastically altered so as to yield a version of early Jewish history which is not true. The manipulation of the Hebrew writings by the Jewish priests had for its object to represent the Jewish priesthood, and its rights and customs, as having been established in the days of Moses. Deuteronomy and Leviticus have been classed as priestly forgeries. Nearly every occurrence, from the creation of the world to the death of Moses, is related twice and, in some cases, three times; and as the Pentateuch is supposed to have been written by Moses one must assume that Moses had double and triple vision.

Chronicles, Ezra, and Nehemiah are impudent forgeries of the fourth century, giving a totally false version of the events. The Martian finds that the terms used for these fabrications are "redaction" or "recension," but, in his understanding, he finds the word most descriptive of the process to be forgery. "The main point is that practically all the experts assure you that in scores of material points the Old Testament history has been discredited, and has only been confirmed in a few unimportant incidental statements; and that the books are a tissue of inventions, expansions, conflations, or recensions dating centuries after the event."

The Martian in his analysis becomes aware of instances related in the Old Testament that oh his planet would have to be termed forgeries,—deliberate falsifications or fabrications of documents or of the signature to them. "Now the far greater part of the more learned clerical authorities on the Bible say that many books of the Old Testament pretend to be written by men who did not write them; that many books were deliberately written as history when the writers knew that they were not history; and that the Old Testament as a whole, as we have it, is a deliberate attempt to convey an historical belief which the writers knew to be false. But these learned authorities do not like the word forgery. It is crude." (*Joseph McCabe, "The Forgery of The Old Testament"*) They veil the meaning of this word in the elegance, the subtlety, the resources, of diplomatic language. They talk of certain books in terms of "their legendary character," "their conformity to a scheme," and "their didactic purpose." To the Martian these are but an extremely polite description of what he would call a forgery.

A theologian in speaking of David states that "Keen criticism is necessary to arrive at the kernel of fact," and, "the imaginative element in the story of David is but the vesture which half conceals, half discloses certain facts treasured in popular tradition." The Martian thinks this is polite language, but the word forgery is much more concise and to the point, and he finds an excellent example of this described by Joseph McCabe in "The Forgery of the Old Testament." He states, "Some time ago we recovered tablets of the great Persian king, Cyrus, and Professor Sayre gives us a translation of them, and he compares them, as you may, with the words of Daniel, 'In that night was Belshazzar, the king of the Chaldeans, slain, and Darius the Median took the kingdom.' The tablets of Cyrus describe the taking of Babylon, and are beyond the slightest suspicion. The Persians had adopted the Babylonian custom of writing on clay, then baking the brick or tablet, and such documents last forever. And these and other authentic and contemporary documents of the age which 'Daniel' describes show:

1. That Belshazzar was not the king of Babylon.

2. That the name of the last king was Nabonidos.

3. That the city was taken peacefully, by guile, not by bloodshed.

4. That is was Cyrus, not Darius the Median, who took it.

5. That Darius, who is said (XI, 1) by Daniel to have been the son of "Ahasuerus" (Xerxes), was really his father.

6. That all the Babylonian names in Daniel are absurdly misspelt and quite strange to the writer.

7. That the writer described the Chaldeans in a way that no writer could have done before the time of Alexander the Great.

It is now beyond question that the man who wrote Daniel, and pretended to be alive in 539 B.C. (when Babylon fell), did not live until three or four centuries later. The book is a tissue of errors, as we find by authentic documents and by reading the real Babylonian names on the tablets."

The Martian discovers glaring instances of forgery in the book of Isaiah and the Psalms of David, which, while they pretend to have been written by Isaiah and David, are really compilations by various writers. Similarly, he finds that the Book of Esther has been pronounced by scholars as a clumsy forgery of the second century, and that the story of the slaying of Goliath by David is not consistent with the unlegendary tradition that the slayer of Goliath was Elhanan, and the period of this adventure not in Saul's but in David's reign. The Book of Psalms, although attributed to King David, was not written by King David; and the Book of Proverbs, although attributed to Solomon, was not written by King Solomon.

The Book of Genesis relates the mythical traditions of the Hebrews from the creation of the world to the death of Joseph. "A French physician of the eighteenth century, Astruc, was the first scholar to point out that the two principal designations of God in Genesis, Elohim and Jahveh, are not used arbitrarily. If we place side by side the passages in which God is called Elohim, and those in which he is called by the other name, we get, two perfectly distinct narratives, which the author of the Pentateuch, as we possess it, has juxtaposed rather than fused. This one discovery suffices to discredit the attribution of these books to Moses, who could not have been an unintelligent compiler, and also discredits the theory of the divine inspiration of the Bible text. A comparison of the two narratives shows that all which relates to the creation of Eve, the Garden of Eden, and Adam's transgression, exists only in the Jehovist text. Thus it is evident that two versions of the Creation are given in Genesis. But there are traces in the Old Testament of a third legend, akin to that of the Babylonians, in which Marduk creates the world by virtue of a victory over the waters of chaos (Tiamat). This conception of a conflict between the creator and hostile forces was contrary to the monotheistic thesis, and has disappeared from our two versions of Genesis; but the suppression sufficiently proves that it was very ancient and had long been accepted."

The Martian finds that theologians have attempted to crawl out of desperate situations in their interpretation of the Old Testament by a method of reading into a passage or extracting out of it ideas altogether foreign to its original intent. This method they call "Allegory." By means of this process they have been able to extract any meaning which suits, their purposes, and by this method of juggling could prove anything. A classic example is that licentious piece of literature called the "Song of Solomon," in which it is claimed that a woman's breasts, thighs, and belly are the symbols of the union of Jahveh and the Synagogue.

Continuing his researches, the Martian notices a number of passages in the Old Testament that lead him to the conclusion that the Hebrews were originally polytheists. The name Elohim, he finds, is plural (singular, Eloah), meaning the gods. Again, in another passage of Genesis, God is described as saying, "Let us make man in our image (I, 26)," and further on, "The man is become as one of us." It becomes evident to him that the Hebrews, like their neighbors, worshiped "baalim" or the gods of the heathens. The "teraphim," the etymology of which is unknown, were little portable idols which seem to have been the Lares of the ancient Hebrews. David owned some (I Samuel XIX, 13-16), and the prophet Hosea, in the eighth century before Christ, seems still to have considered the "teraphim" as indispensable in worship (Hos. III, 4). These evidences of polytheism and fetichism in the people of Israel destroy, in the mind of the Martian, the claim of these people to have been faithful from their earliest origin to a spiritual monotheism. Rather does he find that they took the religions of other peoples with whom they came in contact.

The Old Testament contains numerous instances of the practice of magic. Moses and Aaron were magicians who rivalled Pharaoh's magicians (Ex. VII, 11-20); and Balaam was a magician who pronounced incantations against Israel and afterwards passed over to the service of Jehovah. Jacob resorted to a kind of sympathetic magic to procure the birth of a speckled sheep (Gen. XXX, 39). "Thou shalt not suffer a witch to live," is written in Exodus XXII, 18, and this phrase offered an affirmation of the reality of witchcraft during the period of the Witchcraft Delusion. The Martian notes that the sentence, "Thou shalt not suffer a witch to live," has caused more suffering, torture, and death than probably any other sentence ever framed. His mind revolts at the stupidity and the slavish adherence to so-called authority of the human mind, which is manifested in this example of what occurred in the period of the Witchcraft Delusion, when the words of an ignorant and barbaric Hebrew were taken by Christian followers to be the words of a god. And yet our Martian guest recognizes that in this day all men are aware of the fallacy of this utterance in a book which is still claimed to be infallible.

The Martian then considers the many ancient Hebrew rites and religious taboos that have come down through the ages, and are still practiced in a modified form by the modern Hebrew. Thus, in the Old Testament, there are numerous instances recorded of the practices of slaughtering of innocent animals who were offered as peace offerings to Yahveh. As time passed, the practice of slaughtering and then burning the sacrificial animal gave way to the practice of only giving the blood of the animal as an offering. This custom has come down to the present day in the modern worship of Jehovah; the blood of animals is still forbidden to the modern Hebrew. Therefore, the orthodox Jew has the neck of the chicken slit by a "Shochet" who allows the blood to drip to the ground—a modern blood offering to the Gods. The explanations given by the rabbis of our day are spurious. Similarly, the orthodox Jew of our time still persists in salting the meat before cooking, a process which is intended to remove the blood, which is the portion of the Gods.

The reason that the pious Jew abstains from pork leads to the consideration of Totemism as found in the Old Testament. Totemism is a kind of worship rendered to animals and vegetables considered as allied and related to man. The worship of animals and plants is found as a survival in all ancient societies and is the origin of the belief in the transmigration of souls. Totemism seems to have been as widespread as the animism from which it is derived, and has been closely intertwined in the development of religious beliefs. Totemism in a modified form is found in the Old Testament where animals speak on occasion, as the serpent in Genesis, or Balaam's ass. In the most remote periods it is probable that every clan had at least one totem animal which might no more be killed or eaten than the human individuals of the clan. The totem was protected by taboo. The totem was sacred and in this capacity it was looked upon as a source of strength and holiness, and to live beside it and under its protection was considered as a righteous custom. In certain communities the idea that it was necessary to abstain from eating certain totems survived the progress of material civilization. The cow is taboo to the Hindus, the pig is taboo to the Mohammedans and to the Jews. The pious

Jew abstains from pork because his remote ancestors, five or six thousand years before our era, had the wild boar as their totem. This is the origin of this alimentary taboo; among the ancient Hebrews it arose, and only comparatively recently has it been suggested that the flesh of these taboo animals was unwholesome. In the eighteenth century, philosophers propagated the erroneous notion that if certain religious legislators had forbidden various aliments, it was for hygienic motives. Even Renan believed that dread of trichinosis and leprosy had caused the Hebrews to forbid the use of pork. To show the irrational nature of this explanation, it will be enough to point out that in the whole of the Bible there is not a single instance of an epidemic or a malady attributed to the eating of unclean meats; the idea of hygiene awoke very late in the Greek world. To the Biblical writers, as to contemporary savages, illness is supernatural; it is an effect of the wrath of spirits.

Primitive man ascribed all diseases either to the wrath of God, or the malice of an evil being. The curing of disease by the casting out of devils and by prayers were the means of relief from sickness recognized and commanded by the Old Testament. The hygienic explanation of an alimentary prohibition as still insisted upon by the rabbis is entirely erroneous and marks the expounder of such an explanation as one who is entirely ignorant of the evolution of religious beliefs. The entire matter is well stated in one sentence by

Reinach, "Nothing can be more absurd, generally speaking, than to explain the religious laws and practices of the remote past by considerations based on modern science."

The Martian is able to trace some curious customs that were exhibited by the ancient Hebrews as well as most other ancient peoples, and which have persisted to this day. The customs remain the same, the meanings have become lost in the blind adherence to custom. It is known that the old Jewish mourning customs originated with, the desire for protection from the liberated spirit of the deceased. The loud cries uttered by the mourners were thought to frighten away the spirits. The change of dress, the covering of the head with ashes and the shaving of the hair of the mourners were done with the purpose of making themselves unrecognizable to the spirits. Hence, the custom still prevails of wearing the mourning veil. The covering of mirrors where death occurs in the household may well be an attempt to prevent the spirit from lingering in the vicinity Similarly, even today, the orthodox Jew, in case of grave illness in his family, changes the given name of the sufferer. To confuse the evil spirit causing the disease?

Further survivals of totemism as found in the Old Testament are illustrated by the worship of the bull and the serpent. Portable gilded images of bulls were consecrated and Hosea protested against the worship of the bull in the kingdom of Israel (Hos. VIII, 5; X, 5) The famous golden calf of the Israelites, which was the object of Moses' anger, was a totemic idol. The worship of the serpent was practiced by Moses himself (Num. XXI, 9). A brazen serpent was worshiped in the temple of Jerusalem, and was only destroyed by Hezekiah about 700 B.C. (2 Kings XVIII, 4).

The ancient Hebrews, as well as their neighbors, were phallic worshipers. To primitive people it is but a natural phase to have the phallus become the exponent of creative power, and as such to be worshiped. To these primitive minds there was nothing immoral in genuine phallic worship. Signs of phallicism among the ancient Hebrews can be clearly pointed out; the serpent was a phallic symbol. "That the serpent was the phallus is proved by the Bible itself. The Hebrew word used for serpent is 'Nachash,' which is everywhere else translated in the Bible in a phallic sense, as in Ezekiel XVI, 36, where it is rendered 'filthiness' in the sense of exposure, like the 'having thy Boseth naked' of Micah." (*J. B. Hannay, "Christianity, the Sources of its Teaching and Symbolism."*) The ark itself was a feminine symbol, and phallicism would explain why Moses made an ark and put in it a rod and two stones. "The Eduth, the Shechina, the Tsur, and the Yahveh were identical; simply different names for the same thing, the phallus. They occupied the female ark with which they formed the double sexed life symbol. The Hebrew religion had thus a purely phallic basis, as was to be expected from a ritual and symbolism derived from two extremely phallic nations, Babylon and Egypt." (*J.*

B. Hannay, Ibid.) An intelligent reading of Exodus XXXIV, 13, and 1 Kings XIV, 23 and 24, will prove the above contention.

Once more our Martian guest is besieged by the Hebrew Zealot to examine the divine revelation of his religion. This time the Martian notes, "I, Yahveh, thy God, am a jealous God, visiting the iniquity of the fathers upon the children unto the third and fourth generations" (Deut.), which seems to him to savor of a cruel and monstrous being. He cannot perceive of a just being favoring slavery (Ex. XI), or of a merciful father ordering human sacrifice (Ex. XIII), (Lev. XXVII, 29), (Num. XIII, 3). He is dumbfounded to find references to cannibalism (Lev. XXVI, 14-16-28; Deut. XXVIII, 53-58; Jer. XIX, 9; Ezek. V, 10; Kings VI, 26-29-33). A Benevolent Being, he reasons, would not sanction war and destruction of the captured enemy, yet there are instances of this (Deut. XXI, 10-14; Deut. XX, 13-14; Deut. VII, 1-2-16). The reading of Numbers V, 11-29, and Deuteronomy XXII nauseated him. The Hebrew Zealot, observing the utter disgust with which the reader was regarding his revelation, is obliged to explain to the bewildered barbarian unbeliever that the Old Testament is the foundation for all of our morals and that without it we would have developed into a very shocking and immoral race.

Since the visitor wishes to remain courteous he proceeds,

but with a great deal of hesitation, to further examine the revelation of God. At this point he is assured that this work is read in most schools and taught to small children. However, our guest is again disillusioned; for no sooner does he arrive at Genesis, XII, 11-20, than he finds that Abraham, good Abraham, the pure, the father of all Hebrews, makes of the sacred relationship of marriage a means of personal gain and safety by betraying his own wife. Now it is the Martian's turn to inquire of the Hebrew whether the latter had ever read this story to his own daughter? Or, the story of Abraham's affair with Hagar, his hand-maiden? Was the Hebrew's young daughter aware that Isaac son of Abraham, was as ready and willing to prostitute his wife for protection for himself as was his father Abraham?

The Martian is puzzled by the word "sporting" in Genesis, XXVI, 8-11, and is informed of its meaning. A few moments after reading Genesis XIX, 1-7, he informs his would-be converter that if Lot had lived in Mars and had offered his daughters to appease the mob, the account of that incident would never have found its way into any work on morals. Moreover, he failed utterly to see how the account of Lot's daughters getting him into a drunken state, followed by a statement such as, "Thus were both the daughters of Lot with child by their father," could ever have any moral value.

The story of Jacob, Leah, and Rachel does not appeal

to this infidel Martian, since he still believes that integrity and faithfulness are virtues. Yet, in his endeavor to respect the courtesy due to his host, he reaches for pencil and pad, and notes the various moral lessons he had derived thus far from the Old Testament. He wrote lust, incest, infidelity, and prostitution; arriving at the story of Dinah, Genesis XXXIV, 1-2, he wrote that in addition to those vices already listed, rape should be given a prominent place. The stories of Joseph and Potiphar's wife, Judah and Tamar, King David and his wives, the rape of Tamar by her brother Ammon, did not impress the Martian as stories for the delectation of children, since he was crude enough to hold that anything which would shock the mind of a child, could not have any moral value and would thus be automatically excluded from any religion. He, therefore, returned the volume to the Hebrew with the remark that as an adult he found the stories of De Maupassant and Balzac more interesting, even though they belonged to the same genre.

Our guest now repaired to one of our golf courses where, during the interval of a few hours, the fresh air, the sunshine, and exercise dispelled the mental nausea which the reading of the Old Testament had occasioned in him. Returning to his quarters, he is approached by one of the Christian Brethren and the New Testament is placed in his hands with these remarks, "The Christian recognizes that in the Old Testament the Jews have given to the Christian world its greatest heritage." The fact that in exchange for this priceless heritage, the Christians have given to the Jews a series of persecutions unequaled in the annals of human warfare is explained by the quality of the Brotherhood of Man that naturally manifests itself after a complete conversion to the Bible's precepts. The Old Testament contains the first revelations of God; the New Testament, the last revelations. Our Christian Brother "forgets" to remind the visitor that the difference of opinion regarding these two Testaments of God has caused more sorrow bloodshed, harm, devilment, misery, and devastation than any other single item in the life and history of the human race.

The Martian is hard pressed to reconcile the fact that Mohammedanism six hundred years after the appearance of Christianity triumphed over Christianity in a great portion of the earth's surface; yet he is informed that Christianity is *the* religion of God, that Allah made the Mohammedans, Jehovah the Jews, the Trinity the Christians, and the rest of the believers were illegitimate children of the above gods, was the only conclusion he could reach. In a few moments the myth of Christ begins to unfold itself before his eyes in the Gospels of Matthew, Mark, Luke, and John, the Acts of the Apostles, and the Apocalypse. He finds, "The so-called Messianic texts which are supposed to prefigure Jesus in the Old Testament have all been either misunderstood or deliberately misinterpreted. The most celebrated is that in Isaiah VII, 14, which predicts that a virgin shall bear a son, Emmanuel, but the word, Almah, which the Septuagint rendered "virgin" means in Hebrew a young woman, and this passage merely deals with the approaching birth of a son to the king or the prophet himself. This error of the Septuagint is one of the sources of the legend relating to the virginal birth of Jesus. As early as the second century A.D. the Jews perceived it and pointed it out to the Greeks, but the Church knowingly persisted in the false reading, and for over fifteen centuries she has clung to her error."

His attentive reading convinces him that not one of the Gospels is the work of an eyewitness to the scenes recorded; a little side investigation reveals that there were a great many writings called Gospels, from which the Church finally adopted four, guaranteeing their inspiration and absolute veracity, no doubt because they were in favor in four very influential churches, Matthew at Jerusalem, Mark at Rome or at Alexandria, Luke at Antioch, and John at Ephesus. Moreover, what the Gospels tell him, he perceives is what different Christian communities believed concerning Jesus between the years 70 and 100 A.D. In Matthew XXVI, 39, Mark XIV, 35, and Luke XXII, 42, there are words such as those Jesus is supposed to have uttered during the slumber of these very same Apostles. This occurrence enlightens him as to what St. Augustine meant when he wrote, "I should not believe in the Gospel if I had not the authority of the Church for so doing." If the documents are stuffed with the authority of the Church, these Gospels cannot be utilized for a history of the real life of Jesus.

A study of the Epistles of St. Paul reveals that St. Paul taught that sin and death came into the world by Adam's fall. In spite of a diligent search the Martian found no mention of this in the words ascribed to Jesus. From St. Paul's utterances he learns that Christ came to redeem mankind by his voluntary oblation of himself. He was the Son of God! Paul, not knowing that in the future a special form of conception would be superimposed on Jesus, states that he was of human birth. The Martian determined to ascertain what effect the teachings of St. Paul have had on Christianity. He learns that, "Ever since St. Paul, the ruling idea of Christianity has been that of the redemption of man, guilty of a prehistoric fault, by the voluntary sacrifice of a superman. This doctrine is founded upon that of expiation; a guilty person must suffer to atone for his fault; and that of the substitution of victims, the efficacious suffering of an innocent person for a guilty one. Both are at once pagan and Jewish ideas; they belong to the old fundamental errors of humanity. Yet, Plato knew that the punishment inflicted on a guilty person is not, nor should it be, a vengeance; it is a painful remedy imposed on him for his own benefit and that of society. At about the same period Athenian law laid down the principle that punishment should be as personal as the fault, thus St. Paul founded Christian Theology on two archaic ideas which had already been condemned by enlightened Athenians of the fourth century before our era, *ideas which no one would dream of upholding in these days, though the structure built upon them still subsists."*

In chapter V of the first Epistle of St. John, these words strike the visitor, "There are three that bear witness in heaven, the Father, and the Word, and the Holy Ghost, and these three are One." If these two verses are authentic, they would be an affirmation of the doctrine of the Trinity, dating from the first century, at a time when the Gospels, the Acts, and St. Paul ignore it. It was first pointed out in 1806 that these verses were an interpolation, for they do not appear in the best manuscripts, notably all the Greek manuscripts down to the fifteenth century. The Roman Church refused to bow to evidence. The Congregation of the Index, on January 13, 1897, with the approbation of Leo XIII, forbade any question as to the authenticity of the text relating to the "three heavenly witnesses." It appeared strange to the Martian that a god should need the lies of his disciples to be incorporated in a divine revelation. But his confusion was even greater when he read, "We worship one God in Trinity, and Trinity in Unity, neither confounding the Persons nor dividing the substance— and yet, they are not three Eternals, but One Eternal, not three Almighties, but One Almighty. So, the Father is God, the Son God, and the Holy Ghost God, and yet they are not three Gods, but One God. . . . The Father is made of none, neither created nor begotten. The Son is of the Father alone, not made, nor created, but begotten. The Holy Ghost is of the

Father and of the Son, neither made nor created, nor begotten, but proceeding. . . . And in this Trinity, none is afore or after the other; none is greater or less than another; but the whole three Persons are coeternal together and coequal."

He thought this would make a great puzzle, truly an insoluble conundrum, to take back to bewilder his Martian friends. However, he was able to comprehend the remarks of Vigilantius, "who returned from a journey in Italy and the Holy Land disgusted with official Christianity. He protested vehemently against the idolatrous worship of images, the legacy of Paganism to the Church, a practice directly opposed to that of the Mosaic law which Jesus came, not to destroy, but to fulfill. It was idle to reply that these images were the Scriptures of the illiterate, that they were not the object of, but the stimulus to, worship. Experience showed that the majority of the faithful confounded (as indeed they still do) the sign with the thing signified." (*Salomon Reinach, "Orpheus."*)

The result of the critical examination of the New Testament by the Martian is that just as most of the Old Testament books are not only anonymous but highly composite productions, that as certain writings traditionally ascribed to Moses, David, Solomon, Daniel, and others are utterly lacking in the necessary evidences in support of authorship, but bear unmistakable evidence of having gone through a long compilatory process; so does each gospel, despite its seeming unity, give evidence of being a composite literary product. Scholars have agreed that Mark first set forth the doings of Jesus and "it was out of Mark that both Matthew and Luke took the framework of their own writings, cleverly fitting into its arrangement their own distinctive material and coloring the whole by their own individual treatment." (*Trattner, "Unravelling the Book of Books."*) It is estimated that Mark was written shortly before the Romans destroyed Jerusalem in 70 A.D. "This means that a chasm of 30 or 40 years separates Mark's written document from the ministry of Jesus—a long enough time to create a plastic body of oral teachings and a highly colored tradition embellished with fanciful stories."

Luke was a Greek physician living somewhere on the shores of the Ægean Sea. He had been a friend of Paul, just as Mark had been with Peter. Luke had no personal acquaintance with Jesus and had to get his information from what others said, or from what the friends of "eyewitnesses" had seen.

The Gospel of "Matthew" is an anonymous composition which, on analysis, has been found to incorporate nearly fifty per cent of what is found in Mark. It is now believed by many scholars to have been written between the years 75 and 80 A.D. at Antioch not, of course, by the Apostle Matthew, but by some unknown editor.

The Fourth Gospel, the Gospel of John, is vastly different in style, arrangement, and in the description of the words, actions, and general spiritual character of Jesus. Many scholars believe that it was written in the city of Ephesus, somewhere around the year 100 A.D. "Church tradition ascribed it to the Apostle John, the son of Zebedee, one of the fishermen whom Jesus called to be a disciple. Years ago this view was easily entertained, but there now exists too much refractory evidence against assigning this Greek Gospel to an Aramaic-speaking Galilean. That an untutored fisherman could have written so elaborate and so highly philosophical an account of Jesus has always presented a thorny problem. And so to most scholars John's authorship of the Fourth Gospel is unthinkable."

Not one of the Gospels is the work of an eyewitness, and the four Gospels do not complete each other; they contradict each other; and when they do not contradict, they repeat each other. The Christ of John is a totally different person from the Christ of Mark, Matthew, and Luke. Loisy, in his *"Quelques Lettres,"* states, "If there is one thing above others that is obvious, but as to which the most powerful of theological interests have caused a deliberate or unconscious blindness, it is the profound, the irreducible incompatibility of the Synoptical Gospels, and the Fourth Gospel. If Jesus spoke and acted as he is said to have spoken and acted in the first three Gospels, he did not speak and act as he is reported to have done in the fourth."

The Martian is forced to the conclusion that the New

Testament, with its version of the Virgin Birth, Elizabeth, the cousin of Mary, Zacharias and the Angel Gabriel, Jesus and the Sinner, are on par with the eroticism of the Old Testament. The interpolations, the myth, and fable also compare with the first revelation, and, in his opinion, he prefers Andersen's Fairy Tales, or Æsop's Fables.

Meanwhile, a Protestant Brother mentions the name of Luther, and the conclusions he draws are that the exciting cause of the Reformation was an extravagant sale of indulgences conceded to the German Dominicans. The Augustinians grew jealous of the Dominicans, and an Augustinian Monk, Martin Luther, affixed to the door of Wittenberg Cathedral ninety-five articles against the abuse of indulgences. This started the fray in Germany with Luther at the head of this heresy. The gravest difference of opinion had to do with the Communion. "Luther retained one-half of the mystery, and rejected the other half. He confesses that the body of Jesus Christ is in the consecrated element, but it is, he says, as fire is in the red-hot iron. The fire and the iron subsist together. This is what they called impanation, invincation, consubstantiation. Thus, while those they called Papists ate God without bread, the Lutherans ate God and bread; soon afterwards came the Calvinists, who ate bread and did not eat God." In short, Luther was in harmony with the Roman Church in nothing but the doctrines of the Trinity, Baptism, the Incarnation, and the Resurrection. Luther thought it was time to abolish private mass. He pretended the devil had appeared to him and reproached him for saying mass and consecrating the elements. The devil had proved to him, he said, that it was idolatry. Luther declared that the devil was right and must be believed. The mass was abolished in Wittenberg, and soon afterwards throughout Saxony; the images were thrown down, monks and nuns left their cloisters, and, a few years later, Luther married a nun called Catharine von Bora. This tale did not greatly impress our guest.

A Catholic Brother, not to be outdone, extols the glories of his Universal Church, and the Martian again sets out to investigate. This time he finds:

The quotations in the New Testament which the Catholic creed interprets as giving divine authority to its representatives on earth is a late interpolation; the Trinity as stated above is a paradox which no rational being can understand, and its dogmas and idolatry are consistent with a civilization of 4000 years ago.

A study of the lives of its popes put to shame the statement that they could possibly be the earthly representatives of a Benevolent Being. "In the ninth and tenth centuries the papacy passed through a period of shameful disorder. The Rome of John X was a cloaca in which the Popes set the example of the worst misconduct." (For a good short account of the lives of the popes, see Draper's, "History of the Intellectual

Development of Europe.")

During the complete control by the Church of civilization in Europe, it has retarded the progress of humanity for at least 2000 years, and its precepts and fundamental principles are today detrimental to the advance of mankind. It has to its credit a long series of judicial murders for differences of opinion. The Crusades, instigated by the popes and seconded by the monks, cost millions of lives and exhausted the resources of Christian Europe; they aggravated fanaticism, exaggerated the worship of saints and relics to the point of mania, and encouraged the abuse of and traffic in indulgences. There had never been a single opinion persecuted by the Church in the Middle Ages the adoption of which would not have brought about a diminution of her revenues; the Church has always primarily considered her finances. The papacy was responsible for the Inquisition, and it actively encouraged and excited its ferocity. It gave birth to the Witchcraft Mania. The first Grand Inquisitor, Torquemada, received the congratulations of the Pope. It diabolically applauded the St. Bartholomew Massacre, and instigated the numerous religious wars that tore Europe asunder, and was the cause of the loss of hundreds of thousands of lives and incalculable suffering. With such savage alacrity did it carry out its object of protecting the interests of religion that between 1481 and 1808 it had punished three hundred and forty thousand persons, and of these, nearly 32,000 had been burnt.

"It is perfectly certain that the Catholic Church has taught, and still teaches that intellectual liberty is dangerous, that it should be forbidden. It was driven to take this position because it had taken another. It taught, and still teaches, that a certain belief is necessary to salvation. It has always known that investigation and inquiry led, or might lead, to doubt; that doubt leads, or may lead, to heresy, and that heresy leads to Hell. In other words, the Catholic Church has something more important than this world, more important than the well-being of man here. It regards this life as an opportunity for joining that Church, for accepting that creed, and for the saying of your soul. If the history of the world proves anything, it proves that the Catholic Church was for many centuries the most merciless institution that ever existed among men. We, too, know that the Catholic Church was, during all the years of its power, the enemy of every science. It preferred magic to medicine, relics to remedies, priests to physicians. It hated geologists, persecuted the chemists, and imprisoned the naturalists, and opposed every discovery of science calculated to improve the condition of mankind. There is no crime that the Catholic Church did not commit, no cruelty that it did not reward, and no virtue that it did not persecute. It was the greatest and most powerful enemy of human rights. In one hand, it carried an alms dish, and in the other, a dagger. It argued with the sword, persecuted with poison, and convicted with faggot." R. G. Ingersoll, *"Rome or Reason."*

"From the time of Newton to our own day, the divergence of science from the dogmas of the Church has steadily increased. The Church declared that the earth is the central and most important body in the Universe, that the sun and moon and stars are tributary to it. On these points she was worsted by astronomy. She affirmed that a universal deluge had covered the earth; that the only surviving animals were such as had been saved in the Ark. In this, her error was established by geology. She taught that there was a first man who, some 6000 or 8000 years ago, was suddenly created or called into existence in a condition of physical and moral perfection, and from that condition he fell. But anthropology has shown that human beings existed far back in geological time, and in a savage state but little better than that of the brute. . . . Convicted of so many errors, the papacy makes no attempt at explanation. It ignores the whole matter. Nay, more, relying on the efficacy of audacity, although confronted by these facts, it lays claim to infallibility."

The persecutions of Bruno, Galileo, and Copernicus, together with the facts hitherto stated, did not impress the Martian with the "infallibility" of the Church. The only great spiritual power that could have interposed to prevent the outbreak of the World War was the papacy. Pope Pius X had his Nuncio admonish the Austrian emperor, but he failed even to get an audition from that old imbecile. The next Pope, Benedict XV, was under the influence of a majority of pro-

German cardinals. He strove to remain neutral. He attempted to solace the Belgians with words, but he did not reprove the murderous invaders. He protested against the new and devilish methods of warfare but he did not condemn, he did not excommunicate those that used them. Had the papacy lost its much-used power of commanding kings and nations, and had it lost its greatest threat, a threat which hitherto could have thrown the masses of its adherents into a panic, the threat of excommunication? No, the papacy still blessed the banners of the armies, just as it did during the middle ages, and sent its adherents out to slaughter; but first took great care that the minds of the devout be completely drugged with the poison of its creed. A creed that told its followers that do what you might, no matter how dastardly that act might be, so long as you repent and confess your sins, life everlasting will be the reward. What is the value of a church that has claimed the moral leadership of the world when such things can happen?

Now that the Martian has become acquainted with the three major religions which dominate the world, Judaism, Christianity, and Mohammedanism, and has been amazed and shocked at the significance of their teachings in the history of civilization, his curiosity is further aroused, and he decides to obtain some information of the respective personalities responsible for the amassing of devotees to these creeds, all "infallible," and all detrimental to progress. This time his interest leads him to ancient and contemporary sources, of a literal rather than verbal nature; sources dealing with the three most influential prophets in the history of mankind, Jesus, Moses, and Mohammed.

CHAPTER III

THE PROPHETS MOHAMMED, JESUS, AND MOSES CHARLATANS OR VICTIMS OF MENTAL AND PHYSICAL DISEASE

The prophet or seer is a man of strong imaginative powers, which have not been calmed by education. The ideas which occur to his mind often present themselves to his eyes and ears in corresponding sights and sounds. . . . Prophets have existed in all countries and at all times; but the gift becomes rare in the same proportion as people learn to read and write.

WINWOOD READE.

RELIGIOUS apologists are forever reminding us that we must interpret both the lives and the works of their prophets and recorders in the spirit and meaning of the ages in which they lived. To this I agree; but the apologists have so mutilated the meaning of the words of the seers and built about them such a mass of nonsense, myth, and fable that it becomes nearly impossible after the lapse of centuries to differentiate the actual

78

man from the fabled man. But there are certain facts that do come down to us recorded by disinterested observers from which can be derived finally some conception of their mode of life, and the content and significance of their teachings.

Although time causes great changes in customs and manners, it only effects a negligible variation in the vast majority of diseases which affect the body and mind of man. We know from the examination of the skeletal remains of prehistoric man that the diseases of the bone of thousands of years ago were similar in their manifestations to those same diseases of bone of today. From the writings of the early Egyptian, Greek, and Roman physicians we identify diseases by their symptoms, and recognize that the symptoms of these diseases, have not changed throughout the ages. Therefore, with the knowledge of the signs and symptoms of various diseases which we have today, we can safely assert that if an ancient complained of the same group of signs and symptoms (which is now termed a "disease complex"), he was suffering from the same disease which we can identify in modern man.

What applies to physical disease is just as applicable to mental disease. In speaking of mental disease, it is important for the layman to keep in mind a few fundamental principles held by the physician. The physician in speaking of mental disease means a more or less permanent departure from the normal or usual way of thinking, acting, or feeling. In the examination of a patient with mental disease the physician looks for delusions, illusions, and hallucinations.

A delusion is a false belief, concerning which the individual who holds it is unable to admit evidence such as would be admitted by ordinary individuals.

An illusion is a deception of the senses, a misinterpretation of sensory impressions; the normal person can be convinced of this deception. The mirage, for example, is an optical illusion which has a starting point in an external stimulus.

A hallucination is a deception of any of the five senses, in which there is no starting point but it is fabricated in a disordered mind. Illustrations of hallucinations are the hearing of voices when none are present, smelling of odors, the seeing of visions in a vacuum.

With the elementary understanding of fundamental symptoms of mental diseases as a point of departure, let us consider the cases of Mohammed, Jesus, and Moses, three of the most influential prophets in the history of civilization.

MOHAMMED

Of the three, Mohammed should be considered before the others for several reasons. First, there is no question regarding the actual existence of Mohammed. We know that he was born at Mecca about 571 A.D. and died at Medina on June

8th, 632 A.D. From the facts of his life and the religion which he founded we are able to see the manner in which legend and superstition were superimposed on its original simple form. The historical records of his life and teachings are easier of access since he is nearer our time than the other two prophets, and we can get a better understanding of his character.

It was Gibbon who said, "It may be expected that I should balance his faults and his virtues, that I should decide whether the title of enthusiast or impostor more properly belongs to that extraordinary man. . . . At the distance of twelve centuries, I darkly contemplate his shade through a cloud of incense."

In attempting to peer through this cloud of religious incense we find the following facts: In the city of Mecca, probably in August, in the year 571, Mohammed, the Prophet of Allah, was born. There seems little doubt that he was descended from those lofty Koreish, whose opposition, which at first nearly succeeded in holding his name in perpetual oblivion, eventually caused him to emerge into the light of deathless fame.

His birth was surrounded by all manner of signs and omens, we are told. The labor of his mother, Amina, was entirely painless, earthquakes loosed the bases of mountains and caused great bodies of water, whose names were unfortunately not specified, to wither away or overflow; the sacred fire of Zoroaster which, under the jealous care of the

Magi, had spouted ceaseless flames for nearly a thousand years, was extinguished. All the idols in the world except the Kaaba tumbled to earth. Immediately after the babe was born an ethereal light dazzled the surrounding territory, and, on the very moment when his eyes were first opened, he lifted them to heaven and exclaimed: "God is great! There is no God but Allah and I am his Prophet!" All these poetic fancies have been appropriately denounced by Christian scribes, who have claimed that nature would never have dignified the birth of a pagan like Mohammed with such marvelous prodigies as undoubtedly attended the advent of Christ.

However, Mohammed was born shortly after the death of his father. At the age of six his mother died also, and he spent the first ten years among the Bedouins under the care of a foster-mother named Halima. At the age of four it was noticed that the child had signs of convulsive seizures which later commentators thought were of an epileptic nature. He was brought up under the care of his uncle Abu Talib, and his early manhood was spent in caring for the flock and in attending caravan expeditions.

When the prophet was twenty-five years old, his uncle secured for him a position with a caravan owned by a wealthy widow, Khadija. Thanks to Mohammed's keen business sense the caravan was highly successful, and he was induced to personally report his success to Khadija. That lady, a wealthy widow of forty years, and the mother of three children, was highly pleased at Mohammed's story. As she listened to the proof of his business ability and fondly scanned his large, nobly formed head, his curling coal-black hair, his piercing eyes, and his comely form, it naturally occurred to her that this vigorous and handsome young fellow would make an excellent successor to her deceased husband. She had her way and they were married. During the next fifteen years Mohammed led a tranquil life. His future was provided for and he had plenty of leisure to occupy himself as he chose. In these years Mohammed and his wife continued to be conventional worshipers of idols, who nightly performed rites in honor of various gods and goddesses, among whom were Allah and his female consoler Al-Lat. And so, by the year 610, Mohammed, at the age of forty, was nothing more than a respectable but unknown tradesman who had experienced no extraordinary crises, whose few existing utterances were dull and insipid, and whose life seemed destined to remain as insignificant and unsung as any other Arab's.

At this time, he began to retire for days at a time to a cave in the foothills of Mount Hira, a hill several miles north of Mecca. Meanwhile his business languished. As the months passed, he still continued to act in the same incomprehensible manner; it was noticed that little by little certain members of his immediate family attended him to his refuge or gathered with him in some one of their houses. This continued for several years until, it was rumored that Mohammed, the camel driver, was confidently claiming the honor of having made a great discovery; namely, that "There is no God but Allah, and Mohammed is His Prophet."

By what process of thought had Mohammed come to exalt Allah not merely above all Arabian gods, but above the gods of all times? Furthermore, why was he so certain of his own intimate association with Allah? We can understand this if we consider Mohammed in the light of a victim of mental disease.

One account informs us that as Mohammed was wandering near the cave at Mount Hira, "an angel from the sky cried to him, 'O Mohammed, I am Gabriel!' " He was terrified and hurried home to impart his experience to his wife.

"I see a light," he said to his wife, "and I hear a sound. I fear that I am possessed." This idea was most distressing to a pious man. He became pale, haggard; he wandered about on the hill near Mecca crying for help to God. More than once he drew near the edge of the cliff and was tempted to hurl himself down, and so put an end to his misery at once. He lived much in the open air, gazing on the stars, watching the dry ground grow green beneath the gentle rain. He pondered also on the religious legends of the Jews, which he had heard related on his journeys; and as he looked and thought, the darkness was dispelled, the clouds disappeared, and the vision of God in solitary grandeur rose within his mind, and there came upon him an impulse to speak of God. There came upon him a belief that he was a messenger of God sent on earth to restore the religion of Abraham, which the pagan Arabs had polluted with idolatry, the Jews in corrupting their holy books. At the same time he heard a Voice, and sometimes he felt a noise in his ears like the tinkling of bells or a low deep hum, as if bees were swarming round his head.

At this period of his life the chapters of the Koran were delivered in throes of pain. The paroxysms were preceded by depression of spirit, his face became clouded, his extremities turned cold, he shook like a man in an ague, and he called for coverings. His face assumed an expression horrible to see, the vein between his eyebrows became distended his eyes were fixed, his head moved to and fro, as if he was conversing, and then he gave forth the oracle or Sura.

The hitherto mentally and emotionally normal trader, husband, and father was thus suddenly swept off his feet and carried irresistibly away on a mighty tide. His perturbed spirit now soared to the heights of Heaven, now plunged into the chasms of hell. Moments of ethereal bliss would be followed by periods of profoundest melancholy.

"It is related that the Angel Gabriel, who thus far had labored only in the field of Christian endeavor, was chosen by Allah as bearer of the divine revelation to Mohammed. One day, while the trader-poet was wrestling with his doubts among the foothills of Mount Hira, he saw a wondrous apparition floating downward on celestial wings. 'Thou art God's Prophet, and I am Gabriel,' announced the awe-inspiring guest before he departed to receive the blessing of Allah for having so successfully executed the heavenly command. Gabriel was a very valuable ambassador, for through the to-and-fro journeying of this indefatigable messenger Allah was able to remain at ease in heaven, thus keeping up the appearance of intangible, majestic remoteness so necessary for dignified gods. And thus Mohammed came into his own. From that moment Mohammed looked upon himself as Allah's vice regent, through whom Allah's incontestable decrees were to be given to man." (*Mohammed—R. F. Dibble.*) Mohammed's every doubt had now vanished, his soul was completely at ease, and from his lips there burst the wildly exultant chant, "There is no God but Allah and Mohammed is His Prophet."

The obliging Gabriel, he said, had borne him on a winged steed over Medina to the Temple of Jerusalem, and from there he continued his celestial journey until he was carried completely out of this world to those ethereal realms of bliss where the Seven Heavens are. Up and up he flew, while he carefully noted the order of precedence of those prophets whose model he had proclaimed himself to be. Jesus and John were in the second or third—he was not quite sure which—Moses was in the sixth, while Abraham alone had the supreme distinction of residing in the Seventh Heaven. There, at the apex of indescribable glory, Mohammed had entered the awful presence of his Maker, Who, after some chit-chat, charged him to see that all Moslems should hereafter prostrate themselves in prayer toward the Temple of Solomon five times a day. The truth of this narrative rests upon two solid facts: from that day to this, all devout Moslems have continued to bow themselves five times daily in prayer, and sceptics may still see, upon the rock where stands the Mosque of Omar in Jerusalem, the identical print of the Prophet's foot where he leaped upon the Heavenly Charger.

His thoughts, whether conceived in a white heat of frenzy, or with deliberate coolness and sly calculations for the main chance, were probably not written down in any definite manner during his lifetime. It is not even certain whether he could read or write. He delighted in the appellation, "The Illiterate Prophet," possibly on account of his humility and possibly because he knew that inspired ignorance had been the indisputable prerogative of all successful prophets in the past. Indeed, the very fact that he was unlearned was rightly supposed to increase the miraculous nature of his revelations. As he tossed the divine emanations from his lips, they were sometimes recorded by hireling scribes upon palm leaves, leather, stones, the shoulder blades or ribs of camels and goats. But often they were not immediately written down at all; the Prophet would go around spouting forth his utterances to his followers, who, trained from infancy to memorize verses and songs of every sort with infallible precision, would piously commit them to memory. Such is the Koran, and through its instrumentality, Allah the Wise, The Only Wise, revealed his immutable decrees: to the good, the rewards of a Paradise that utterly beggared the Christian Heaven; to the bad, the punishments of a Hell that contained an infinity of such refined tortures of heat, and even of cold as neither the most imaginatively gifted Jew or Christian had yet conceived.

Reinach aptly states, "It is humiliating to the human intellect to think that this mediocre literature has been the subject of innumerable commentaries and that millions of men are still wasting time in absorbing it." Over one hundred and sixty million are adherents of the Koran.

In an objective analysis, excluding the emotional factors of religious bias, Mohammed would as unquestionably be considered a victim of mental disturbances as an individual living in our own day and manifestng the same symptoms.

Mohammed was the subject of illusions, hallucinations, and delusions. He had suicidal tendencies, and he had alternating periods of exhilaration and depression. To simply assert that he was an epileptic does not explain these symptoms. For epileptics cannot throw a fit at will. However, we know that ten per cent of epileptics develop mental diseases, no particular psychosis but a loss of mental and moral sense.

There are two types of individuals who can produce seizures such as Mohammed was wont to evoke at will. One type is the hysterical, and the other is that degraded individual who for the sake of collecting alms will place a piece of soap in his mouth, enter a crowded street, fall to the ground, and proceed to foam at the mouth and twist and contort himself as an epileptic does. That is the charlatan, the faker, and that brings us to the second aspect of his (Mohammed's) character.

"Outside of Arabia, Paganism was in general disrepute. The dissolute and declining Romans were cracking lewd jokes in the very faces of their gods, the myriad followers of Confucius, Buddha and Zoroaster were either too remote or too helpless to matter in one way or another. Talmudic Judaism and Oriental Christianity despised idolatry and worshipped the same Jehovah, even though they disputed with each other, and indeed, among themselves, concerning the various attributes, amorous pursuits, and lineal descendants of the Godhead. Now, to one who chose to regard himself as a prophet, Monotheism had distinct advantages over Polytheism." (*Mohammed—R. F. Dibble.*)

In the first place, it was rather confusing to attempt to obey the behests of conflicting deities; in the second place, the different prophets of Jehovah in Judaism and Christendom had, so far as Mohammed knew, been uniformly successful, for he was familiar with the glorious history of Abraham, Moses, and David, and he always held to the perverse conception that Jesus was not crucified. However deep in the dumps prophets may have been on occasion, they have invariably believed one thing: victory for their particular cause would inevitably come. Neither an unbroken series of worldly failures nor the chastisement of his god have ever shaken the faith of a first-class prophet in himself or, as he would doubtless prefer to say, in his Divinity. Arabia, broken, unorganized, inglorious, idolistic Arabia, obviously lacked one Supreme Being whose prerogative was greater than all other Supreme Beings, and that Being, in turn, needed a messenger to exploit His supremacy. The messengers who had served Jehovah had certainly prospered well; but Jehovah Himself appeared to be on the decline. His Unity was steadily disintegrating into a paradoxical Trinity. Why, therefore, not give Allah, the leading icon in Arabia, an opportunity? Such considerations quite probably never entered the head of Mohammed with any definiteness; yet his behavior for the rest of his days seems to indicate that these, or similar conceptions, were subconsciously egging him on.

Of certain facts, moreover, he was definitely aware. He may have had little or no formal education, but his memory was retentive and capacious, and his caravan journeys, together with the scores of conversations he had held at the yearly fairs, as well as at Mecca, with many cultivated strangers, had packed his mind with a mass of highly valuable matter. In these ways he had learned both the strength and the weakness of the Jews and Christians; their fanatical enthusiasm and despairs; their spasmodic attempts to proselytize as well as the widespread defection from their faiths. "Since his conception of religion was largely personal, for he looked upon Moses, Jesus, and the rest of the prophets as merely capable men who had founded and promulgated religions; and since Arabia had no pre-eminent ruler, why should he not seize the reins of power and carry on the great tradition of prophethood? What a magnificent opportunity beckoned, and how fortunate that he had been the first to recognize the call! By keeping only what was best of the Arabic faith, the Kaaba and the Black Stone, and by a judicious selection of the most feasible ideas which lay imbedded in Jewish and Christian precepts, he might establish a code that would supersede all others, and then might dictate to all Arabs alike. What prophets had done, he would also do and do better." (*Mohammed—R. F. Dibble.*)

Such are the thoughts of a charlatan and a demagogue. If Mohammed actually had such ideas, we can never know; but a study of his further actions and conquests surely shows that he must have had something of the same trend of thought in mind.

His "fits" before the oncoming of a new Sura have been mentioned. Eventually, he so perfected his technique that he could throw a cataleptic fit and produce a message without any previous preparation. He would drum up a crowd with his ludicrous snortings and puffings until the resounding cry, "Inspiration hath descended on the Prophet!" assured him that he had a sufficiently large audience to warrant the out-spurting of a new Sura. While in a room that was obviously empty, he declared that all seats were occupied by angels; he cultivated suave and benign expression; he flattered and astounded his followers by telling them facts which he had presumably acquired through private information; he took the most painstaking care of his person, painting his eyes and perfuming his entire body daily, and wearing his hair long. Ayesha, one of the Prophet's wives, remarked that the Prophet loved three things: women, scent and food, and that he had his heart's content of the first two, but not of the last. In fact, Mohammed, himself, argued that these two innocuous diversions intensified the ecstasy of his prayers. In the Koran's description of heaven so much emphasis was put on food that a jolly Jew objected on the grounds that such continual feasting must of necessity be followed by a purgation. The Prophet, however, swore that it would not even be necessary to blow the nose in Paradise, since all bodily impurities would be carried off by a perspiration "as odoriferous as musk."

When his wife Khadija was dying he comforted her with the assurance that she, together with three other well-known women, the Virgin Mary, Potiphar's wife, and "Kulthum," Moses' sister, would occupy his chamber in Paradise.

On Mohammed's escape to Medina, a long series of holy wars began which, like all holy wars, were characterized by extreme brutality. The Koran of the period contains such pacific doctrines as these: "The sword is the key of Heaven and Hell; a drop of blood shed in the cause of God, a night spent in arms is of more avail than two months of fasting or prayer; whosoever falls in battle, his sins are forgiven. At the day of Judgment his wounds shall be resplendent as vermilion, and odoriferous as musk; and the loss of limbs shall be supplied by the wings of angels and cherubim . . . God loveth not the Transgressors; kill them wheresoever ye find them."

Mohammed, no less than many other religiously-minded emperors and tsars, appears to have conducted himself in battle according to the wise principle that a head without a halo is infinitely more desirable than a halo without a head. Yet he was profoundly convinced that the ultimate victory of Islam depended upon the sword. The Koran of this period breathes defiance against the enemies of Islam on almost every page. Its profuse maledictions, once confined to the evildoers of Mecca, now include all unbelievers everywhere. When Mohammed once had captured a fortress inhabited by a tribe of Jews, his judgment was, "The men shall be put to death, the women and children sold into slavery, and the spoil divided amongst the army." Then, trenches were dug, some seven hundred men were marched out, forced to seat themselves in rows along the top of the trenches, beheaded, and then tumbled into a long gaping grave. Meanwhile, the Prophet looked on until, tiring of the monotonous spectacle, he departed to amuse himself with a Jewess whose husband had just perished.

He continued these conquests until, at his death, in 632, he was the master of nearly all Arabia and revered almost as a god. Yet, when Omar, his first lieutenant, captured Jerusalem in 636, he ensured the conquered Jews and Christians free exercise of their religion, and the security of their persons and their goods. But when the Crusaders took Jerusalem in 1099, they massacred all the Mohammedans, and burnt the Jews alive. It is estimated that 70,000 persons were put to death in less than a week to attest the superior morality of the Christian faith.

The successors of Mohammed, the Caliphs, in less than a century conquered Syria, Egypt, Babylonia, Persia, Turkestan, Spain, Northern Africa, Sicily, and Southern France. Today, 160,000,000 are followers of Mohammed,—a man who began as a humble religious leader, and ended as an adroit politician and powerful general; a man who hid during battles, who often broke faith with friend and foe alike, a charlatan and demagogue of general intellectual incompetency, and a victim of mental disease.

JESUS

When we come to consider the life of Jesus, a far different

and more intricate problem is met with. None but the most illogical and purposely ignorant of religious apologists will admit that the life of Jesus has been misrepresented by his followers to suit their particular aims. Had the followers of the moralist Epictetus or the Rabbi Hillel written lives of these two teachers they would be quite similar to the reputed life of Jesus. The moral sentiments attributed to Christ in the Gospels were borrowed from the Jewish rabbis and the numerous cults that flourished in that age. The birth, death, and resurrection of Christ is quite similar to the myths of that time concerning the savior gods Adonis, Isis, Osiris, Attis, Mithra, and a multitude of others. (*For a full exposition of the subject, the reader is referred to E. Carpenter, "Pagan and Christian Creeds."*)

The evidence for the point of view that Jesus was actually a historic character is so slight that such scholars as J. M., Robertson, Prof. W. B. Smith, Professor Drews, Dr. P. L. Couchoud, and many others deny the historic reality of Christ on the ground that the Gospels are totally unreliable as history, that Paul bears no witness to a human Jesus, and that the pagan and Jewish writers are strangely silent about the Messiah Jesus.

There are in existence only twenty-four lines from Jewish and Pagan writers referring to Jesus. These include a reference in Tacitus' Annals, and brief references by Suetonius and Pliny the Younger. These three references are considered spurious by many scholars, and even if they were all to be accepted it would mean that the total pagan testimony as to the historicity of Jesus is confined to three very vague and brief references written a century after the reputed time of Jesus. The longest reference to Jesus is in the writings of the Jewish historian, Josephus. The passage referring to Jesus in his "Jewish Antiquities" has been considered as spurious even by conservative scholars. A group of scholars has always deemed it very probable, however, that this spurious reference may have replaced an unfavorable reference to Jesus in the original. Working on this theory, Dr. Eisler has purged of interpolations this work by a painstaking and scholarly investigation.

However, it must be pointed out that with regard to Jesus' actual existence, what divided the Christians and non-Christians was not the question whether or not Jesus existed; but the vastly more pertinent and essentially different question whether or not the obscure Galilean carpenter, executed by a Roman governor as king pf the Jews, was really a superhuman being who had overcome death, the longed-for-savior of mankind, foretold by the Prophets, the only-begotten Son of God Himself.

To the Jews, Jesus was indeed a heretic and an agitator of the lower orders; to the pagans, he was a magician who through sham miracles and with subversive words had incited the people to rebellion, and as a leader of a gang of desperate men had attempted to seize the royal crown of Judæa, as others had done before and after him. The non-Christian waiters referred to Jesus as a wizard, a demagogue, and a rebel.

We are fortunate, at this date, to have brought to our attention a masterful work by Dr. Robert Eisler, a work which will be as revolutionary to the study of Christianity as was Darwin's "Origin of the Species" in the realms of science; and, similarly, the former work will be the basis upon which much progress will be made in a great field. Dr. Eisler unfolds a great mass of hitherto unknown information concerning the life, the actual appearance, and the doings of Jesus. He definitely establishes the proof of Jesus' actual existence, and makes clear many hitherto obscure utterances and deeds of this Prophet.

The descriptions which follow are based on the material in this work of Dr. Eisler, "The Messiah Jesus."

In the complete statement of Josephus on Pilate's governorship, we find, "At that time there appeared a certain man of magical power, if it is permissible to call him a man, whom certain Greeks call a Son of God, but his disciples, the True Prophet, said to raise the dead, and heal all diseases. His nature and his form were human; a man of simple appearance, mature age, small in stature, three cubits high, *hunchbacked*, with a long face, long nose, and meeting eyebrows, so that they who see him might be affrighted, with scanty hair but with a parting in the middle of his head, after the manner of the Nazarites, and with an undeveloped beard. Only in semblance was he superhuman for he gave some astonishing and spectacular exhibitions. But again, if I look at his commonplace physique, I, for one, cannot call him an angel. And everything whatsoever he wrought through some invisible power, he wrought through some word and a command. Some said of him, 'Our first law giver is risen again, and displays many healings and magic arts. Others said, 'He is sent from God.' Howbeit in many things he disobeyed the law and kept not the Sabbath according to our fathers' custom.

"And many of the multitude followed after him and accepted his teachings, and many souls were excited, thinking that thereby the Jewish tribes might be freed from Roman hands. But it was his custom most of the time to abide over against the city on the Mount of Olives, and there, too, he bestowed his healings upon the people. And there assembled unto him of helpers one hundred and fifty, and a multitude of the mob.

"Now, when they saw his power, how he accomplished whatsoever he would by a magic word, and when they had made known to him their will, that he should enter into the city, cut down the Roman troops, and Pilate and rule over us, he disdained us not. And having all flocked into Jerusalem, they raised an uproar against Pilate, uttering, blasphemies alike against God and against Cæsar.

"And when knowledge of it came to the Jewish leaders, they assembled together, with the high priests and spake, 'We are powerless and too weak to withstand the Romans. But seeing that the 'bow is bent,' we will go and impart to Pilate what we have heard, and we shall be safe, lest he hear of it from others and we be robbed of our substance and ourselves slaughtered, and the children of Israel dispersed.

"And they went and imparted the matter to Pilate, and he sent and had many of the multitude slain. And he had that wonder-worker brought up, and after instituting an inquiry concerning him, he passed this sentence upon him, 'He is a malefactor, a rebel, a robber thirsting for the crown.' And they took him and crucified him according to the custom of their fathers."

Such is the history of Jesus as contrasted with the myth of Jesus in the New Testament. This description of the actual appearance of Jesus for the first time gives us a clue to the mental and physical characteristics of this Prophet.

It must be borne in mind that at the time that Jesus achieved manhood, his people and his nation were under the complete domination of Rome, and oppressed by a race whom the Jews looked upon as cursed barbarians and idolaters. The country was overrun with religious zealots who stormed over the cities and villages preaching the immediate destruction of the world and the proximity of the long-awaited coming of the Messiah.

The fact that Jesus had to bear the hard fate of a deformed body may go far in helping to explain this remarkable character. It is common knowledge how frequently weak and deformed children have to suffer from the cruelty and neglect of environment, a factor which cannot but produce a peculiar reaction on the childish mind which has a far-reaching effect in later life. This accounts for Jesus' indifference towards his mother and brothers; of a delicate constitution, he must have suffered from insults a great deal more than the others, which throws some light on the severe punishment demanded by Jesus for comparatively harmless insults. Under such circumstances it is easy to explain how every "neighbor," and next-of-kin, although to the weak naturally an "enemy," came to be included in the sphere of that all-embracing love which is the nucleus of Jesus' teaching. For the cripple has to face the dilemma either of warping everything into a powerful, misanthropic hatred, or else to overcome this feeling of revenge for the high moral superiority of a Plato, Mendelssohn, or a Kant. Jesus chose the latter of the two courses, and we may well imagine that it was not at Golgotha that he had the first occasion to cry out, "Father, forgive them for they know not what they do!"

In the case of Jesus, the whole paradoxical thought of his

being the vicarious sin-offering and world redeemer can best be understood as the solution, proposed in the Deutero-Isaiah, of the question which had occupied Job—to wit: Why must the innocent suffer? If the maimed in body refuse to consider himself as forsaken by his God, as a sinner punished for some guilt of which he is unconscious, he cannot but assume that there is such a thing as a vocation to suffering, and believe in the inscrutable plan of salvation in which his own life and sufferings are called upon to play some part. Nothing but this conviction of being thus elected can afford him the desired compensation for his depressed and hampered ego.

A repressed nature of this type will, in seeking such a compensation, escape from the harsh reality into the realm of dreams. This is the basis of what the physician recognizes in hysteria, and in the mental disease termed "Dementia Præcox." The glorious daydreams of the millennium, the time of bliss when all strife and all hate will disappear from the earth, when all the crooked will be made straight, find their best explanation in this peculiarity. They console the suffering and heavy-laden for the bitter reality which, in the light of the old messianic prophecies, appears only as a nightmare, promptly to be chased away by the dawn of a new day, a new, a perfect era. The Davidic Jesus, in spite or rather because of his servile form, feels that he is himself the secret incognito king of that wonderful realm, the monarch whom God some time in the future, nay, right here and before the passing of the present generation, will transform while at the same time "revealing" his kingdom.

It is but natural that in the mental development of such individuals they should seek to be great, glorious, and to achieve the supernatural, since they, themselves, are denied the ordinary satisfactions. If, in addition, such individuals believe that they have had a divine call, if the disability of the body so preys on the mind that the sensitive structure gives way to delusions, then there results an aberration from the normal and usual processes of thought,—to be sure not the rabid, violent form of mental disease, but yet a deviation from the normal manner of thinking. Such was the case with the Prophet Jesus.

Afflicted in body but endowed with a sensitive mind, exposed to an unusual environment of seething unrest and political ferment, and firmly convinced in the current fancies regarding the approaching destruction of the world, the conquest of the Evil Power, and the Reign of God, Jesus became the subject of a delusion that he was the only true Messiah who had been presaged by the prophets of old.

The greatest difficulty encountered in every attempt to present the life and work of Jesus according to the evidence of his own words preserved in the sources is the sharp, irreconcilable contradiction between the so-called "fire and sword" sayings on the one side, and the beatitudes on the peacemakers and the meek, the prohibition to kill, to be angry, to resist wrong, and the command to love one's enemy, contained in the Sermon on the Mount, on the other.

In the early period of his messianic career, the period of the Sermon on the Mount, Jesus was a thorough quietist. But if we realize that the delusion that he was "The Messiah" had entered his mind so vehemently that he firmly believed that the end of the world was imminent, and that it was his duty to save as many as possible, we can understand his acquiescence to the violence which followed.

Moreover, he was clearly forced to the fatal road by the idea that he must set on foot a movement of hundreds of thousands, the picture of the exodus from Egypt with the fantastic figures given in the Old Testament. The Messianic rising he was to initiate could not be regarded as realized if he left the country with a band of some hundred elect. If he wished, however, to put at least two-fifths of the population in motion, the method of sending out messengers had proved altogether unsatisfactory. He must try the effect of his own words in a place where, and at a time when, he was sure to reach the greatest multitude of his people. That could only be in Jerusalem, at the time of the great pilgrimage at the feast of the Passover. Moreover, the desired result could only be obtained of course if he openly proclaimed himself to be the Messiah.

Then it was that the Prophet of quiet reversed his words and armed his disciples. Jesus was fully aware of the illegality of this arming of his disciples and of his own direction to purchase a weapon; none the less, he saw no escape from this bitter necessity. The prediction of the prophet must be fulfilled, according to which the righteous servant of the Lord must be numbered among the lawless transgressors. True it is that he did not lead the revolt himself, but tarried with his disciples at the Last Supper at a house near by the fighting. When he becomes aware that his secret hiding place on the Mount of Olives has been betrayed, Jesus hopes for a miracle from God up to the last. Captured, he is led away to the palace of the high priest's family on the Mount of Olives, where, while Jesus is questioned by the high priest, Peter, unrecognized, warms himself at the fire in the courtyard and thrice denies his master. He was then taken to the Roman governor's court-martial, where sentence was passed and he was led off to the place of execution and there deserted by all his followers except a few Galilean women. Then was heard the last despairing cry of the desolate, dying martyr, "My God, My God, why hast thou forsaken me?"

Thus ended the career of this deformed Prophet with the sensitive deluded mind; a martyr who attempted only to effect reforms amongst his own people, in his own small locality.

MOSES

With regard to the life, the deeds, and the words of the Prophet Moses we have no history; only myth and legend. The existence of Moses is not demonstrated by the Biblical books which are falsely ascribed to him, yet we cannot be certain that such a character did not exist. In any event, we must judge his character from the writings ascribed to him.

The legend of the child cast upon the waters is to be found in the folklore of all nations. This legend, concerning Moses, relates that one day Pharaoh's daughter, while bathing with her maids in the Nile, found a Hebrew child exposed on the waters in obedience to a new decree. She adopted the boy, gave him an Egyptian name, and brought him up in her palace as a prince. She had him educated and the fair inference is that he was schooled in the culture of the Egyptians. The royal lady made of the Hebrew slave-child an Egyptian gentleman.

Yet, although his face was shaved, and outwardly he appeared to be an Egyptian, at heart he remained a Hebrew. One day, when he was grown, Moses went slumming among his own people to look at their burdens, and he spied an Egyptian smiting a Hebrew. He was so overcome by passion at this scene that he killed the man on the spot. The crime became known, there was a hue and cry raised, and the king had a search made for Moses with the intention of slaying him. With all hope of a career in Egypt ended. Moses escaped to the Peninsula of Sinai, and entered the family of an Arab sheik.

The Peninsula of Sinai lies clasped between two arms of the Red Sea. It is a wilderness of mountains covered with a thin, almost transparent coating of vegetation which serves as pasture to the Bedouin flocks. Among the hills that crown the high plateau there is one which at the time of Moses was called the "Mount of God." It was holy ground to the Egyptians, and also to the Arabs, who ascended as pilgrims and drew off their sandals when they reached the top. Now is it strange that Sinai should have excited reverence and dread? It is indeed a weird land. Vast and stern stand the mountains, with their five granite peaks pointing to the sky. Avalanches like those of the Alps, but of sand, not of snow, rush down their naked sides with a clear tinkling sound. A peculiar property resides in the air, the human voice can be heard at a surprising distance and swells out into a reverberating roar, and sometimes there rises from among the hills a dull booming sound like the distant firing of heavy guns.

Let us attempt to realize what Moses must have felt when he was driven out of Egypt into such a harsh and rugged land. Imagine this man, the adopted son of a royal personage, who was accustomed to all the splendor of the Egyptian court, to the busy turmoil of the streets of the metropolis, to reclining in a carpeted gondola or staying with a noble at his country house. In a moment all is changed. He dwells in a tent, alone on the mountain side, a shepherd with a crook in his hand. He is married to the daughter of a barbarian; his career is at an end.

He realizes that never again will he enter that palace where once he, was received with honor, where now his name is uttered only with contempt. Never again will he discourse with grave and learned men in his favorite haunts, and never again will he see the people of his tribe whom he loves and for whom he endures this miserable fate. They will suffer but he will not help them; they will mourn, but he will not hear them. In his dreams he hears and sees them. He hears the whistling of the lash and the convulsive sobs and groans. He sees the poor slaves toiling in the fields and sees the daughters of Israel carried off to the harem with struggling arms and streaming hair. He sees the chamber of the woman in labor, the seated, shuddering, writhing form, the mother struggling against maternity, dreading her release, for the king's officer is standing by the door, ready, as soon as a male child is born, to put it to death.

The Arabs who gave him shelter were also children of Abraham, and they related to him legends of the ancient days. They told him of the patriarchs who lay buried in Canaan with their wives; they spoke of the God whom his fathers had worshiped. Then, as one who returns to a long lost home, the

Egyptian returned to the faith of the desert, to the God of Abraham, Isaac, and Jacob. As he wandered on the mountain heights, he looked to the west and saw a desert; beyond it lay Canaan, the home of his ancestors, a land of peace and soon to be a land of hope. For now, new ideas rose tumultuously within him. *He began to see visions and to dream dreams.* He heard voices and beheld no form; he saw trees which blazed with fire and yet were not consumed. He became a prophet and entered into the ecstatic stage. *That is, he began to have illusions and hallucinations.*

Dwelling on the misery and suffering of his people, his mind becomes deluded with the idea that he has been chosen by his new-found God to liberate his people from the tyranny of their oppressors.

Meanwhile the king had died, and a new Pharaoh had ascended the throne. Moses returns to Egypt to carry out the great designs which he had formed. He announces to the elders of his people, to the heads of the houses, and the sheiks of the tribes that the God of Abraham had appeared to him in Sinai and had revealed his true name. It was Jehovah. He had been sent by Jehovah to Egypt to bring away his people, to lead them to Canaan.

In company with his brother, Aaron, Moses asked Pharaoh to liberate the children of Israel, but after several vain attempts to dazzle Pharaoh with his skill as a magician, he was met with an obstinate refusal. Moses before Pharaoh descends to the level of a vulgar sorcerer, armed with a magic wand, whose performances only draw our smiles. This charlatanry having been unsuccessful, the wizard connives with his accomplice Jehovah to have inflicted upon the Egyptians the ten plagues. Then the loving and kind Father, having killed innumerable Egyptians, as the story relates, so terrorizes the minds of his other children in Egypt, that Pharaoh is finally convinced that he must allow the Chosen People to leave his domain. The Israelites quitted Egypt carrying away with them the gold and silver of their oppressors. They then entered the desert.

The magic art of Moses enabled them to pass dry-footed through the Red Sea, whereas the Pharaoh who was pursuing them was engulfed with his whole army. Again the Chosen People are liberated by means of the death of multitudes of Egyptians. Truly, Jehovah at that time must have loved them well, or did some other Deity form the Egyptians? It matters not that the crossing of the Red Sea and the drowning of Pharaoh are romantic incidents, not only unknown to the Egyptian texts, but even to the earliest of Hebrew prophets. It matters not, for the story is the important thing, even though it is an inspired story, inspired by the Jehovah who tortured and killed the Egyptians to show how well he loved *his* people.

This Wild West story, with its multitudes of slaughters,

proceeds to the wilderness of Sinai; and there again, the Prophet Moses goes into a secret seance and finally announces that God had delivered laws to him, which had been issued from the clouds.

What a great showman was this Prophet! Barnum must have been a devoted admirer of Moses, for Moses was the first to create the two-ring circus; for these laws given by Jehovah are described in two places, and the circus varies in both places. Exodus XX and Exodus XXXIV are the two texts which differ considerably.

To further convince the Children of Israel, Moses tells them the story of how he had cajoled Jehovah into allowing him to see what no man had hitherto seen, the form of Jehovah, for it appears that Jehovah was so pleased with this murderer, charlatan, and wizard that he allowed him to glimpse His hind quarters. At least, Jehovah had a sense of humor!

What a bag of tricks this Prophet had at his command! The Prophet waves his arms and tugs at his gown, and lo and behold! The Lord has spoken! The following is a specimen of the revelations which the Lord is supposed to have dictated to Moses. (Leviticus XIV, 25.)

"The priest shall take some of the blood of the trespass offering and put it upon the tip of the *right* ear of him who is to be cleansed and upon the thumb of his *right* hand, and upon the great toe of his *right* foot, and the priest shall pour of the oil into the palm of his own *left* hand and shall sprinkle with his *right* finger some of the oil that is in his *left* hand seven times before the Lord."

Surely, it must have been a God with a superior mentality who dictated this, for it surpasses our feeble comprehension. And we can well imagine Jehovah's wrath when the priest confuses his *right* and *left*.

Twirling his arms again, Moses gives forth this oracle (Numbers XV, 37-41): "And the Lord spake unto Moses, saying, 'Speak unto the Children of Israel, and bid them that they make them a fringe upon the corner of their garments throughout their generations, and that they put upon the fringe of each corner a cord of blue, etc., etc."

Jehovah chooses Blue as the divine color. Royal Purple. Divine Blue. Then there is the familiar myth of the Prophet's tapping of the rock to bring forth water in the desert; the story of the manna; the tale of the doves.

Thus can the fabled life of Moses be divided into two stages, the early period of illusions, hallucinations, and delusions, and the later stage of wizardry, charlatanry, and demagoguery. Neither must we think that we moderns are the first to peer through this sham, for what the Israelites thought of these laws appears from the bitter criticism of Moses and Aaron, which the Haggadah put into the mouth of the rebel Korah.

"When we were given the ten commandments, each of us

learnt them directly from Mount Sinai; there were only the ten commandments and we heard no orders about 'offering cake' or 'gifts to priests' or 'tassels.' It was only in order to usurp the dominion for himself and to impart honor to his brother Aaron, that Moses added all this."

Moses, Jesus, and Mohammed—these prophets whose adherents number hundreds of millions, about whom there has been built up those vast systems of theology,—what is there of the divine in their characters? What supernatural in their deeds? What wisdom poured forth from their lips which did not come from other philosophers? What immense structures have been founded on these shifting sands, on this morass of ignorance and childish fable? How long can these structures endure, aided by the bolstering up of the theologists, and how long must it be before the light of reason will pierce these foundations of blindness and force them to topple over? How much longer before humanity can begin to build on a sound foundation?

Moses, Jesus, and Mohammed; revolutionists three. Moses at the head of a weak, squabbling, and disgruntled group of Hebrew desert marauders. Jesus sanctioning the insurrection against Rome. Mohammed at the head of his Arabian marauders.

If the freethinkers firmly believe that in them dwell the hope for a better humanity, for an exhilarated progress, for universal freedom and liberty for all mankind, and emancipation from fear and superstition, then they, too, must destroy. They must first undo the wrong before they can proceed to build on a right foundation. They must build on the corner stone that all religion is human in its origin, erroneous in its theories, and ridiculous in its threats and rewards. Religion is the greatest impediment to the progress of human happiness.

CHAPTER IV

SOUNDNESS OF A FOUNDATION FOR A
BELIEF IN A DEITY

It is better to bury a delusion and forget it than to insult its memory by retaining the name when the thing has perished.

F. H. BRADLEY.

A thousand miraculous happenings have been honoured by the testimony of the ancients, which in later times under a more exacting and sceptical scrutiny can no longer be believed. Inherent in man's nature is his disposition to be gulled. . . . Emotion is encouraged to supplant cool reason, fanaticism to supplant tolerance. Not by such means can our race be saved.

LLEWELYN POWYS.

OUR interplanetary visitor is firmly convinced that all religion, no matter what, its antiquity or its modernity may

114

be, is an invention of our groping earthly minds. It occurs to him that it would be interesting and proper to lay aside all theology, all creed, all the superficial trappings placed by man about his conceptions of a deity, and consider only the basic God-idea. The literature on the subject revealed to him that even on this broad and basic principle not all religionists were agreed. He found a threefold classification:

(1) Those who held to the belief in an anthropomorphic personal God who was benevolent, omniscient, and omnipotent.

(2) Those who saw in the constitution of our universe an impersonal Supreme Power, who had created the universe, but who had not given us any revelation, and thus has no need for worship by prayer and sacrifice.

(3) Those who very recently conceived of the deity as a "cosmic force," an "ultimate," or as a mathematical or physical law. Such are the hypotheses of Jeans and Eddington. The Martian set about, therefore, with the principle that, "God is a hypothesis, and as such, stands in need of proof."

(1) The belief in a personal God:

The Martian, as our guest, had by this time had ample opportunity to survey our civilization, and to acquaint himself with the things with which God in His goodness had endowed His earthly children. A proponent of a personal God informs him that his deity is an infinite personal being of consciousness, intelligence, will, good, unity, and Beauty; the Supreme, the infinite personality, who was loving, benevolent, omnipotent, and omniscient. Like the American from Missouri, the visitor hastened to see for himself the marvelous workings of such an exalted being, for surely such a being, with such attributes as he was credited with, would certainly be in an excellent position to bestow great gifts upon his earthly children.

The Martian is informed that the vast majority of our inhabitants, no matter what their geographical distribution may be, are suffering from a "financial depression" brought on by the last World War. War and cruelty are synonymous in the mind of our seeker for God; and immediately, there arises a conflict between the conception of an omnipotent, all-wise and loving God and one who would permit war and cruelty. Fearing that he has not comprehended the meaning of an omnipotent being, he turns to the lexicon for verification, only to learn that it means an all-powerful being. How, then, could an omnipotent being permit wholesale and private murder? Is He not rather a demon than a God? On the other hand, if this being is not omnipotent, then He is a useless god, and there is no need for all the fears which religion breeds, no need for creed and worship. Every war, particularly this last one, is an indictment of God. "God's in His Heaven, all's right with the world," is seemly only to minds drugged with an irrational creed.

"If there is a God, he is quite careless of human well-being or human suffering. The deaths of a hundred thousand men mean no more to him than the deaths of a hundred thousand ants. A couple of million men locked in a death struggle on the battle-field is only a replica of the struggle that has been going on in the animal world throughout time. If there be a God, he made, he designed all this. He fashioned the hooks for the slaughter, the teeth for the tearing, the talons for destruction, and man with his multiplied weapons of destruction has but imitated his example. A world without God, and in which humanity is gradually learning the way to better things, is an inspiration to renewed effort after the right. A world such as this, with God, is enough to drive insane all with intelligence enough to appreciate the situation." (*Chapman Cohen: "War, Civilization and the Churches."*)

When the Martian investigated the annals of the World War he found, despite the opportunities Providence had had of showing its benevolence, the affair of the sinking of the *Lusitania*, the torpedoing of hospital ships, vessels that were not engaged in fighting but in bringing home wounded men who had fought in "God's Cause." He found descriptions of the slaughter of men and women and children in air raids, and he naturally concludes that the "providence of God" is an insult to the earthly intelligence.

Greatly disturbed, he picks up one of our newspapers and

the stories of hate and racial antagonism rear their ugly heads. These, together with jealousy and fear, seem to him to be the outstanding features of our attitudes. A benevolent, loving, omnipotent father, guiding our destinies, yet allowing such monstrosities to exist! The conundrum grows deeper as he proceeds.

It is a bright day, and the Martian is aware of a headache brought on by the effort to understand the ways of earthlings, and therefore decides to drive through the city streets. Yet this drive affords him no relaxation, for on every side two diametrically opposed sights meet his keen eyes—luxury and poverty. Poverty and starvation, yet the Lord's Prayer: "Our Father which art in Heaven, give us this day our daily bread!" No Martian father would allow his children to starve; if he did, the law would fine him and imprison him. Since these earthlings are neglected by their Heavenly Father, and are powerless to indict him, the least they could do would be to stop paying tribute to him. If the God of these earthlings bothers not about them, why should they trouble about God? The Son of God who could once create a miraculous batch of fish to satisfy a few fishermen, can do nothing to help these starving millions! Aloud he muses, "Is there no place on Earth which is free from this contradiction?"

His automobile happens to stop in front of an immense edifice marked "Hospital," and his curiosity is sufficiently aroused to cause him to alight and enter. The physician in charge courteously asks his distinguished visitor to inspect this refuge for those suffering with pain. He remembers that a religionist had told him that disease is a visitation of the Lord for our sins, in the same breath with which he had added that the Lord was loving and compassionate. If that were so, then this was the ideal place to witness the infinite goodness and compassion of the Creator of all earthlings. But, the first scene to meet his gaze was that of a woman in childbirth. The torture the excruciating pain, and the mental anguish of the human female before his eyes, defied his Martian power of expression. This process of birth, it was explained to him, was not a pathological one, nor a disease, but a physiological function. To this, the Martian could no refrain from replying, "From your own words, Doctor it is readily understood that your women experience a torture more acute, more nerve-wracking, and of longer duration than your Jesus experienced during his crucifixion. And your world commiserates and sheds oceans of tears when they contemplate the anguish of Jesus on the cross; but no mention is made of the agony which is the fate of every woman who brings another human being into this 'best of worlds.' "

"But, my dear Martian," exclaims the physician, "the Heavenly Father has ordained that in anguish shall woman bring forth her young." The other deliberated on the compassion of the Benevolent Father in silence and continued on his rounds through the hospital.

Nearby was the crib containing a baby of a few days suffering with a congenital heart disease. The infant's lip were blue, so was the body blue, and the gasping for breath and heaving of the small chest were pitiful to behold.

"This infant," nonchalantly remarked the physician "was born with a greatly defective heart. It will live for a few days, it will thirst for air, it will have intense air hunger, the lungs will fill with fluid and then it will drown in its own secretions."

The Martian recalled the time he had plunged under the water and remained there too long; vividly, he remembered the thirst for air, the seeming bursting of the lungs, the compression, and vise-like grip of the muscles of the throat and chest, and he could not help exclaiming, "Benevolent, Compassionate Being!"

The physician continued, "This child," pointing to a beautiful, robust boy of ten years, "was in perfect health, until he fell in the street and received a minor cut which the parents treated with home remedies, but which in a few days was diagnosed as Tetanus." And the doctor went on to explain that the compassion of the Lord is great when this occurs, for the child gets convulsions, the jaws become locked, and beads of cold sweat stand out on the child's forehead in his anguish; the convulsions increase in severity and in duration so that finally they are continuous and the child lies with the heels and back of the head only touching the bed, the rest of the body is arched. The convulsions then become so severe that the body is so bent backwards at times that the head and trunk touch the-heels. The misery of such a child is sufficient to cause a physician, to lose his reason. Again the Martian murmurs, "Verily, the compassion of the Lord is beyond understanding."

The child in the next bed had just become paralyzed by an attack of poliomyelitis (infantile paralysis). The Martian observes how the Lord in His compassion saved a certain number of these children upon whom he vents His anger for their sins, by inflicting upon them this hideous disease. He saves their lives, but to serve as an everlasting reminder, as a covenant between them and their Lord, He paralyzes their limbs. The spectacle of these children attempting to move, making intense effort to move paralyzed limbs, was the most revolting and heart-breaking sight that he had ever witnessed. This time, too, the Martian remarked, "Verily, the Lord in His infinite wisdom and goodness strange tasks does perform."

The physician then informed him of the many men and women who have died of cancer. A large number of these individuals had reached a period in life where they could just afford to relax from their struggles for mere sustenance; men and women who had reached a calm lake after journeying through troubled and tortuous waters; who had fought the "good fight," and had won the just reward of resting after their labors. But no, the Lord must trouble them for their sins.

A group of these sufferers is shown to the Martian, and the normal course of this disease is explained. This time all he can do is to protest that he firmly asserts that not one of our savage chiefs, even were he of the most primitive tribe, of the cruelest imagination, of the most base and insane nature, would nor could conceive of such torture as the Loving Father conceived when he decided upon cancer as a visitation for our sins. The roasting of a witch alive is but a mere trifle compared to the long-drawn-out agony, the slow wasting, the anguish of a cancer patient watching himself sink to death. And when death mercifully releases this sufferer from his hellish torture the preacher murmurs, "Lord, thy will be done."

The Martian talks for a few moments with a sufferer from this disease and ascertains that the latter is a devout and true religionist, that he has been a good, moral church-goer, and has lived strictly according to the tenets of his creed, that he firmly and passionately believes that he has lived so that he will merit the reward of heaven, an everlasting sojourn in a land where there is no pain and suffering. And yet, this devout religionist, when he was informed that he had an incurable cancer, traveled the length and breadth of his land, from one surgeon to another, allowing himself to be cut to pieces, in order that he might remain on this earth but a moment

122

longer. To stay and suffer the tortures of the damned when he might go to heaven and get his reward in the land where there is no pain!

"I wonder," mused the Martian, "did the grim spectre of death finally instill a grain of scepticism into his mind?"

Later, in the quiet of his chambers, he reviews the day's impressions—cruelty, hate, fear, jealousy, racial antagonism, poverty, luxury, disease, pain, superstition, church, religion, and intolerance.

"If we suppose that the universe is the creation of an Omnipotent and Benevolent God, it becomes necessary to ask how pain and evil arise. Pain and evil are either real or unreal. If they are real then God, who, being omnipotent, was bound by no limitations and constrained by no necessities, willfully created them. But the being who willfully creates pain and evil cannot be benevolent. If they are unreal, then the error which we make when we think them real is a real error. There is no doubt that we believe we suffer. If the belief is erroneous, then it follows that God willfully called falsehood into existence and deliberately involved us in unnecessary error. It follows once again that God cannot be benevolent.

"If we regard pain and evil as due to the wickedness of man and not as the creation of God, we are constrained to remember that man himself is one of God's creations (God being conceived as all creative), and received his wickedness, or his capacity for it, from whom? If we say that man had no wickedness to begin with but willfully generated wickedness for himself, we have to face the double difficulty of accounting for: (a) How man, who is an emanation from God, can will with a will of his own which is not also a piece of God's will; and (b) how a benevolent God could, assuming pain and evil to be a purely human creation, deliberately allow them to be introduced into a world that knew them not, when it was open to Him to prevent such introductions." (*C. E. M. Joad, "Mind and Matter."*)

He had seen that crime and immorality exist now, just as they had existed before the belief in one personal God, and just as they promise to exist beyond our time. He had scrutinized evidence revealing the incontestable fact that most criminals were religious, and absolutely and proportionately, a smaller number of criminals were non-believers in a personal deity. Judging by these alone, a belief in a benevolent, loving, omniscient, omnipotent, and compassionate Being could not be sustained. Furthermore, if such a God ever existed, he certainly would have revealed his true religion to the first man, Adam. If he required prayer to satisfy his vanity, he surely would have told Adam how, when, why, and where to pray. Then again, once having neglected to inform his first model about all this, since He is omnipotent, he would certainly have instilled into the minds of men "the" true creed so that no doubt could have ever entered into any one's mind. What a universe of suffering He would have saved!

The Martian is aware that a great number of earthlings hold that every event must have a cause, therefore the Universe must have had a cause, which cause was God. Everything as it now exists in the universe is the result of an infinite series of causes and effects. Everything that happens is the result of something else that happened previously and so on backwards to all eternity. Applying this reasoning that everything is the effect of some cause, and that a cause is the effect of some other causes, the theists work back from effect to cause and from cause to effect until they reach a First Cause. By predicating a First Cause, however, the theist removes the mystery a stage further back. This First Cause they assume to be a cause that was not caused and this First Cause is God. Such a belief is a logical absurdity, and is an example of the ancient custom of creating a mystery to explain a mystery. If everything must have a cause, then the First Cause must be caused and therefore: Who made God? To say that this First Cause always existed is to deny the basic assumption of this "Theory." Moreover, if it is reasonable to assume a First Cause as having always existed, why is it unreasonable to assume that the materials of the universe always existed? To explain the unknown by the known is a logical procedure; to explain the known by the unknown is a form of theological lunacy.

The effect noted in any particular case is not of necessity

related to a single cause, and science gives no assurance that causes and effects can be traced backward to a simple First Cause. A man is so unfortunate as to contract pneumonia. What is the cause? An infection of the respiratory tract by the pneumococcus. It is not quite so simple as to ultimate causation. The person afflicted was harboring these germs in his nose and throat, and his resistance was weakened by wetting his feet. The day was cold and his shoes were thin. The humidity and temperature were such that rain fell. The temperature and humidity were caused by air currents hundreds of miles distant from the scene, and so ad infinitum. In this series of complications where may we discern a first cause? When applied to the much more difficult problem of physical phenomena, we can conceive of an endless cycle of causes, but we cannot conceive of a First Cause. "Cause and effect are not two separate things, they are the same thing viewed under two separate aspects. . . . If cause and effect are the expressions of a relation, and if they are not two things, but only one, under two aspects, 'cause' being the name for the related powers of the factors, and 'effect' the name for their assemblage, to talk, as does the theist, of working back along the chain of causes until we reach God, is nonsense." (*Chapman Cohen: "Theism or Atheism."*)

A great many theists attempt to deduce the existence of an invisible creator and ruler of the universe from the visible features of nature such as the design, regularity of movement and structure, and the various aspects of beauty which one may find in studying natural objects. This argument from design in nature has been overruled by a study of the evolutionary processes. Paley based his argument on the assertion of a mind behind phenomena, the workings of which could be seen in the forms of animal life. The theists no longer use Paley's original arguments, but a great deal of the theistic arguments are still based on his assumptions. From the humanistic point of view, and the theist bases his entire arguments from design in nature from the humanistic view, an understanding of the merciless character of organic evolution shows clearly that the forces at work in nature are full of waste, there are numerous plans that are futile, there is an unrelenting preying of one form of life upon the other, and it is not always the "higher" form that is victor; there are myriads of living organisms coming to life only to perish before reaching an age at which they can play their part in the perpetuation of the species; and there is a universe of pain and misery that serves no useful purpose. The impartial eye of science observes ugliness as well as beauty, disorder as well as order, in nature. If there is evidence of design in a rose, there is at least as much evidence of design in the tubercle bacillus, and the tetanus bacillus. Whatever in nature produced the peacock produced the itch-mite; whatever produced man produced the spirochete of syphilis. If this earth is evolving for the better, the past is still vivid in all its cruelty. The old and familiar argument from design and beauty in nature is so inconsistent with the facts at hand, that most theists have abandoned this attitude, and the retreat from this position has been turned into a veritable rout by the steady advance of scientific knowledge. God could by exercising His omnipotence reveal His existence with overpowering conviction at any moment; yet, men have been searching for centuries for just the slightest evidence of His presence.

The Martian, moreover, holds that the entire argument is irrelevant, for even if he grants that there is a supernatural being that fashions that which we behold at work in the universe, how can we say that he designed all this without first knowing what his intention was? Only by knowing the intention in the mind of a supernatural being before the act, can we infer that something was designed. When the theist finds intention and design in nature he is but reading his own feeling and desires into nature. Considering the universe as a whole, the Martian fails to find anything that suggests a conscious and purposive god, and certainly nothing to suggest a being that considers the welfare of man. The individual is not much interested in God as manifested in nature, what he is vainly seeking is *God as Providence;* he is seeking an intelligence that his clergy tell him is devoted to his welfare, an intelligence that will guide his stumbling efforts, that will relieve him from war and misery, that will shield the innocent from pain and poverty. He finds that his clergy cannot point to one clear trace of the action of God in human affairs. In the whole long record of man's career the finger of God cannot be found pointing to one well-substantiated fact.

The Martian considers the theistic argument that it would be impossible to have an orderly universe merely resulting from the inherent properties of natural forces, and that "directivity" is necessary to keep the universe on its present track. Keeping in mind the scientific conception of the universe and the knowledge at hand concerning the atoms and their properties, it is inconceivable that any other arrangement than the present one should have resulted. The Martian cannot marvel as most earthlings do that the present order exists as it does; the marvel to him would be if any other order should be or that any radical alteration in it should occur. He perceives that the state of the universe at any moment is the result of all the conditions then prevailing, and that the natural forces possess the capacity to produce the universe as we see it. It matters not what the ultimate nature of these forces may be, electrons, protons, electricity, or wave energy; these material forces possess the capacity to produce the universe as we see it. If these forces do not possess this capacity it is indeed difficult for the Martian to conceive in what way even a "directing and supreme mathematician" an "ultimate," or any supernatural power however designated could produce this capacity. Unless the capacity for producing the universe as we see it existed in the atoms themselves, no amount of direction could have produced it. The property of the atom and its combinations to produce the material universe is therefore inherent in the atoms themselves and does not necessitate the operation of a deity. The order manifest in the universe is the necessary consequence of the persistence of force. If a supernatural, intelligent force existed, the Martian believes that the claims of the theist could in no way be better substantiated than if this controlling force would in some way manifest an inhibitive influence and prevent certain things occurring which would have transpired but for his interference. Such manifestations have not occurred. It is impossible for the theist to show any instance in which the normal consequences of known forces did not transpire in which the aberration could not be accounted for by the operation of other known forces.

A "law" of nature is not a statute drawn up by a legislator; it is the interpretation and the summation which we give to the observed facts. The phenomena which we observe do not act in a particular manner because there is a law; but we state the "law" because they act in that particular manner. It cannot be said that the laws of nature are the result of a lawmaker; it cannot be affirmed that a supreme intelligence told things in nature to act just that way and no other. If the theist claims that a supreme intelligence issued laws for his own pleasure and without any reason, then he must admit that there is something which is not subject to law and the train of natural law is interrupted. If it is claimed that a supreme intelligence had a reason for the laws which he gave, the reason being to create the best possible universe, then it follows that God himself was subject to law and there is no advantage in introducing God as an intermediary. This contention would make it appear that there is a law outside and anterior to the divine edicts, and God does not serve the purpose of the theist since he is not the ultimate lawgiver.

The anthropomorphic conception of God, our Martian finds, is now denied by most cultured theists; nevertheless, they still maintain a belief in a deity endowed with consciousness. Professor H. N. Wieman states that, "God is superhuman, but not supernatural. He is a present, potent, operative, observable reality . . . He is more worthy of love than any other beloved . . . He is one to whom men can pray and do pray, and who answers prayer." This can be understood to be not greatly removed from the fundamentalists' conception of God, but when he continues to say, "God is that interaction between individuals, groups, and ages which generates and promotes the greatest possible mutuality of good," and "it responds to prayer and is precisely what answers prayer, when prayer is answered," the personal "He" has suddenly changed to the unpersonal "It." Emotions and intelligence are connected with nerve structures in all sentient beings that we have experience and knowledge of. How can we attribute these qualities to a being who is described to us as devoid of any nerve structure?

In former ages the theist saw God in the color and construction of a flower, in the starry heavens, and in a sunset or sunrise. The biologists have driven the theists from this misconception, the physicists have explained the phenomena of sunset and sunrise, and with the advance of astronomy the heavens no longer proclaim the glory of God, and the theistic arguments have shifted from worlds to atoms. At the present moment the vision of God has narrowed down to a perception of the divine intelligence noted in the design of the atom. Astronomy, physics, geology, chemistry, medicine, psychology, ethics, aesthetics, and the social sciences have left no room for a theistic explanation of the universe. The mystics who proclaim God in their intuitive trances are being crowded out into the light of reason by the researches of psychologists. There are still many gaps in our knowledge, and if the theist persists in finding the manifestation of a supreme being in these vague zones of our present ignorance, he is at the mercy of the science of the future. Science is concerned with mind as much as it is with the material aspects of atoms and stars, hence the sciences of psychology, ethics, and aesthetics. The entire universe is the province of science and it is rapidly providing a scientific interpretation of all the contents of the universe. It may well be a few more centuries before the scientific explanation is partially complete, but it must be kept in mind that science as we conceive the term is less than 2500 years old, and out of this infantile period, at least 1000 years must be deducted for the intellectual stagnation of the dark ages.

In tracing the retreat of the clergy from the arguments from the First Cause, the arguments from design, causation, and directivity, the Martian recalls the words of Vivian Phelips, "How is it that God allowed earnest and learned divines 16 commit themselves to arguments in proof of His existence, the subsequent overthrow of which has been a potent cause for unbelief?"

"The finite mind cannot expect to understand the Infinite," retorts a theist to our Martian. "What manner of reasoning is this," asks our Martian, "that denies my finite mind the right to question the 'proofs' of the existence of an Infinite, when these same 'proofs' are derived by finite minds? The theist cannot infer God from the cosmic process until he can discover some feature of it which is unintelligible without him."

(2) The belief in a deity, but the rejection of revelations, theology, priestcraft, and church.

To the Martian the opinion held by these individuals presented two difficulties. First, if the adherents of this hypothesis considered their deity as a providence which took an active part in the life of this world, then the objections heretofore stated against belief in a personal god are still valid. Secondly, if they considered this being as only a creator, who then leaves this world to its own resources, they are only assuming a philosophical existence behind phenomena. Such a being, they believe, they deduce intellectually. But actually who created this creator? They assume a god who remains always hidden behind phenomena, but such a god has no connection with the God that the religious man worships and to whom he prays for guidance and for blessings, for actual interference in the life of this world. Such theories impress our visitor as but a feeble attempt at new concepts of the same hypothetical deity, and it seemed to him that we already had sufficient ideas of God to trouble our earthly minds.

(3) The god of the Physicists.

It was brought to the Martian's attention that two scientists, Sir Arthur Eddington, a British astronomer, and Sir James Jeans, a mathematical physicist, had still another concept of God.

According to Eddington, "Phenomena all boil down to a scheme of symbols, of mathematical equations." He admits that this mathematics of nature does not explain anything. They do not define reality, they only define the relations that exist between the phenomena of reality. So far does he go, and then his limited mind, our Martian perceives, meets an obstacle that he cannot explain. He, therefore, abandons the formula and returns to the human mind which has conceived this formula. From the "spiritual essence of Man's nature," he assumes the spiritual nature of the cosmos itself, which he finds in what religion has known for centuries as God. To him, it is impossible to explain the universe except in terms of spirit.

Professor Jeans insists that in the equations which reveal the relations between phenomena, there may reside also the revelation of the ultimate which these phenomena express. He believes that there may exist "a great architect of the universe who is a pure mathematician."

However, the Martian argues, "Is it not a fact that in your earthly experience, you have created your gods in your own image? Your savages created God in the only fashion their mental capacities could supply, in the shape of an idol; now the modern physicist creates his god in the light of his own intimate vision, which is that of a mathematician! This is just another attempt to formulate an hypothetical existence of a supernatural being."

The theologians, by this time thoroughly aroused, lay down a verbal barrage, and learned Jesuits place before the visitor a recent publication entitled, "The Question and Answer" by Hilaire Belloc. The author, acting as the mouthpiece of the Roman Catholic Church, attempts to prove two things: namely, whether God is, and that the witness to Revelation is the Roman Catholic Church. Were it not for the fact that the work was published by permission of the Church, one could logically suppose from its arguments that the author was attempting to give the answer, "No," to the question propounded, as to whether God is. There is one sentence, however, to which the Martian agrees: this one, "But religions, though not very numerous, considering the vast spaces of time over which we can study them, and the vast number of millions to which they apply, differ and contradict each other; on which account, any one approaching this problem for the first time, and being made acquainted at the outset with the variety of religions, would naturally conclude that every religion is man-made, and every religion an illusion."

On reading the opening remarks, the Martian exclaims, "This earthling plainly tells us at the beginning that he will make his theories fit in with his conclusion! He informs us that he does not seek the truth, no matter where it may lead, but he only deems it necessary to fit ideas, no matter how distorted, in order that the final conclusion will simulate what he deliberately sets out to prove."

Mr. Belloc's statement, "How many men will agree that wanton cruelty, treason to family or the state, falsehood for private gain, breach of faith, are admirable?" strikes the Martian as absurd when viewed in the light of the historical annals of the Church itself. Mr. Belloc's creed must have considered these very vices as virtues, judging from the actions of his Church.

In calling the Roman Catholic Church the witness to

revelation, the author continues with, "Yet, that it should suffer from men's hatred and persecution." If God has divinely ordained this institution as His Church on earth, and in His omnipotence and omniscience allows this Church to be hated, then how do the religionists assume that their god is a god of love? The author tells us that He is a god of hate, such a god as was conceived of by the barbarians and the Hebrews—cruel, vengeful, and monstrous. Does not this apologist confuse his god with his devil? Then again, has it not occurred to this apologist that he is in all futility attempting to prove something which is a contradiction within itself? If God is, and is benevolent, is it not logical to assume (since the theologians assume all sorts of attributes to this deity) that he would not have constructed the minds of men when He created them so as to desire to doubt His being; would not have tortured the minds of men with cruel doubt as to His existence?

If He is omnipotent, it would have been just as easy to instill into the minds of men only the strongest desire to believe in His reality; and even that would not be necessary had He so arranged matters that by His everlasting presence He would reveal Himself or His deeds to man in such a conclusive manner that even the feeblest of intellects could not doubt His existence.

If He is omniscient, as the parable asserts, that not a hair falls from the head of man, not a sparrow dies without His knowledge, it must therefore be apparent that He created man with the foreknowledge that man would doubt His existence. This is a contradiction in itself.

The Martian notes that in the entire length of the work not a reference is made to the time-worn theological defense, "the revelation" which the Church has always claimed for its scriptures.

Appended as an afterthought, as an apology, as it were, for the philosophical defense and not the theological, the Jesuit father reminds the reader of its messiah, Jesus and the New Testament. The Jesuit states, "The New Testament writings, considered merely as trustworthy historical documents, inform us that—" but at this point the Martian interrupted the speaker, for the audacity of any learned man terming the New Testament writings "historical" was beyond his comprehension. It brought forcibly to his attention the great change which the apologies for the Church had undergone, and the new methods which they assumed. The old theological defense of the deity was gone; not even philosophy was deemed strong enough support for the present day. How the Church had fallen! The Church which had persecuted, anathematized, burned, and tortured the scientist, the geologist, the astronomer, the geographer, the biologist, the chemist, and the physician; this same Church in its last extremus, casts aside theology as its weapon and its appeal to the minds of the sceptics whom they aim to convert. The Church casts aside its own theology, having learned by bitter experience and recanting of opinions, bulls, and infallible statements by infallible popes, and now succumbs to the opinions it has formerly anathematized. In the present age the Church calls science to its aid, and utterly disregards its obsolete theology which it still practices, and attempts, by means of the misinterpretation of scientific facts and statements of a few men such as Eddington and Jeans, to force science into some illogical and unscientific concordance with the conception of a supreme being.

Ironically it occurs to the Martian that the shades of Hypatia, Bruno, Galileo, Copernicus, Vanini, Darwin, and the vast numbers of Waldenses, Albigenses, Huguenots, Jews, and the victims of the Inquisition and the Witch Hunt, must, as they contemplate the present tactics of that Holy Institution, the Church, find some consolation in the depths of that hell to which the Church consigned them. The Martian logically deduces that by employing science for its defense, the Church admits the impotence of "divine revelation," in this age, to convince even its own adherents of the problematical existence of a divine being. *Theology is no longer recognized as authoritative even by theologians!*

Will the theologians now discard their theology based on the supernatural, and build a system of theology based on science? Is this all that is left to the theologian: that he must use the pitiful "Theology of Gaps"? That is, wherever there are gaps in scientific knowledge, the theologians insert their idea of God! This is but the replacing of the question mark with a meaningless label.

CHAPTER V

THE PERSISTENCE OF RELIGION

We believe what we believe, not because we have been convinced by such and such arguments, but because we are of such and such a disposition.

C. E. M. JOAD.

The mind of the ordinary man is in so imperfect a condition that it requires a creed; that is to say, a theory concerning the unknown and the unknowable in which it may place its deluded faith and be at rest.

WINWOOD READE.

Generations followed and what had been offered as hypothetical theological suppositions were through custom and

141

tradition taken for granted as unquestioned truth.

LLEWELYN POWYS.

THE Martian has had his attention drawn to the statement that religion in some form or other has existed from most primitive times down to the present day. The theologians point to this as a proof of the existence of a supreme being. An investigation of this assertion leads the Martian to the conclusion that religions have continued to exist mainly because of the power which inherited superstitions wield over mankind. Men are born with a marked tendency towards superstitions.

Certain isolated families of men are born with an inherited tendency towards tuberculosis. Most of these are born, not with an active tuberculosis, but some as yet imperfectly understood tendency, a defect in their protons plasmic make-up that renders them an easy prey to the tubercle bacillus if they are exposed to it. Similarly, generations of men have been born with a weakened mental vitality towards superstition; a weakened mental capacity that renders their minds an easy prey to that fear which manifests itself in superstition, creed, religion—the God-idea. It was Karl Marx who remarked that, "The tradition of all the generations of the past weighs down like an Alp upon the brain of the living."

Since the days of our racial childhood, our beliefs have

been handed down from generation to generation, and they have persisted since in all ages it was forbidden to question their existence. Man has persuaded himself that it is so just because he has said it for so long and so often. The force of repetition is great; it is, in fact, taken by a vast majority of men as the equivalent of proof.

Most men have to accept their religions ready made. Their daily tasks leave them no time or opportunity for a personal search. The toil for bread is incessant, there is not sufficient leisure to verify the sources of their religious beliefs. Moreover, the ecclesiastic's answers to the riddles of life are easier, by far, to grasp than the answers of science. These two factors, of innate mental inertia and force of repetition, are well manifested by the present tactics of advertising. The manufacturer of any product well knows that constant repetition and the dangling of his product before the eyes of the public will lead to a widespread acceptance of the advertising slogans propounded for his article.

The force of so-called authority has aggravated this mental inertia. It takes a tremendous amount of will power and mental courage for any individual to assert an opinion that runs counter to the accepted mode of thinking. It is much easier and much more pleasant to give oneself passively to that delusion of grandeur, that delusion that pleasantly drugs the mind with the assumption that there is a supreme being who is personally interested in our well-being; a providence who, like a school master, at his pleasure dispenses rewards and punishments; as immortality, Heaven and Hell. So firmly has this become entrenched in the minds of men that the irrationalities which manifest themselves against such a conception make no impression. Schopenhauer well states, "Nothing is more provoking, when we are arguing against a man with reasons and explanations, and taking all pains to convince him, than to discover at last that he *will* not understand, that we have to do with his *will*"

The Martian, knowing the widespread extent of religious beliefs and their supposed influence in our daily lives, is prepared to find in our annals a vast literature that would attest to the overwhelming benefits that mankind had derived from his religious beliefs.

He is amazed to find that the little good which religion had accomplished, had occurred at the time when our race was in its infancy. Just as fear is instilled into the mind of the child to protect it from the dangers of its environment before the child has reached the age when it can use its reason for protection, just so had religion, by its implantation of fear, served its purpose in the days of our racial childhood. The child, however, as soon as it learns to reason, replaces those fears by a logical comprehension of the laws governing his environment. But in religious matters this fear has clung to man tenaciously; and while at first serving a protective function, at the present stage of civilization constitutes an embryonic impediment. The assertion of ecclesiastics that without the aid of religious learning and influence our civilization would have been retarded is a statement that a study of the development of man shows to be directly opposed to the facts; that religion has been the greatest impediment in the road to progress. This will be shown in the subsequent chapters. The oft-repeated assertion that, during the Middle Ages, ecclesiastic influence was the saving grace is well refuted by Dr. William J. Robinson:

"We are told by the Church apologists that during the Middle Ages the priests and monks kept up the torch of learning, that, being the only literate people, they brought back the study of the classics. Historically speaking, this is about the most impudent statement that one could imagine. It was the Church that retarded human progress at least one thousand years, it is the Church that put a thick, impenetrable pall over the sun of learning and science, so that humanity was enveloped in utter darkness, and if the priests and monks later learned to read and write (from the Arabs, Jews, and Greeks exiled from Constantinople after 1453), it is because they wanted to keep the power in their hands; the people they did not permit to learn either to read or write. *Even the reading of the Bible, bear in mind, was considered a crime.* We are told that the priests and monks built hospitals and gave alms to the poor. Having gotten enormous tracts of the best land into, their hands, so that the people, were starving, they were willing to throw a bone occasionally to the latter. It cost them nothing and it gave them a reputation for charity. They built enormous monasteries with well filled cellars, and lived on the fat of the land, while the people lived in wretched hovels, working their lives away for a crust of bread. The beasts, the domestic animals lived a more comfortable life than did the men, women, and children of the people. And the Church never, never raised a finger to ameliorate their condition. It kept them in superstitious darkness and helped the temporal lords—for a long period the spiritual were also the temporal lords—to keep them in fear, subjection and slavery."

The Martian being an impartial observer examined what had been done by Christianity for the intellectual and material advancement of humanity during her long reign, and what had been done by science and purely secular knowledge in its brief period of activity, the period when science and secular knowledge had partially liberated themselves from ecclesiastical domination. He came to the conclusion that in instituting a comparison he had established a contrast.

CHAPTER VI

RELIGION AND SCIENCE

Science, then, commands our respect, not on the basis that its present assumptions and deductions are absolutely and for all time true, but on the ground that its method is for all time true— the method of discovery, the method of observation, research, experimentation, comparison, examination, testing, analysis and synthesis.

MAYNARD SHIPLEY, "The War on Modern Science."

In the bare three and one-half centuries since modern science began, the churches had conducted an unremitting crusade against it. That much of this crusade had turned into a rear-guard action was due less to the weakness of the defenders of the faith than to the invulnerability of their non-resistant victim.

HORACE M. KALLEN, "Why Religion?"

SOME sixty years ago in the "Dogmatic Constitution of the Catholic Faith," the Church stated, "But never can reason be rendered capable of thoroughly understanding mysteries as it does those truths which form its proper subject. We, therefore, pronounce false every assertion which is contrary to the enlightened truth of faith . . . Hence, all the Christian faithful are not only forbidden to defend as legitimate conclusions of science those opinions which are known to be contrary to the doctrine of faith, especially when condemned by the Church, but are rather absolutely bound to hold them for errors wearing the deceitful appearance of truth. Let him be anathema . . .

"Who shall say that human sciences ought to be pursued in such a spirit of freedom that one may be allowed to hold true their assertions even when opposed to revealed doctrine."

Can anything stronger be said to discourage research, investigation, experiment, and retard progress? And only sixty years ago! It is but the restatement of what the Church has uttered so many times and for so long—that all knowledge, material as well as spiritual, is to be found in the Bible as interpreted by the Church. It was this myth which had stultified the mind of man for 1500 years (during the period in which the Church was dominant); it was this that had killed the urge to search and seek for the truth, which is the goal of all science, the means by which humanity is set on the road to progress. This was the damnable precept foisted on the minds of men which enslaved them throughout the ages, and from which we are just emerging. This was the precept that plunged the world into the Dark Ages, and retarded the advance of mankind for centuries.

This is the reason that it is utterly impossible for the intellectually honest scientist, and for that matter any individual, to reconcile science with religion. On the one hand, that of religion, we have the forces of intolerance, superstition, and the endeavor to besmirch, repress, and ridicule every advance favorable to mankind; to cloak with meaningless words obsolete rites, to stand in the way of human progress, because it does not permit men to think boldly and logically. Science, on the other hand, does not hesitate to tear down old conceptions, and has only one motive, the ultimate truth. Religion has the purpose of keeping the masses in the narrow and false path of only accepted doctrines. The true scientist is the man with the open mind, one who will discard the worthless and accept only the proven good. The religionist closes his mind to all facts which he is unwilling to believe, everything which will endanger his creed. Religion teaches the individual to place all hope, all desire, in a problematical hereafter. The stay on earth is so short compared to the everlasting life to come, that of what interest is this life; all things are vain. The misery, the suffering, of his fellow men leave him cold; he can only think of living in the light of his narrow creed so that he may gain his future reward. How well this philosophy has fitted in with the schemes of the select few for the control of the many!

Truth to the scientific mind is something provisional, a hypothesis that for the present moment best conforms to the recognized tests. It is an evolving conception in a constantly changing universe. It is not that science has attained true conclusions; not that the evidence at hand must remain immutable; but that the scientific method of analyzing and formulating assumptions on the basis of discovery, on ascertained facts, is a superior method to the closed "infallible" method of "revelation." These assumptions, based upon the known facts, lead to a working hypothesis which in turn develops into a theory. If the theory is adopted it must account for the facts known. But the theory is not held as final, it is always changed or abandoned if necessary to conform to the new discovered data. Science welcomes the critical attitude that leads to the refinement of its theories. There may be today various theories held by scientists in which they are mistaken, but the question of the *method* by which they arrive at conclusions can no longer be under consideration with regard to its validity.

To the scientific mind, knowledge is something to be arrived at by study and research. To the religionist, knowledge is something that is contained in an infallible and supernatural statement or insight. Religion exalts the transcendental; science manipulates only the material. To the consistent religionist, his belief, as such, determine the fact; to the scientist it is the evidence that establishes the fact. To the religionist truth is something that is unchanging, that is fixed, final, and heretical to question. Confronted with a constantly changing universe, he would delude himself that his inner convictions give him a finality concerning his evolving environment. It is therefore not so much Science that the religionist is fighting, but the *scientific method.* This scientific method of approach, he rightly perceives, has so pervaded our mode of thinking that it is the subtle and most disintegrating force that is shattering the religious foundations.

Dr. James T. Shotwell, speaking of the scientific method, concludes, "But whatever strictures philosophy may pass upon the *conclusions* of science, as merely relative and provisional, there is no clearer fact in the history of thought, that its *attitudes* and *methods* have been at opposite poles from those of religion. It does no good to blink the fact, established as it is by the most positive proofs of history and psychology. Science has made headway by attempting to eliminate mystery so far as it can. Religion, on the other hand, has stressed mystery and accepted it in its own terms. Science is the product of bold adventure, pushing into the realm of the mysterious to interpret its phenomena in terms of the investigator; religion enters this same realm to give itself up to the emotional reactions. Science is the embodiment of the sense of control, religion yields the control to that power which moves in the shadow of the woods by night, and the glory of the morning hills . . .

"Science does not justify by faith, but by works. It is the living denial of that age-long acceptance which we accord to the mystery—as such. It renounces authority, cuts athwart custom, violates the sacred, rejects the myths. It adjusts itself to the process of change whose creative impulse if itself supplies. Not *semper idem* but *semper alterum* is the keynote of science. Each discovery of something new involves the discarding of something old. Above all, it progresses by doubting rather than by believing." (*James T. Shotwell: "The Religious Revolution of To-day."*)

There has never been an advance in science of widespread importance which in some manner or other endangered some mouldy religious concept, that the Church has not bitterly opposed; an advance which in time has proven of inestimable benefit for all mankind. A glance at the history of human progress will reveal scores of such instances.

The two rival divisions of the Christian Church, Protestant and Catholic, have always been in accord on one point, that is, to tolerate no science except such as they considered to be agreeable to the Scriptures. It was the decree of the Lateran Council of 1515 that ordered that no books should be printed but such as had been inspected by the ecclesiastical censors, under pain of excommunication and fine.

It is easily understood that having declared the Bible to contain all knowledge both scientific and spiritual, and then passing a decree ordering no books to be printed which did not agree on all points with the Church's interpretation of the Bible, the Church was in absolute control of all thought, both written and spoken.

It was to no advantage for the scholar to investigate any new fields, for all knowledge which was possible for the mind to discover had already been revealed in the Scriptures. Thus declared the Church. We understand why it was that Copernicus did not permit his book to be published until he was dying. We understand also that when Galileo and Bruno had the courage of their convictions, and gave voice to their beliefs, they were persecuted. Galileo was made to recant a discovery that the youngest of children now takes for granted. Bruno was burnt at the stake.

We know that astronomy was at a standstill under Church domination, chemistry was forbidden, and the study of natural philosophy was contradicted; while anthropology, which showed on what mythical foundations the story of the fall of man rests, was squelched. The attitude of the Church on geography was hostile to the truth, as witness the persecutions of those who dared to venture that the earth was round.

Botany, mathematics, and geometry, as well as the natural sciences, slumbered. Geology, which proved that the earth was more than 6000 years old, was anathematized; archeologists had the greatest difficulty to expound the truth concerning the antiquity of the human race. In purely civil matters, the clergy opposed fire and marine insurance on the ground that it was a tempting of Providence. Life insurance was regarded as an act of interference with the consequence of God's will. Medicine met the most strenuous of opposition.

It is impossible in this short study to analyze the specific forms of retardation which the Church exhibited to all of these branches of learning, whose only endeavor it was to search for the truth, to state the facts, and to alleviate and make more bearable man's sojourn on this earth. However, a few of the many instances of retardation on the part of the Church will be pointed out.

CHAPTER VII

RELIGION AND MEDICINE

Now, when physiologists study the living brain of an ape, they have no grounds for supposing that they are dealing with a dual structure. The brain is not a tenement inhabited by a spirit or soul. The spirit or soul is but a name for the manifestations of the living brain. The leading neurologists of the world are agreed that the same is true of the human brain. It was only when they abandoned the dual conception—an inheritance from the dark ages of medicine—that they began to understand the disorders of man's mind and how to treat them.

Modern medicine thus strikes at the very root of Christian doctrine. For, if man is truly mortal, if death ends all, if the human soul is but the manifestation of the living brain, as light and heat are the manifestations of a glowing bar of steel, then there can be no resurrection of the dead. Man has the seeds of immortality in him, but the gift is for the race, not for the individual.

SIR ARTHUR KEITH.

155

MEDICINE and religion have been closely associated from the most pristine time. Primitive medicine had its origin in conjunction with the most primitive of religious conceptions, namely, animism; an illusion that made primitive man recognize in all things, and everywhere, spirits such as his supposed spirit; a belief that the world swarms with invisible spirits which are the cause of disease and death. And thus primitive medicine is inseparable from primitive modes of religious belief. All these phenomena which we consider today natural—the rustling of leaves in a forest, the crash of thunder, the flash of lightning, winds, clouds, storms, and earthquakes—were to primitive man the outward and visible signs of angry gods, demons, and spirits. Similar spirits caused disease and death, and these evil spirits that produced disease and death were to be placated and cajoled by man, just as he did his other deities, by magic, by burnt offerings, and sacrifice.

The first holy man, the first priest, was the "shaman," and it was his duty not only to placate and cajole the spirits that were thought to control the physical well-being of the individual members of the tribe; but it was his duty also, by the exercise of his magic, to alleviate and cure illness by exorcism. The "shaman" was therefore the first medicine man, the first witch doctor, the first physician. He relied chiefly upon psychotherapy as does the modern witch doctor of Christian Science.

Medicine could not begin to be medicine until it was disassociated from magic, religion, and theology. This struggle has been going on from the time of the "shaman" to the present moment. Primitive medicine stands midway between magic and religion, as an attempt to safeguard health by control of so-called supernatural processes, and the warding off of evil influences by appeal to the gods.

In all primitive societies, priest, magician, and medicine man were one and the same; and medicine remained stationary until it could divorce itself completely from religion. Primitive medicine, then, springs from folklore, legends, credulity, and superstitions; the same forces that give rise to all forms of religious beliefs.

Huxley has stated, "Science commits suicide when it adopts a creed," and from the earliest of times those men who had a scientific trend of mind realized this, however vaguely, and have attempted to divorce science from religion. The science of medicine has been divorced from superstition, but its twin brother religion lies as firmly bogged in the mire of superstition today as it did in the days of the incantations of the first theologist, the "shaman." And it is due to this close association of religion and medicine that ideas of the greatest scientific moment have been throttled at birth or veered into a blind alley through some current theological lunacy. Medicine has advanced through its disassociation with supernaturalism, while religion still remains the last refuge of human savagery.

And so it had been that throughout those long, sterile, and barbarous ages primitive man ascribed all diseases either to the wrath of God, or the malice of an Evil Being. With the rise of the Greek philosophers, the human mind for the first time began to throw off the fogs of superstition. In Greece, 500 years before Christ, Hippocrates developed scientific thought and laid the foundations of medical science upon observation, experience, and reason. Under his guidance, medicine for the first time was separated from religion. He relieved the gods of the responsibility for disease and placed it squarely upon the shoulders of man. His findings were passed on to the School of Alexandria, and there medical science was further developed. At this stage of history all advances stopped, and for the following reason:

With the coming of Christianity this science, as well as all others, was stultified. A retrogression took place to the ideation of the most primitive of men, namely, the conception of physical disease as the result of the wrath of God, or the malice of Satan, or by a combination of both. The Old Testament attributes such diseases as the leprosy of Miriam and Uzziah, the boils of Job, the dysentery of Jehoram, the withered hand of Jeroboam, the fatal illness of Asa, and many other ills, to the wrath of God, or the malice of Satan. The New Testament furnishes such examples as the woman "bound by Satan," the rebuke of the fever, the casting out of the devil which was dumb, the healing of persons whom "the devil oftimes casteth into the fire," and various other episodes. Christian theology then evolved theories of miraculous methods of cure, based upon modes of appeasing the divine anger, or of thwarting satanic malice. The curing of disease by the casting out of devils, by prayers, were the means of relief from sickness recognized and commanded by the Bible. Thus Christianity perverted the beginning of a science of medicine to a system of attempted cure of disease by fraud.

The treatment of disease descended to the cures found in holy and healing wells, pools, and streams; in miracles and the efficacy that was to be found in the relics of saints. Instead of reliance upon observation, experience, and thought, attention was directed toward supernatural agencies. In contrast to the Greek physicians who were attempting to lay a scientific foundation, we have the Christian idea prevailing that the water in which a single hair of a saint had been dipped was to be used as a purgative; water in which St. Remy's ring had been dipped cured lunacy; oil of a lamp burning before the tomb of St. Gall cured tumors; wine in which the bones of a saint had been dipped cured fevers; St. Valentine cured epilepsy; St. Christopher cured throat disease; St. Eutropius, dropsy; St. Ovid, deafness; St. Vitus, St. Anthony, and a multitude of other saints. the maladies which bear their names.

"In the year 1585, in the town of Embrun, France, the male generative organ of St. Foutin was greatly revered. A jar was placed beneath his emblem to catch the wine with which it was generally anointed; the wine was left to sour, and then it was known as the 'Holy Vinegar.' The women drank it in order to be blessed with children." (*Joseph Lewis, "Voltaire."*)

Enormous revenues flowed into various monasteries and churches in all parts of Europe from relics noted for their healing powers. The ecclesiastics perceived that the physician would interfere with these revenues and gifts of the shrines, and deemed it the will of God to persecute and condemn physicians. St. Ambrose declared, "The precepts of medicine are contrary to celestial science, watching and prayer." St. Augustine declared, "All diseases of Christians are to be ascribed to these demons, chiefly do they torment fresh baptized Christians, yea, even the guiltless, new-born babe." Gregory of Nazianzus declared that bodily pains are provoked by demons, and that medicines are useless, but that they are often cured by the laying on of consecrated hands. St. Niles and St. Gregory of Tours gave examples to show the sinfulness of resorting to medicine instead of trusting to the intercession of saints.

Even as late as 1517, Pope Leo X, for a consideration, issued tickets bearing a cross and the following inscription, "This cross measured forty times makes the height of Christ in His humanity. He who kisses it is preserved for seven days from falling sickness, apoplexy, and sudden death."

The Council of Le Mons, in 1248, forbade monks to engage in surgery. At the beginning of the twelfth century, the Council of Rheims forbade monks to study medicine; and shortly after the middle of the twelfth century, Pope Alexander III forbade monks to study or practice medicine. In the thirteenth century, the Dominican Order forbade all ecclesiastics to have any connection with medicine; and when we remember that the policy of the Church had made it impossible for any learned man to enter any other profession, the only resource left for a scholar was the Church; so effectively did the Church kill all scientific endeavors.

The Reformation made no sudden change in the sacred theory of medicine. The Church of England accepted the doctrine of "royal touch," and in a prayer book of that period is found a service provided for that occasion which states that "They (the kings), shall lay their hands on the sick, and they shall recover."

Pestilences were taught to be punishments inflicted by God on society for its shortcomings. Modern man has no conception of the ravages of infections and epidemics that swept over Europe in the Middle Ages, and to a lesser extent, until less than fifty years ago. Tacitus described the plague in Rome thus: "Houses were filled with dead bodies, and the streets with funerals. . . . Alike, slaves and plebeians were suddenly taken off amidst lamentations of their wives and children, who, while they mourned the dead, were themselves seized with the disease, and, perishing, were burned on the same funeral pyre."

In 80 A.D. an epidemic swept Rome causing 10,000 deaths daily. During the ages until the present century, wave after wave of pestilence swept over Europe. The plague in 1384 A.D. took no less than 60 million lives. It was estimated that twenty-five per cent. of the population of the then known world perished in that one epidemic. Between 1601 and 1603, 127,000 died of the plague in Moscow. The epidemic of 1630 took 500,000 lives in the Venetian republic; Milan alone lost 88,000. In 1605, London lost 69,000; 70,000 died in Vienna in 1679; the following year Prague lost 83,000, all from this disease. The horrors of such visitations are beyond description, and can scarcely be imagined. For a time, attempts were made to collect and bury the dead. Wagons would pass through the streets at night collecting the victims. The drivers, benumbed with drink, frequently failed to ascertain whether death had occurred. Living patients, desperately ill, were piled into the wagons with corpses beneath, about, and on them. These gruesome loads were dumped pell-mell into huge pits hastily dug for the purpose. In some instances, living victims crawled out of these pits and survived to tell the tale. As the epidemics progressed, attempts to dispose of the dead were abandoned. Putrefying bodies were everywhere. Whole cities were left desolate, the few survivors having fled.

It is not to be wondered at that such epidemics swept over Europe when it was taught that these were the vengeance of God. How could it be discovered that the real causes were the crowded conditions and bad sanitation of the cities, the squalor, the misrule, and gross immorality occasioned by the Holy Wars, when hordes of soldier-bandits plagued the countryside? The devout continued to live in their squalor, to trust in the Lord, and to die by the millions.

In all pestilences down to the present time, the Church authorities, instead of aiding and devising sanitary measures, have preached the necessity of immediate atonement for offenses against the Almighty. The chief cause of the immense sacrifice of lives in these plagues was of course the lack of hygienic precautions. But how could this be discovered when, for ages, living in filth was regarded by great numbers of holy men as an evidence of sanctity!

St. Hilarion lived his whole life long in utter physical uncleanliness. St. Athanasius glorifies St. Anthony because he had never washed his feet. St. Abraham's most striking evidence of holiness was that for fifty years he washed neither his hands nor his feet; St. Sylvia never washed any part of her body save her fingers; St. Euphraxia belonged to a convent in which the nuns religiously abstained from bathing; St. Mary of Egypt was eminent for filthiness; St. Simeon Stylites was in this respect unspeakable—the least that can be said is that he lived in ordure and stench intolerable to his visitors. For century after century the idea prevailed that filthiness was akin to holiness.

Another stumblingblock hindering the beginnings of modern medicine and surgery, was the theory regarding the unlawfulness of meddling with the bodies of the dead. The dissection of the human body was prohibited since the injury to the body would prevent its resurrection on the Last Day. Andreas Vesalius was the pioneer in the movement for increased knowledge of anatomy, and in 1543, when his work appeared, he was condemned to death by the Inquisition as a magician. He escaped this fate by undertaking a pilgrimage to Jerusalem only to be shipwrecked on the Island of Zante when he attempted to return, and there died in misery and destitution.

In the year 1853, cholera, after having committed serious ravages in many parts of Europe, visited Scotland. It was evident to most thinking people that, due to the extreme poverty and squalor of most of the Scottish towns at that time, a great number of people would necessarily succumb to this disease unless stringent sanitary measures were instituted immediately. Instead, the Scotch clergy proposed to combat this scourge with prayer and fasting, which would have lowered the resistance to this disease by producing physical exhaustion and mental depression. They proposed the ordering of a national fast day in which the people were to sit the whole day without nourishment in their churches and retire to their beds at night weeping and starved. Then it was hoped that the Deity would be propitiated, and the plague stayed. To give greater effect to this fast day, they called upon England to help them, and the Presbytery of Edinburgh dispatched a letter to the English minister, requesting information as to whether the queen would appoint a national fast day. The English minister, to his credit, advised the Presbytery of Edinburgh that it was better to cleanse than to fast, and cleanse they must swiftly or else, in spite of all prayers and fastings of a united but inactive nation, the cholera would devastate them.

There are today, in this twentieth century, two pestilences which could be wiped from the face of the earth. "There are two pestilences which thus unfortunately involve moral conceptions. They are the plagues of Syphilis and Gonorrhea. Against them medicine has developed methods of control. They could be eradicated, but as yet civilization has not advanced entirely beyond the ancient idea that disease is imposed by God as a measure of vengeance for our sins. It still rejects protection, when without it these plagues will continue to exact death and suffering on a scale which probably exceeds that of any one of the medieval plagues. Those who today look upon Syphilis and Gonorrhea as punishment for sin have not progressed beyond the ideas of medieval Europe.

"Ignorance and bigotry are the twin allies of the plagues of Syphilis and Gonorrhea. Medicine and civilization advance and regress together. The conditions essential to advance are intellectual courage and a true love for humanity. It is as true today as always in the past that further advances or even the holding of what has already been won, depend upon the extent to which intellectual courage and humanity prevail against bigotry and obscurantism." (*Haggard, "Devils, Doctors, and Drugs."*)

As a result of the lack of control of these plagues there are in the world at the present moment thousands of children suffering from congenital syphilis who would never have been born but for the desire of Christians to see sinners punished. With regard to the spread of sex knowledge, the clergy's attitude is dangerous to human welfare. The artificial ignorance of sex subjects which orthodox Christians attempt to enforce upon the young is extremely dangerous to mental and physical health. The young are much less likely to act wisely when they are ignorant, than when they are instructed.

These two venereal diseases are no more controlled under the moral standards of today than they were two centuries ago, and yet medical science offers for these diseases what it can offer for few others; both a prevention and a cure. And it is due to the ignorance and the bigotry of the theists that the spread of sex knowledge is hampered so that a sane conception of sex and the prevention of venereal disease does not eradicate these diseases. The theists have, therefore, without sense or justice, founded their morality on disease; neglecting the fact that all disease is immoral in the widest sense, since it is detrimental to the happiness of man, and that no one disease is more so than another. The morality of the body is health—not disease. So much for the actual facts and reality. In passing to the theoretical, we again see the truth of the statement that religion is the last resort of human savagery.

To postulate that a supreme being is omnipotent, omniscient, and all-loving, and then to assume that he inflicts disease on his children as punishment for sin is a sadistic mental aberration. In his omniscience he full well knows beforehand what each of his children will do. He foreordains their sins and then punishes his children for sins that he wills them to commit. It is just as if a syphilitic father should punish his syphilitic child because the child has that congenital disease for which the father is responsible. If the theist insists that his deity is all that he claims him to be, then it is only logical that instead of man asking his god for forgiveness, what actually should be is that God should ask the forgiveness of man for his bungling and error.

Christianity has attempted from its inception to eradicate the sexual instinct and in so doing has antagonized an instinct that is as fundamental as that of self-preservation. All it has accomplished is a distortion. The church, by claiming that it alone was privileged to regulate sexual desires, has done one of two things to each of its adherents. It has either made him a hypocrite or driven him insane. Much of the insanity in this country could be overcome were religion and sex permanently divorced; and an immediate amount of inestimable good could be accomplished when one considers that fifteen per cent of all mental disease is caused by syphilis.

Physical disease having been considered as a malicious trick of Satan, it was but natural that the disease of the mind was also attributed to satanic intervention. The conception that insanity was a brain disease, and that gentleness and kindness were necessary for its treatment, was throttled by Christian theology for fifteen centuries. Instead the ecclesiastic burdened humanity with a belief that madness was largely possession by the Devil. Hundreds of thousands of men and women were inflicted with tortures both physical and mental. It was not until 1792 that the great French physician Penel, and William Tuke in England, placed the treatment of mental disease on a rational and scientific basis. And this, in spite of such ecclesiastical attacks as were seen in the *Edinburgh Review* of that period. These two men, Penel and Tuke, were the first acknowledged victors in a struggle of science for humanity which lasted nearly two thousand years.

The clergy resisted Jenner when he introduced vaccination, and yet the application of this measure of defense against disease has probably saved more lives than the total of all the lives lost in all wars. The clergy maintained that "Smallpox is a visitation from God, and originates in man, but Cowpox is produced by presumptious, impious men. The former, heaven ordained, the latter is perhaps a daring and profane violation of our holy order."

In the seventeenth century, the Jesuit missionaries in South America learned from the natives the value of the so-called Peruvian Bark in the treatment of ague. In 1638, quinine, derived from this bark, was introduced into Europe as a cure for malaria. It was stigmatized as "an invention of the Devil." The ecclesiastical opposition to this drug was so strong that it was not introduced into England until 1653.

The medieval Christians saw in childbirth the result of a carnal sin to be expiated in pain as defined in Genesis. Accordingly the treatment given the child-bearing woman was vastly worse than the mere neglect among the primitive peoples. Her sufferings were augmented by the fact that she was no longer a primitive woman and child-bearing had become more difficult. In these "Ages of Faith" which could be better called the "Ages of Filth," nothing was done to overcome the enormous mortality of the mother and child at birth. Attempts, however, were made to form intra-uterine baptismal tubes by which the child, when it was locked by some ill chance in its mother's womb, could be baptized and its soul saved before the mother and child were left to die together. But nothing was done to save their lives. No greater crimes were ever committed in the name of civilization, religious faith, and smug ignorance than the sacrifice of the lives of countless mothers and children in the first fifteen centuries after Christ among civilized mankind.

Approaching our own time, we have the example of Dr. James Y. Simpson, professor of obstetrics at the University of Glasgow about 1850, first administering an anesthetic to alleviate the pain of childbirth. He was bitterly opposed by the clergy on the ground that it was impious to attempt to escape from the curse pronounced against all women in Genesis. It was Dr. Simpson who, in defending this humanitarian practice, asserted that opposition, particularly on theological grounds, had been presented against every humane innovation in the past.

When Paul Ehrlich, in 1910, announced his discovery of salvarsan for the treatment of syphilis, the clergy again were horror-struck that man should interfere with a visitation of the Lord.

The resistance to the spread of information concerning contraception, commonly known as birth control, is an example of the Church's dominance of government today;

and yet this information is as vital to the welfare of humanity as is the control of cancer.

In 1926, our newspapers carried conspicuous headlines, "Episcopal Church Joins Catholic to Gag Birth Control"; four years later, 320 bishops of the Episcopal Church met in London, and by a majority of 3 to 1 voted in favor of contraception when "there is morally sound reason for avoiding complete abstinence." The bishops had by this time become well aware of the insistence of secular opinion towards this movement, and having done their best to prevent this progressive movement for the past one hundred years, they finally accepted defeat, proving once again that religion has never accepted anything that science has shown to be a fact or of benefit to humanity until it was compelled to do so to save its face. The infallible Church, however, still persists in its opposition and in the Encyclical of Pope Pius XI, published in January, 1931, it is said, "The conjugal act is destined primarily by nature for the begetting of children. Those who, in exercising it, deliberately frustrate its natural power, and purpose, are against nature and commit a deed which is shameful and intrinsically vicious." So speaks the infallible Pope, but the great majority of physicians hold that there are few things more perilous to mental health, intellectual efficiency, moral equanimity, and physical well-being than prolonged denial of the sex urge for the average, normal human being. Every physician can furnish numerous case histories to substantiate the statement that continual sexual abstinence is prejudicial to the health and happiness of the man and woman, and is the causation of hundreds of semiderelicts and psychoneurotics. Furthermore, the rising tide of insanity in this country would be stemmed were religion and sex permanently divorced.

Today the modern clergy still endeavor to explain natural phenomena by supernatural theories, and while they do not assign preternatural powers to witches and demons, they yet persist in attempting to pervert facts of science, and delude themselves with faith in some supernatural force. The clergy state that the physician cures disease through the mediation of God, the physician merely playing the part of the agent of God, through whom the real cure is effected. Is anything more ridiculous and at the same time more contradictory, than to suppose that an all-powerful god should have to appoint an intermediary to perform his work? And if it is only by God's will and aid that a cure takes place, then it follows that God must be willing for the individual to be cured; why in the name of reason, did He not prevent the initial step, the contracting of the disease? What a mass of suffering, of mental anguish might thus have been spared us! Thus, this omnipotent being either did not desire to spare us this misery and suffering, in which case he must surely be a monster incarnate; or, on the other hand, he is powerless to halt it, and thus cannot be omnipotent.

While the clergy maintain that a cure is only effected by God's will, the physician knows otherwise. The physician accomplishes his cures alone, and definitely cures and saves the lives of human beings by his own skill, intelligence, and application of methods which have been developed by the exercise of secular knowledge, not theological nonsense. When man is so unfortunate as to contract an infection of the appendix, and that inflammation succeeds to pus-formation so that this diseased and nonessential part of the human anatomy is on the point of rupturing and causing a fatal peritonitis, it is not by God's will and intervention that a cure is effected, but by the intervention of the surgeon who removes the diseased part. If man depended upon God's will to save him, as he did in the past, the appendix would rupture, peritonitis would set in, and despite prayers and sacrificial offerings, the Deity would exact his life.

When an innocent infant, in the first few weeks of life, develops an intussusception (an infolding of the bowel which causes an acute obstruction), the prayers and supplication of the parents avail not a particle; if the surgeon did not save the infant's life by operating and removing the obstruction, the benevolent being would allow the child to die.

The adult who develops a hernia, which is due to a defect in the construction of the human body, which is assigned to an omniscient being who still persists in forming bodies that are defective, and this hernia becomes strangulated (twisted), the deity sits calmly by in omnipotent inaction, while the prompt interference of the surgeon saves the individual's life.

When the surgeon observes a superficial cancerous growth, or an internal growth which can be removed in its entirety, does he trust to the Lord to halt this pernicious development? No, the surgeon does not consult God, but resorts to his own knowledge and skill to save a human life.

The diphtheritic child who is strangling to death with a diphtheritic membrane in its throat is not permitted by the physician to be left to the benevolent being's will, nor to the prayers of the parents. The physician's prayer is the diphtheria antitoxin, which in his hands is the life-saving device.

When the physician administers quinine for malaria, or salvarsan for syphilis, he effects cures for these diseases by using agents to which the clergy strenuously objected when they were first introduced. And when the ecclesiastic attributes to the Deity whatever laws man has been able to evolve out of his own experience and wisdom, he establishes, fallaciously, the corollary that if God is responsible for the cures, He is also responsible for the non-cures. Then what of the countless number that died of disease before man evolved those cures, and what of the wholesale murder of His children in the past ages?

Do certain diseases still baffle the physician? Surely it is less often than the pestilences of old which baffled sacrifice and prayer. The cruelest laws ever devised by man have more equity and benevolence in them than the appalling and irrational jurisprudence of the Deity.

Do certain diseases as yet remain to plague man? Then it is only because religion has for the past 2000 years been the greatest obstacle in the development of cures for these diseases. Every single individual, in the past 2000 years, who has succumbed to a disease for which medical science has no cure, has died directly at the hands of religion. The obstruction which religion has placed on the development of medical science has laid at its feet the responsibility for the deaths of countless millions throughout the ages.

The religionist replies that man's mind cannot fathom the will of God. Which is an irrational statement for it is a well established fact, and indeed, a criterion of insanity, that when the deranged are confronted with facts which are conclusive and with creations of the imagination, they cannot differentiate fact from fancy, and maintain, instead, that fancy is the real fact. The religionists are guilty of the same breach of reason. They suffer with what may be termed, "dementia religiosa." The remarkable feature of the latter disease is its wide prevalence.

Dr. Haggard in his book, "Devils, Drugs, and Doctors," declares, "The early and Medieval Christians accepted the doctrine of the power of demons in the lives of men; they saw this power particularly in the demoniac production of diseases. They believed in miracles and especially in the miraculous healing of diseases. The demonological belief of the Christians was inherited from the doctrine of the Jews, who were believers in demons and the 'possession by the devil.' Jesus himself cured by casting out of devils. Following his example, Christians everywhere became exorcists. Jewish demonology was continued among Christian converts, and the belief in supernatural interpositions in human affairs was widely accepted. *Nothing has retarded the growth of scientific medicine during the past 2000 years so much as the iron grip of theology in maintaining practices based on belief in this supernatural origin of disease."* The fabled curing of disease by casting out devils, and the New Testament recordings of Jesus's conviction that disease was caused by evil spirits, have had an inestimable detrimental result on the development of medical science. The fact that Jesus believed in the demoniacal production of diseases and cured them by exorcism was deemed so important by the author of the Gospel according to Mark that he has actually recorded the Aramaic words Jesus was reported to have used in addressing his patients. In Mark V: 41, Jesus is reported to have given the command "Talitha cumi" to a little Jewish girl whom her parents believed dead. In Mark VII: 34, Jesus is reported as uttering the magical word "Ephphatha," as he "put his fingers into his ears, and he spit, and touched his tongue" in behalf of "one that was deaf, and had an impediment in his speech."

An excellent and timely illustration of what occurs when secular knowledge has not yet replaced ecclesiastical ignorance and bigotry, particularly in the field of medicine, is furnished by an article from one of Philadelphia's leading newspapers, *The Evening Bulletin*, of December 23, 1932. We quote it verbatim:

"Faith Healers Arrested; Two Charged with Choking to Death 5-Year-Old Girl, Linden, Texas, Dec. 23, 1932. Despite a purported confession, officers to-day continued an investigation of the death of a five-year-old girl, allegedly at the hands of two itinerant preachers who sought to 'drive out the devil' they believed responsible for her partial paralysis. Murder charges were filed against Paul Oaks and his brother, Coy Oaks, and precautions taken to prevent possible mob vengeance. Sheriff Nat Curtright said the accused men admitted they had choked the child to death in an attempt to cure her. Officers said the preachers had been conducting meetings in rural communities and had preached on the subject of faith healing. George Wilson, a neighbor, officers said, found the two men kneeling over the prostrate form of the child. They ordered him to leave, declaring he was a 'devil.' He said the child's father was in the room."

Medieval exorcism still practised in one of the leading

nations of the world! In America, which prides itself on its scientific advances, towards whom the rest of the world looks for guidance in scientific discoveries and practices!

To have retarded the growth of medicine for the past 2000 years! Think of the strides made in medicine in the past hundred years, and dwell on the comfort humanity derives from it, in contrast to the filth, misery, and pestilences of the fourteenth, fifteenth, and sixteenth centuries. Would so much progress have been possible had man still persisted in the belief that disease was due to demoniac intervention, and that the sum total of all knowledge humanly possible was contained in the Bible?

It is no longer necessary for children to choke to death with diphtheria. Yellow fever, and small pox in civilized countries are, or could be, wiped from the face of the earth. Malaria is controlled; tuberculosis will shortly be a rarity; typhoid fever and cholera have been eradicated wherever there is sanitation; erysipelas can be controlled; hydrophobia prevented; childbirth fever has lost its tremendous mortality; tetanus can be checked; syphilis and gonorrhea can be controlled; diabetes and pernicious anemia can be controlled; surgery is reclaiming vast multitudes and restoring to useful and happy lives thousands who would have hitherto died. So much has been done; but it is especially true that there is as much, at least, yet to be done. But all this has been achieved so recently.

What might not have been won had not the minds of men been polluted from infancy, warped by the first professional holy men, the religionists, the priests? Had the idea of a supernatural force been allowed to die in the Dark Ages, as it surely would have, as man's mind expanded and developed, humanity would today find itself more advanced on the road to progress. But as it was, the myth of religion was foisted on the superstitious brain, and man resigned himself to his fate, and lived in such a manner as to please this hypothetical supernatural being. The inevitable result was the abject misery, both material and spiritual, of Europe during the period when the Church was in absolute control.

If this myth and mystification had died with the dead ages, as it should have done, what a fitter place to live in this world would be today! Consider the needless misery and the agony of those who died of the various plagues; and think of the advanced stage of medicine of Alexandria, three hundred years before the Christian era, where the physicians were welcomed to the famous library by the emperors. The state gave them their livelihood and their duties were to advance medicine by study and research. Anatomy was studied and dissection was allowed. With the coming of Christianity, the remnants of this library were destroyed, and with them went all progress in that field. If such had been the enlightened state in Egypt three hundred years before Christianity appeared, then why had not science made the same progress then as it does now?

Because, to the knowledge stored in the library at Alexandria had not been added a progression of learning, a continued process of research; if this had not been halted by Christianity, how much vaster would our achievements be today?

It was not necessary for all of those millions to have been the victims of plagues, of inquisitions, of witchcraft burnings, of religious persecutions and wars. The sorrow and pain brought to untold numbers throughout the centuries could have been prevented; and would have been if man had been interested in the welfare of his fellowmen instead of the glorification of an almighty being. Future generations may well declare religion to have been the curse of humanity. The Church had cursed the human intellect by cursing the doubts which are the necessary consequence of its exercise. She had cursed even the moral faculty by asserting the guilt of honest error.

Medicine which has for its sole objects the alleviation of man's sufferings, to cure them when possible, to relieve more often the pains and ills which make this life a living hell, what might it not have accomplished ages ago had religion not interfered with its progress? Whatever cures are known, and preventions that are practiced now, could have been common knowledge centuries ago. And what of the multitudes that perished who might have been saved, and what of the misery which might have been prevented, had not this curse fallen upon man?

Since 1906, there have been only five deaths from yellow fever in the United States. Outbreaks of cholera and plague are unknown. In former years, puerperal fever took the lives of from five to fifty of each one hundred parturient mothers. At present, an average of one out of 1250 mothers dies of this infection following childbirth. Deaths from many diseases are less than one-tenth of their former number. These include wound infections, diphtheria, scarlet fever, malaria, dysentery, typhoid, small pox, and many dietary and metabolic diseases. Since 1880, the medical sciences have accomplished a total net saving of human life from all diseases which, if equally distributed among the population, would add sixteen years to the life span of each person. In 1880, the average duration of human life, that is, the average age at which death occurred, was 41.78 years. In 1925, the average duration of life was 58.29 years. In other words, those born at this time live on the average 16.5 years longer than those born at any time prior to 1880. In a population of 120,000,000 this would mean a total of 1,920,000,000 additional years of life. Such a figure is as difficult to conceive of as are the interstellar spaces. This is one contribution, numerically expressed, which medical science and its offspring, preventive medicine, have made to humanity in the short space of fifty years.

Indeed if, as the religionists believe, there is a god, he could not have punished his subjects more than by instilling in them the "dementia religiosa." If the Church had not taught that the sum total of all knowledge was contained in the Bible, and prohibited, on pain of death and confiscation of property, the promulgation of any discoveries, men would have reasoned as they are accustomed to at the present day, and we would not be 2000 years behind in all branches of learning.

But there has never been an advance in science of widespread importance, which in some manner endangered some mouldy religious concept, that the Church has not bitterly opposed; an advance which in time has proven of inestimable good for all mankind. (A glance at the history of human progress will reveal scores of such instances.) The opposition to medicine, as previously noted, is only one of many examples which might have been chosen. In proportion, as the grasp of theology upon education tightened, medicine declined, and in proportion, as the grip relaxed, medicine developed.

CHAPTER VIII

RELIGION AND ASTRONOMY

IN the early Church, astronomy, like other branches of science, was looked upon as futile, since the New Testament taught that the earth was soon to be destroyed and new heavens created.

The heavenly bodies were looked upon by the theologians as either living beings possessing souls, or as the habitation of the angels. However, as time passed, the geocentric doctrine, the doctrine that the earth is the center of the universe and that the sun and planets revolve about it, was the theory that held the highest respect.

Copernicus, in 1543, was first to bring clearly before the world the then astounding theory that the earth and planets revolve about the sun. But not until he was on his deathbed did he dare to publish it, for he well knew the opposition with which it would be met. Even then he published it with an apologetic lie by a friend Osiander, that Copernicus had propounded the doctrine of the earth's movement not as a fact, but as a hypothesis.

"Thus was the greatest and most ennobling, perhaps, of scientific truths—a truth not less ennobling to religion than to science—forced in coming before the world, to sneak and crawl." (*White: "History of Warfare of Science with Theology."*

During the next seventy years the matter slumbered, until Galileo upheld the Copernican doctrine as the truth, and proved it to be the truth by his telescope. Immediately the Church condemned the statements of Copernicus and forbade Galileo to teach or discuss them. All books which affirmed the motion of the earth were forbidden, and to read the work of Copernicus was declared to risk damnation. All branches of the Protestant Church, Lutheran, Calvinist, Anglican, vied with each other in denouncing the Copernican doctrine.

One man, Giordano Bruno dared to assert the truth in the hearing of the Papacy. For this heresy he was hunted from land to land, finally trapped in Venice, imprisoned at Rome, burned alive, and his ashes scattered to the winds!

Against Galileo, the war against the Copernican theory was concentrated. His discoveries were declared to be deceptions, and his announcements blasphemy when, in 1610, he announced that his telescope had revealed the moons of the planet Jupiter.

In 1615, Galileo was summoned before the Inquisition at Rome, and forced to promise that he would "relinquish altogether the opinion that the sun is the center of the world, and immovable, and that the earth moves, nor henceforth to hold, teach, or defend it in any way whatsoever verbally or in writing."

Pope Paul V solemnly rendered the decree that "the doctrine of the double motion of the earth about its axis and about the sun is false and entirely contrary to Holy Scripture."

The climax of this instance of the infallibility of the Church occurred when in his seventieth year Galileo was again brought before the Inquisition; he was forced to abjure under threats of torture and imprisonment by command of Pope Urban a truth which, in this day, is taken for granted by the youngest of children. Galileo was then kept in exile for the rest of his days, died, and was buried ignobly, apart from his family, without fitting ceremony, without monument or epitaph.

As late as 1873 there was published, in St. Louis, a work by a president of a Lutheran teachers' seminary in which he stated that the earth is the principal body of the universe, that it stands fixed, and that the sun and moon only serve to light it.

Astronomy brings forth a noble array of men who have, by their intense desire for the truth, persevered against the Church, and in spite of the vilest opposition of that Church, brought to the attention of man laws that have given a meaning and order to our universe.

Copernicus escaping persecution only by death; Bruno

burned alive; Galileo imprisoned; Kepler reviled, and Newton bitterly attacked. In this manner has religion aided astronomy!

CHAPTER IX

RELIGION AND GEOGRAPHY

THE ancient Greeks, especially the Pythagoreans, Plato, and Aristotle, had evolved theories of the earth's sphericity, which, while vague, were basic for subsequent accurate ideas that developed later.

When Christianity sprang into existence Eusebius, St. John Chrysostom, and Cosmos evolved a complete description of the earth. They considered the earth as a parallelogram, flat, and surrounded by four seas, as a kind of house, with heaven as its upper story and the earth as its ground floor. To the north of the earth was a great mountain; at night the sun was pushed into a pit and pulled out again in the morning, with heaven as a loft and hell as a cellar. In the Atlantic Ocean, at some unknown distance from Europe, was one of the openings into hell, into which a ship sailing to this point, would tumble. The terror of this conception was one of the chief obstacles of the great voyage of Columbus. Luther, Melanchthon, Calvin, and Zwingli held to the opinion that a great firmament, or floor, separated the heavens from the earth; that above it were the waters and angels, and below it, the earth and man.

During the time that the sphericity of the earth was still undecided, another question arose that was considered of far greater importance, namely, the conception of the antipodes and the problem of deciding whether human beings existed on the earth's opposite side. It was Lactantius who asked, "Is there any one so senseless as to believe that there are men whose footsteps are higher than their heads? That the crops and trees grow downward? That the rains and snow and hail fall upwards toward the earth? I am at a loss as to what to say of those, who, when they have once erred, steadily persevere in their folly, and defend one vain thing by another."

St. Augustine insisted that men could not be allowed by the Almighty to live there, since, if they did, they could not see Christ at His second coming, descending through the air.

In the eighth century, a Bishop Virgil of Salzburg dared to assert that there were men living in the antipodes. He was strongly attacked by St. Boniface of Germany, who appealed to Pope Zachary for a decision. The Pope, as the infallible teacher of Christendom, made the following response: He declared it, "Perverse, iniquitous, and against Virgil's soul." And again another infallible statement by the infallible Pope Zachary became a doctrine of the Church.

In Italy, in 1316, Peter of Abano, famous as a physician, promulgated the opposite view to that of the Church, for which he was persecuted by the Inquisition, and barely escaped with his life. In 1327, Cecco d'Ascoli, an astronomer, was burned alive at Florence for daring to assert that men lived in the antipodes.

The difficulties that beset Columbus are well known. How he was hounded both in Portugal and in Spain by the clergy; and even after his discovery of America, the Papacy still maintained its theory of the flatness of the earth and the nonsense of the antipodes. Pope Alexander VI and Pope Julius II attempted to settle the disputes between Spain and Portugal by drawing some remarkable maps that may still be found: but no one dares to disturb the quiet of the ridiculous bulls that the popes issued on this dispute.

In 1519 Magellan made his famous voyage and proved the earth to be round and that men actually lived in the antipodes. But the force of ecclesiastical stultification was so great, as it is today, that men still believed the opposite view for two hundred years after the voyage of Magellan.

CHAPTER X

RELIGION AND CHEMISTRY AND PHYSICS

THE establishment of Christianity, beginning a new evolution of theology, arrested the normal development of the physical sciences for more than 1500 years. The work begun by Aristotle and carried on to such a high state of relative perfection by Archimedes, was stifled by the early Christians. An atmosphere was then created in which physical science could not grow. The general belief derived from the New Testament was that the end of the world was at hand, and the early Church Fathers poured contempt upon all investigators of the science of nature.

Then, too, for science there was established an insurmountable barrier, in that the most careful inductions of science from ascertained facts must conform to the view of nature given in the myth and legends of the Bible. For 1500 years science was forced to confine itself to a system of deducing scientific truth from scriptural texts. It was the accepted word of the clergy that science was futile and dangerous which led to the discrediting of Roger Bacon's works.

In 1163 Pope Alexander III forbade the study of physics to all ecclesiastics, which of course, in that age, meant prohibition of all such scientific studies to the only persons likely to follow them.

Roger Bacon was first to practice extensively the experimental method of science. Through his researches the inventions of clocks, lenses, and the formula for extracting phosphorus, manganese, and bismuth were brought to light. Bitterly attacked by the clergy, he attempted to defend himself by stating that much which was ascribed to demons resulted from natural means. This statement but added fuel to the flame. For in 1278 the authorities of the Franciscan Order assembled at Paris, solemnly condemned Bacon's teachings, and the general of the Franciscans, Jerome of Ascoli, afterwards Pope, threw him into prison, where he remained for fourteen years. At the age of eighty, he was released from prison declaring, "Would that I had not given myself so much trouble for the love of science."

"Sad is it to think of what this great man might have given to the world had ecclesiasticism allowed the gift. He held the key to treasures which would have freed mankind from ages of error and misery. With his discoveries as a basis, with his method as a guide, what might not the world have gained! Nor was the wrong done to that age alone; it was done to this age also. . . . Thousands of precious lives shall be lost, tens of thousands shall suffer discomfort, privations, sickness, poverty, ignorance, for lack of discoveries and methods which, but for this mistaken dealing with Roger Bacon and his compeers, would now be blessing the earth." (*White: "Warfare of Science."*)

Centuries afterwards, for stating the same claim, namely, that much which was attributed to demons, resulted from natural causes, Cornelius Agrippa, Weyer, Flade, Loos, Bekker, and a multitude of other investigators and thinkers, suffered confiscation of property, loss of position, and even torture and death.

In the latter half of the sixteenth century, John Baptist Porta, who was the first to show how to reduce the metallic oxides and thus laid the foundation of several important industries, was summoned to Rome by Pope Paul II, and forbidden to continue his researches.

Both in Protestant and Catholic countries instruction in chemistry and physics was discouraged by Church authorities, and in England the theologians strenuously opposed the Royal Society and the Association for the Advancement of Science.

Francis Bacon and Boyle were denounced by the clergy, and Lavoisier was sent to the scaffold by the Parisian mob. Priestley had his home, his library, instruments, and papers containing the results of long years of scientific research burned by a Birmingham mob that had been instigated by

Anglican clergymen. He was driven into exile, and the mob would have murdered him if they could have laid their hands upon him.

Yet, in spite of the opposition of the clergy, an opposition of such force that one may well wonder how these tender embryonic sciences could have withstood the terrific ecclesiastical onslaughts, the truths of chemistry and physics continued to diffuse themselves among the intelligent observers. The value to humanity of these two sciences is now established as inestimable.

CHAPTER XI

RELIGION AND GEOLOGY, PHILOLOGY AND EVOLUTION

The human race has suffered three grave humiliations: when Copernicus showed that the earth was not the center of the universe; when Darwin proved that man's origin was not the result of direct creation; when Freud explained that man was not the master of his own thoughts or actions.

LLEWELYN POWYS.

IN the writings of the Greek and Roman philosophers are found the germinal concepts of geological truths. But as Christianity took control of the world instead of a steady progression of knowledge in this field there was a distinct retrogression. According to the prevailing belief the earth was soon to be destroyed and the collecting of knowledge was futile and any study of its nature was vain.

St. Jerome stated that the broken and twisted crust of

the earth exhibited the wrath of God against sin. Tertullian asserted that fossils resulted from the flood of Noah. A scientific explanation of fossil remains was attempted by De Clave, Bitaud, and De Villon in the seventeenth century. The theological faculty of Paris protested against the scientific doctrine as unscriptural, destroyed their treatises, and banished their authors from Paris.

In the middle of the eighteenth century Buffon, in France, produced a thesis attempting to state simple geological truths. The theological faculty of the Sorbonne dismissed him from his high position and forced him to print a recantation stating, "I declare that I had no intention to contradict the text of the Scripture; that I believe most firmly all therein related about the creation, both as to order of time and matter of fact. I abandon everything in my book respecting the formation of the earth and generally all which may be contrary to the narrative of Moses!"

The doctrine which Buffon abandoned is now as firmly established as that of the earth's rotation upon its axis. Yet, in his day, it was heatedly asserted by ecclesiastics that the scientific doctrine that fossils represent animals which died before Adam contradicts the theological doctrine of Adam's fall, and the statement that death entered the world by sin—and this objection was further strengthened when the ecclesiastics became cognizant that geology had proved that the earth was vastly older than the 6000 years determined by Archbishop Ussher's interpretation of the Old Testament.

About 1580, there was published by authority of Pope Gregory XIII, the Roman Martyrology, revised in 1640 under Pope Urban VIII, which declared that the creation of man took place 5199 years before Christ. In 1650, Archbishop Ussher announced after careful study that man was created 4004 years before the Christian era. But, this proving too vague, Dr. John Lightfoot, vice-chancellor of the University of Cambridge, assured the world that, "Heaven and earth, centre and circumference, were created together, in the same instant, and clouds full of water . . . and this work took place and man was created by the Trinity on the 23d of October, 4004 B.C. at nine o'clock in the morning."

When the Egyptologists, Assyriologists, archeologists, and anthropologists showed that man had reached a far advanced stage of civilization long before the 6000 years given as the age of the earth, their efforts were ridiculed by the clergy, and these scientists were forced to bring their findings before the world in the face of the well known methods of ecclesiastical opposition.

At a very early period in the evolution of civilization men began to ask questions regarding language, and the answers to these questions were naturally embodied in the myths, legends, and chronicles of their sacred books. Language was considered God-given and complete. The diversity of language was firmly held to be explained by the story of the Tower of Babel; and since the writers of the Bible were merely pens in the hand of God the conclusion was reached that not only the sense, but the words, letters, and even the punctuation proceeded from the Holy Spirit.

At the end of the seventeenth century, the ecclesiastical contention that the Hebrew punctuation was divinely inspired seemed to be generally disproven. The great orthodox body of "religiosa dementia" fell back upon the remainder of the theory that the Hebrew language was the first of all languages which was spoken by the Almighty, given by Him to Adam, transmitted through Noah to the world after the deluge, and that the confusion of tongues was the origin of all other tongues.

It has only been in comparatively recent time, and in spite of the opposition of the clergy, that language has been accepted as the result of evolutionary processes in obedience to laws more or less clearly ascertained. Babel thus takes its place quietly among the other myths of the Bible.

In a purely civil matter, the infallible Church from its inception had displayed a marked hostility to loans at interest. From the earliest period the whole weight of the Church was brought to bear against the taking of interest for money. Pope Leo the Great solemnly adjudged it a sin worthy of severe punishment. In the thirteenth century, Pope Gregory IX dealt an especially severe blow at commerce by his declaration that even to advance on interest the money necessary in maritime trade was damnable usury. The whole evolution of European civilization was greatly hindered by this policy.

RELIGION AND EVOLUTION

Darwinism, which at first was declared by the clergy to be brutal, degrading, atheistic, and anti-Christian, is now included as part of the Bible teaching.

In a similar manner, the Copernican theory, the theory of gravitation, the nebular hypothesis, the theory of uniformity in geology, and every scientific advance has been opposed on the same grounds; that is, that these are against the teachings of the Christian Church. And how many Galileos, Brunos, and Darwins, and other would-be benefactors to the human race have died mute because of this opposition and fear of persecution by the Church?

In 1877, an eminent French Catholic physician, Dr. Constantin James, published an elaborate answer to Darwin's book. He called it, "On Darwinism, or the Ape Man." A copy was sent to Pope Pius IX, who was so pleased with it that he sent the author a reply in which he stated that it "refutes so well the aberrations of Darwinism, a system which is repugnant at once to history, to the traditions of all peoples, to exact science, to observed facts, and even to reason itself, would seem to need no refutation did not alienation from God and the leaning toward materialism, due to depravity, eagerly seek support in all this tissue of fables."

The Protestant clergy were no less vigorous in their opposition. In our own country it was opposed by Dr. Noah Porter, president of Yale College, and most bitterly by the Rev. Dr. Hodge and the Rev. Dr. Duffield, both leading authorities at Princeton University.

Fundamentalism in the United States furnished the spectacle of the trial, in 1925, of a school teacher named Scopes, for teaching the theory of evolution. Dayton, Tennessee, became the laughingstock of the educated world, and the derision with which this effort to obstruct knowledge at this late date was met with by the comments of the press in this country and abroad is at least encouraging. But it is an excellent example of what effect religious obscurantism may exert in backward sections of our country.

Dr. Max Carl Otto, considering the implications of evolution, calls attention to the following: "Take the evolution of living forms. The more we learn about biological history the clearer it becomes that the process has been, from the human point of view, incredibly bungling and wasteful. There have been futile experiments without number; highly successful achievements have been thrown aside; one type of life after another has arisen and has pushed up a blind alley to extinction. If there is a God whose method has been Evolution, then seemingly his slogan was 'We'll fight it out along this line if it takes a billennium' but, unlike Grant, he has always surrendered. In this maelstrom, the human species, as Thomas Huxley said—'plashed and floundered amid the general stream of evolution, keeping its head above water as best it might, and thinking neither of whence nor whither.' Many volumes have been written to give a purposive interpretation of the rise and evolutionary ramifications of living forms. The course of evolution itself is their refutation."

When the Churches could no longer ignore the rising tide of secular opinion, they resorted to compromise and called to their aid a certain number of intellectually dishonest scientists. The attempt to harmonize Christianity and Evolution can only be accounted for in terms of either dishonesty or stupidity.

"And that is true of the whole range of science. Science is, in fact, atheistic or nothing. It knows nothing of God, it does not bother about God, its triumphs are achieved by leaving God out of account." (*C. Cohen.*)

What has heretofore been mentioned is but a mere trifle when one considers the vast number of similar incidents in which religion has played the rôle of barrier to progress. These examples, though few, are sufficient to impress the mind of any clear-minded, intelligent individual with the conviction, in spite of all the sophistry and casuistry of the ecclesiastical apologies, that progress in this world has taken place in direct proportion to the degree that the mind of man has liberated itself from the control of theology and the myth of religion.

CHAPTER XII

RELIGION AND WITCHCRAFT

Better that a man's body should be destroyed than his soul. The worst death of the soul is freedom to err.

ST. AUGUSTINE.

It would be hard to calculate the perilous import of so treacherous an utterance, an utterance the latent sentiment of which has been responsible for I know not how much human agony. Menacing indeed to human happiness was such a claim, and in the course of time when the corporate body of the church became all-powerful in Christendom, it put into tyrannical practice what had been but a theological theory.

LLEWELYN POWYS.

IT is the purpose of this chapter to trace the origin of witches, wizards, and devils, the widespread belief in them at the time of pagan Rome, and the manner in which these were incorporated into Christian theology.

With the rise of Christianity and the gain of political power by its adherents, the perverted pagan idea of witchcraft became the source of the most terrible persecutions in the bloody history of religion. The numerous references to witches and devils in both the Old and New Testaments established the authority for the organized religious mania that scourged both Roman Catholic and Protestant Europe, and extended its tentacles into the New England colonies.

Instigated by ecclesiastics, and carried into effect by the intellectual serfs, their adherents, hundreds of thousands of "witches" were tortured and burned during the sway of the Witchcraft Delusion. With the Bible as an inspiration, the clergy inflamed the superstitious minds of the masses of that time with the conception of a ceaseless strife between the Kingdom of God and the Kingdom of Satan for possession of their souls and their bodies.

We of the present age may readily wonder how such a belief could have had so firm a grasp on the minds of our ancestors. Perhaps we will be tempted to attribute it to the ignorance of that time, particularly to the ignorance of the untutored masses. On the contrary, this does not approximate the actual situation. History reveals that the greatest minds of that age, men eminent in law, letters, and philosophy, not only defended this conception strenuously, but even engaged in the extermination of "witches."

That men of such superior intellect could defend such a barbaric institution, which today is revolting to our senses, necessitates the conclusion formulated at the end of this chapter.

The ancient Greeks and Romans believed that it was possible by supernatural means to inflict evil on their fellowmen, and all the sects of philosophers admitted this, with the exception of the Epicureans, who denied the existence of evil spirits. The magicians, in Greece and Rome, were at times punished because they injured men and not because they offended the gods. During the latter period of pagan Rome, some of the emperors passed laws against the magicians, if it was proven that by casting the horoscope the magicians had ascertained what was, according to their belief, the most auspicious time to start a rebellion against their rule. The emperors, however, notably Marcus Aurelius and Julian, were the patrons of magicians who foretold coming events to them. The public methods of foretelling the future, such as the oracle of the gods, formed part of their religion.

When the first Christians came into Rome and spread Christianity throughout the empire, they were inspired by an intense religious enthusiasm. They thought much less of the civil than of the religious consequence of magic, and sacrilege seemed much more terrible in their eyes than anarchy.

The Christians found in Rome a vast polytheistic religion in contrast to their own in which the entire world was divided into the Kingdom of God and the Kingdom of Satan. For them the world seemed to be teeming with malignant demons, who had in all ages persecuted and deluded mankind. "According to these Christians, the immediate objects of the devotions of the pagan world were subsidiary spirits of finite power and imperfect morality; angels, or, as they were then called, demons, who acted the part of mediators, and who, by permission of the Supreme and Inaccessible Deity, regulated the religious government of mankind. The Christians had adopted this conception of subsidiary spirits, but they maintained them to be not the willing agents, but the adversaries of the Deity; and the word demon, which among the pagans, signified only a spirit below the level of a Divinity, among the Christians signified a devil." (*Lecky.*)

"This notion seems to have existed in the very earliest period of Christianity; and in the second century, we find it elaborated with the most minute and detailed care. Tertullian, who wrote in that century, assures us that the world was full of these evil spirits, whose influence might be descried in every portion of the pagan creed. If a Christian in any respect deviated from the path of duty, a visible manifestation of the devil sometimes appeared to terrify him. The terror which such a doctrine must have spread among the early Christians may be easily conceived. They seemed to breathe an atmosphere of miracles.

Wherever they turned they were surrounded and beleaguered by malicious spirits, who were perpetually manifesting their presence by supernatural arts. Watchful fiends stood beside every altar, they mingled with every avocation of life, and the Christians were the special objects of their hatred. All this was universally believed, and was realized with an intensity which, in this secular age, we can scarcely conceive. The bearing of this view upon the conception of magic is very obvious. Among the more civilized pagans, magic was mainly a civil, and in the last days of the empire, a political crime. In the early church, on the other hand, it was esteemed the most horrible form of sacrilege effected by the direct agency of evil spirits. It included the whole system of paganism, explained all its prodigies, and gave a fearful significance to all its legends. When the Church obtained the direction of the civil power, she soon modified or abandoned the tolerant maxims she had formerly inculcated; and in the course of a few years, restrictive laws were enacted, both against Jews and heretics." (*Lecky.*)

Constantine, after his conversion to Christianity, enacted laws against the magicians. These were made more rigid under Constantius, his son, but suspended under Julian. These persecutions were renewed by Valentinian, spasmodically carried on to a slight extent, and then lapsed. During the period that elapsed between the sixth and thirteenth centuries the executions for sorcery were comparatively rare.

It is to be borne in mind, then, that magic as existing in pagan Rome was part of the religious conceptions of the Romans. The oracle as well as the various demons, which to them signified what the word "angel" signifies to us now, formed an elaborate system of mythology and idolatry. The early Christians coming into contact with these conceptions, at first found an insurmountable difficulty in spreading their beliefs among the rural inhabitants of the Roman empire. Polytheism was dominant while their monotheism was as yet a persecuted belief. The road of least resistance was compromise, and so this vast system of polytheism was perverted, while seemingly accepted into their beliefs, by making these "angels," "demons," as we now understand the word. Since the early Christians were dominated by a belief in constant Satanic presence, these demons were said to be the "Hosts of Satan." It was firmly believed that the arch-fiend (Satan) was forever hovering about the Christians, but it was also believed that the sign of the cross, or a few drops of holy water, or the name of Mary, could put him to an immediate and ignominious flight.

"In the twelfth century, however, the subject passed into an entirely new phase. The conception of a witch, as we now conceive it, that is to say of a woman who had entered into a deliberate compact with Satan, who was endowed with the power of working miracles whenever she pleased, and who was continually transported through the air to the Sabbath, where she paid her homage to the Evil One—first appeared. The panic created by the belief at first advanced slowly, but after a time with a fearfully accelerated rapidity. Thousands of victims were sometimes burnt alive in a few years. Every country in Europe was stricken with the wildest fever. Hundreds of the ablest judges were selected for the extirpation of this crime. A vast literature was created on the subject, and it was not until a considerable portion of the eighteenth century had passed away that the executions finally ceased. The vast majority of those accused of witchcraft were women, and again the Bible furnished the authority for the belief that women were inherently wicked. That the Fathers of the Church believed this is exemplified by the statement of Chrysostom in which he said that women were a 'necessary evil, a natural temptation, a desirable calamity, a domestic peril, a deadly fascination, and a painted ill.' " (*Lecky.*)

At this period the conception of a witch is radically different from that which was prevalent in the era prior to this one. The popular belief of the witchcraft ages, a belief sanctioned by most of the learned men of the time, was that the earth swarmed with millions upon millions of demons. They multiplied by reproduction in the usual way, by the accession of the souls of wicked men, of women dying in childbirth, of children stillborn, of men killed in duels. The air was filled with them, and one was always in danger of inspiring them with the air, of swallowing them in food and drink. Most

Christian writers and legendists said that there were so many of them they could not be counted, but Wierus took a census of them and reported that there were only 7,505,926 divided into seventy-two companies, each commanded by a captain or prince. They could make themselves hideous, or beautiful, as suited their purposes, and assume any shape. While capable of appearing at any time, they preferred the night between Friday and Saturday. Any human being who gave up to them his immortal soul could command their services for a certain time. Occasionally general conferences took place, at the pleasure of Satan, which were attended by all the demons and all the witches.

"These 'sabbaths' were held on the Brocken or other high mountain. Upon the spot where they met, nothing would ever grow afterwards, as their hot feet burnt all the fecundity out of the soil. In France, England, and the American Colonies, it was supposed that witches made their trips on broomsticks; in Spain and Italy it was believed that they twirled on the back of the Devil himself, who, for the occasion, transformed himself into male goat. On no account would a witch, when starting for a sabbath, go out through the open door or window; she would pass through the keyhole or up the chimney. While they were gone, inferior demons assumed their shape, and lay in their beds, feigning illness. Assembled on the Brocken, the Devil, as a double-headed goat, took his seat on the throne. His subjects paid their respects to him, kissing his posterior face. With a master of ceremonies appointed for the occasion, he made a personal examination of all the wizards and witches, to see if they had the secret mark about them by which they were stamped as the Devil's own. This mark was always insensible to pain, and it was the sure proof of witchery when found by the inquisitor. Any witches found by the Devil not so marked received the mark from him then and there, also a nickname. Then they all sang and danced furiously. If a stranger came to be admitted, silence reigned while he denied his salvation, spat upon the Bible, kissed the Devil, and swore absolute obedience to him. Singing and dancing was resumed, a mythical formula being used in the singing. When tired, they sat down and told of their evil deeds; those who had not been bad enough were scourged by Satan himself with thorns and scorpions until they could neither sit nor stand. Then came a dance by thousands of toads who were conjured out of the ground and standing on their hind legs kept time to the music Satan evoked from bagpipes or a trumpet. They could all talk, and asked the witches to give them the flesh of unbaptized babes for food. The witches promised to do so. The Devil told them to remember and keep their word and then stamped his foot, and the frogs disappeared instantly into the earth. Next came a most disgusting banquet except for a few of the most wicked witches, to whom were given rich viands on golden plates and expensive wines in crystal goblets. Then came more dancing; those who did not care for that amused themselves by mocking the sacrament of baptism. For this purpose the toads were again called up and sprinkled with filthy water, the Devil making the sign of the cross, while the witches repeated a formula as absurd as that used in ordinary baptisms. Sometimes the Devil made the witches take off their clothes and dance before him, each with a cat tied around her neck, and another dangling behind as a tail. Sometimes, again, there were lascivious orgies. At cock-crow, all disappeared; the sabbath was over." (*"The Story of the Inquisition"*—*Freethought Press Association.*)

This conception of a witch continued from the twelfth century to the time witch-burning ceased. With this idea of a witch being constantly instilled into the minds of their listeners, the clergy set loose fervidly religious mobs to scourge the countries of innocent women. With the entire world divided into the "Hosts of Heaven" and the "Hosts of Satan," with witches abounding in the air, in the water, and in the food, and with their immortal souls at stake, the frenzied population found evidences of withcraft in all manner of happenings.

"Pope after pope set the seal of his infallibility upon the bloody persecutions. At length came Innocent VIII who, on the 7th of December, 1484, sent forth his bull Summis Desiderantis. Of all documents ever issued from Rome, imperial and papal, this, doubtless, first and last, caused the greatest shedding of innocent blood. Yet no document was ever more clearly dictated by conscience. Inspired by the scriptural command, 'Thou shalt not suffer a witch to live,' Pope Innocent exhorted the clergy of Germany to leave no means untried to detect sorcerers, and especially, those who by evil practice destroy vineyards, gardens, meadows, and growing crops. These precepts were based upon various texts of scripture, especially upon the famous statement in the Book of Job; and to carry them out, witch-finding inquisitors were authorized by the Pope to scour Europe, especially Germany, and a manual was prepared for their use, the Witch-Hammer, Malleus Maleficarum." (*White: "Warfare of Science."*)

Another important and much discussed department was the connection between evil spirits and animals. That the Devil could assume the form of any animal he pleased, seems to have been generally admitted, and it presented no difficulty to those who remembered that the first appearance of that personage on earth was as a serpent, and that on one occasion a legion of devils had entered into a herd of swine. Saint Jerome also assures us that in the desert St. Anthony had met a centaur and a faun, a little man with horns growing from his forehead, who were possibly devils, and at all events, at a later period, the "Lives of the Saints" represent evil spirits in the form of animals as not infrequent. Lycanthropy, however, or the transformation of witches into wolves, presented more difficulty. The history of Nebuchadnezzar and the conversion of Lot's wife were, it is true, eagerly alleged in support of its possibility; but it was impossible to forget that St. Augustine appeared to regard lycanthropy as a fable, and a canon of the Council of Ancyra had emphatically condemned the belief. On the other hand, that belief has been very widely diffused among the ancients. It had been accepted by many of the greatest and most orthodox theologians, by the inquisitors who were commissioned by the popes, and by the Jaw courts of most countries. The evidence on which it rested was very curious and definite. If the witch was wounded in the form of an animal, she retained that wound in her human form, and hundreds of such cases were alleged before tribunals. Sometimes the hunter, having severed the paw of his assailant, retained it as a trophy; but, when he opened his bag, he discovered in it only a bleeding hand, which he recognized as the hand of his wife.

A French judge named Boguet, at the end of the sixteenth century, devoted himself especially to the subject and burnt multitudes of lycanthropes. He wrote a book about them and drew up a code in which he permitted ordinary witches to be strangled before they were burnt, but excepted lycanthropes who were to be burnt alive.

Now let us examine on what authority the popes and afterwards the reformers so rigorously persecuted the "witches." Both the Old and the New Testaments are riddled with references to witches, wizards, and devils. For example, this passage from Exodus XXII 18, "Thou shalt not suffer a witch to live."

From Matthew VIII 28-32, "There met him two possessed with devils coming out of the tombs, exceeding fierce, so that no man might pass by that way. And, behold, they cried out, saying, 'What have we to do with thee, Jesus, Son of God? Art thou come hither to torment us before the time?' And there was a good way off from them a herd of many swine feeding. So the devils besought him, saying, 'If thou cast us out, suffer us to go away into the herd of swine. And he said unto them, 'Go!' And when they were come out, they went into the herd of swine. And behold, the whole herd of swine ran violently down a steep place into the sea and perished in the waters."

The Old Testament, therefore, definitely commands its adherents to kill, and the New Testament gives a brilliant example of its chief magician, Jesus, exorcising devils from men and driving them into swine. There are numerous passages of the Bible which speak of the Devil, the Devil and his angels, spirit of an unclean devil, dumb spirit, foul spirit, unclean spirit, evil spirit, witch, witchcraft, wizards, necromancers, satan, the tempter, prince of the power of the air, prince of devils, etc.

These passages in the Bible were at once the chief source and sanction of the terrible atrocities which extended over several centuries and have come to be known, taken collectively, as the "Witchcraft Persecutions." The Devil, with his subordinate demons and the human beings who sold their souls to him, were supposed to be both capable and guilty of blighting the crops; causing the lightning; bringing destructive storms; withholding the rain; drying up cows; killing domestic and wild beasts; afflicting the nations with pestilence, famine, and war; causing all manner of diseases; betwitching men, women, and children; planting doubts in the mind and weeds in the fields; and in brief, doing about everything that was disagreeable to man in general, or that offended the priests as a caste.

Thus buttressed by the Bible, and with the nearly entire current of Church literature setting in the same direction, it is no wonder that the witchcraft delusion became one of the most appalling, if not the most appalling, fact in the development of the Christian religion.

There is extant no other record of destruction and cruel slaughter growing out of such beliefs in supernatural persons and powers that can ever begin to tell such a story of degradation and mercilessness as the record made by the Christian Church. Theologians laid stress especially upon the famous utterances of the Psalmist that "All the gods of the Heathens are devils," and St. Paul, "The things which the Gentiles sacrifice, they sacrifice to the devils."

Those suspected of heresy and witchcraft must confess; they were to be tortured until they did confess. This made suspicion equivalent to confession and conviction. In the witch "trial" the victim must not only incriminate herself but her accomplices, or all whom she "knew" to be in partnership with the Devil. She was bound to be tortured until she had given the names or described the persons of those she had seen at the "witches' sabbath." Then they would be put to the torture and the process repeated. It was not in human nature long to bear the awful pain; soon the leading questions of the inquisitors would be answered as they wanted them answered. It would be incredible were it not attested by such a multitude of witnesses, that men could honestly believe that testimony so extorted had the slightest value. But it is indisputable that hundreds of thousands of human beings were sent to a cruel death on this utterly worthless "evidence."

As few people realize the degree in which these superstitions were encouraged by the Church that claims infallibility, I may mention that the reality of this particular crime was implied and its perpetrators anathematized by the provincial councils or synods of Troyes, Lyons, Milan, Tours, Bourges, Narbonne, Ferrar, Saint Malo, Mont Corsin, Orleans, and Grenoble; by the Rituals of Autun, Chartres, Perigueux, Evreux, Paris, Chalons, Bologna, Troyes, Beauvais, Meaux, Rheims, etc., and by the decrees of a long series of bishops.

The infection was everywhere—Germany, Spain, Portugal, France, Italy, England, Scotland, and even America was scourged. It has been estimated that one hundred thousand perished in Germany from the middle of the fifteenth century to the middle of the sixteenth century.

Pope Gregory IX wrote a great mass of nonsense to the bishop and other chiefs urging stringent methods against the Stedingers, Frieslanders, inhabiting the country between Weser and Zeider Zee. He wrote, "The Devil appears to them (the Stedingers) in different shapes, sometimes as a goose or duck, and at other times in the figure of a pale, black-eyed youth, with a melancholy aspect, whose embrace fills their hearts with eternal hatred against the Holy Church of Christ. This Devil presides at their sabbath when they all kiss him and dance around him. He then envelops them in total darkness, and they all, male and female, give themselves up to the grossest and most disgusting debauchery."

The infallible pope of Rome!

The result was that the Stedingers, men, women, and children, were slain, the cottages and woods burned, the cattle stolen and the land laid waste. The pope's letter is a fair example of the theological literature of the time; the slaughter of the Stedingers an average illustration of the evangelistic methods of the Church.

Millions of men, women, and children were tortured,

strangled, drowned, or burned on "evidence" that today would be accepted nowhere unless by a court and jury composed of the inmates of a lunatic asylum, if even by them. It is unnecessary to say that the more severe the persecution, the more widespread did witchcraft become. Every person tortured accused others and whole communities went mad with grief and fear and superstition. No amount of human evidence establishing the actual whereabouts of the accused at the time they were asserted by the witness on the rack to have been at the sabbath would avail. The husbands were told that they had seen or held only the devil-created semblance of their wives. The originals were with Satan under the oak. The confessions of tens of thousands of witches are to be found in Europe's judicial records of the period of the Inquisition.

"The Protestant Reformers zealously seconded the exertions of Rome to extirpate witchcraft; they felt that they must prove that they were as orthodox as the Catholics, and were as loyal to the Bible. No one urged their fundamental ideas more than did Luther, Calvin, Beza, the Swedish Lutherans, Casaubon, Wesley, Richard Baxter, the Mathers,—all stood loyally by Rome." (*Lecky.*)

At Lisbon, a horse whose master had taught him many tricks, was tried in 1601 and found guilty of being possessed by the Devil, for which he was burned.

The witchcraft mania proper in England began in the

sixteenth century and reached its climax in the early part of the seventeenth century. Sir Matthew Hale, the great jurist, sanctioned the delusions and passed sentences of death by burning.

Queen Elizabeth made witchcraft a capital offense in England; and King James I wrote a book on the subject, and lent his personal aid and royal support to the persecutions.

Joan of Arc, the noblest of all the victims of this belief, perished by English hands, though on French soil, and under the sentence of a French bishop.

In Scotland, during the sixteenth century, as well as the seventeenth, were seen the most horrible examples of what domination of superstitious minds by ecclesiastics could do.

"Nothing was natural, all was supernatural. The entire course of affairs was governed, not by their antecedents, but by a series of miracles. Going still further, they claimed the power (the clergy) not only of foretelling the future state, but also of controlling it; and they did not scruple to affirm that, by their censures, they could open and shut the Kingdom of Heaven. As if this were not enough, they also gave out that a word of theirs could hasten the moment of death, and by cutting off the sinner in his prime, could bring him at once before the Judgment Seat of God.

"The Scotch clergy preached that, 'Hell was created before man came into the world. The Almighty,' they did not scruple to say, 'having spent his previous leisure in preparing and completing this place of torture, so that, when the human race appeared, it might be ready for their reception.'

"Of all the means of intimidation employed by the Scotch clergy none was more efficacious than the doctrines they propounded respecting evil spirits and future punishment. On these subjects, they constantly uttered the most appalling threats. The language which they used was calculated to madden men with fear and to drive them to the depths of despair.

"It was generally believed that the world was overrun by evil spirits who went not only up and down the earth, but also lived in the air, and whose business it was to tempt and hurt mankind. Their number was infinite, and they were to be found at all places and in all seasons.

"At their head was Satan himself, whose delight it was to appear in person ensnaring or terrifying every one he met. With this object, he assumed various forms. One day he would visit the earth as a black dog, on another day as a raven, on still another day he would be heard in the distance roaring like a bull. He appeared sometimes as a white man in black clothes, and sometimes he became a black man in black clothes, when it was remarked that his voice was ghastly, that he wore no shoes, and that one of his feet was cloven. His stratagems were endless. For, in the opinion of divines, his cunning increased with his age; and having been studying for more than 5000 years, he had now attained to unexampled dexterity. He could, and he did, seize both men and women and carry them away through the air. Usually he wore the garb of laymen, but it was said that, on more than one occasion, he had impudently attired himself as a minister of the Gospel. At all events, in one dress or other, he frequently appeared to the clergy, and tried to coax them over to his side. In that, of course, he failed; but out of the ministers thus tempted, few indeed could withstand him. He could raise storms and tempests. He could work, not only on the mind, but also on the organs of the body, making men hear and see whatever he chose. Of his victims, some he prompted to suicide, others to commit murder. Still, formidable as he was, no Christian was considered to have attained to a full religious experience unless he had literally seen him, talked to him, and fought with him.

"The clergy were constantly preaching about him, and preparing their audiences for an interview with their great enemy. The consequence was that the people became almost crazed with fear. Whenever the preacher mentioned Satan, the consternation was so great that the church resounded with sighs and groans. They believed that the Devil was always and literally at hand; that he was haunting them, speaking to them, and tempting them. The clergy boasted that it was their special mission to thunder out the wrath and curses of the

Lord. In their eyes the Deity was not a Beneficent Being, but a cruel and remorseless tyrant. They declared that all mankind, a very small portion only excepting, were doomed to eternal misery.

"The Scotch clergy taught their hearers that the Almighty was sanguinary, and so prone to anger that he raged even against walls and houses, and senseless creatures, wreaking his fury more than ever, and scattering, desolation on every side.

"The people, credulous and ignorant, listened and believed.

"For in Scotland as elsewhere, directly the clergy succeeded in occupying a more than ordinary amount of public attention, they availed themselves of that circumstance to propagate those ascetic doctrines which, while they strike at the root of human happiness, benefit no one except the class which advocates them; that class, indeed, can hardly fail to reap the advantages from a policy which by increasing the apprehensions to which the ignorance and timidity of men make them liable, does also increase their eagerness to fly for support to their spiritual advisers; and the greater their apprehension, the greater the eagerness." (*Buckle: "The History of Civilization in England."*)

James I of England had become imbued with the idea of witchcraft while in Scotland, and he believed that his stormy passage on his return from Denmark was due to witches. This storm was the origin of one of the most horrible of the many horrible Scotch trials on record. One Dr. Fian was suspected of having aroused the wind and a confession was wrung from him by torture which, however, he almost immediately retracted. Every form of torture was in vain employed to vanquish his obduracy; the bones of his legs were broken into small pieces in the boot. All the torments that Scottish law knew of were successively applied. At last, the king (who personally presided over the tortures) suggested a new and more horrible device. The prisoner, who had been removed during the deliberation, was brought in and "His nails-upon his fingers were riven and pulled off with an instrument, called in Scottish a 'turkas,' which in England we call a 'payre' or 'pincers' and under everie nayle there was thrust in two needles over, even up to the heads. So deeply had the devil entered his heart, that he utterly denied all that which he avouched," and he was burnt unconfessed.

And this from a king of England!

The methods of obtaining a confession were as follows: If the witch was obdurate, the first, and it was said, the most effective method of obtaining confession was by what was termed "waking her." An iron bridle or hoop was bound across her face with four prongs which were thrust into her mouth. It was fastened behind to the wall by a chain, in such a manner that the victim was unable to lie down, and in this position she was sometimes kept for several days, while men were constantly with her to prevent her from closing her eyes for a moment in sleep. Partly in order to effect this object, and partly to discover the insensible mark which was the sure sign of a witch, long pins were thrust into her body. At the same time, as it was a saying in Scotland that a witch would never confess while she could drink, excessive thirst was added to her torments. Some prisoners have been "waked" for five nights, one it is said, even for nine.

The physical and mental suffering of such a process was sufficient to overcome the resolution of many, and to distract the understanding of not a few. But other and perhaps worse tortures were in reserve. The three principal ones that were habitually applied were the "penny-winks, the boot, and the caschielawis." The first was a kind of thumbscrew; the second was a frame in which the leg was inserted, and in which it was broken by wedges driven in by a hammer; the third was also an iron frame for the leg, which was from time to time heated over a brazier. Fire-matches were sometimes applied to the body of the victim. We read in a contemporary legal register, of one man who was kept for forty-eight hours in "vehement torture" in the caschielawis; and of another who remained in the same frightful machine for eleven days and nights, whose legs were broken daily for fourteen days in the boots, and who was so scourged that the whole skin was torn from his body. This was, it is true, censured as an extreme case, but it was only an excessive application of the common torture.

The witches were commonly strangled before they were burnt, but this merciful provision was very frequently omitted. An Earl of Wear tells how, with a piercing yell, some women once broke half-burnt from the slow fire consuming them, struggled for a few moments with a despairing energy among the spectators, but soon with shrieks of blasphemy and wild protestations of innocence sank writhing in agony amid the flames.

But just picture this scene for a moment! The horror of such a scene! What a crime for one human to commit against another! A burnt offering to the gods! How well pleased the Almighty God must have been with the stench of burning human flesh rising to his nostrils. And how well he must have rewarded his faithful servants, for was this not done in His name? "Thou shalt not suffer a witch to live."

As Lecky points out in his famous work on the "History of European Morals," such incidents are but illustrations of the great truth that when men have come to regard a certain class of their fellow creatures as doomed by the Almighty to eternal and excruciating agonies, and when their theology directs their minds with intense and realizing earnestness to the contemplation of such agonies, the result will be an indifference to the suffering of those whom they deem the enemies of their God, as absolute as it is perhaps possible for human nature to attain.

225

It is a historical fact that in 1591, a lady of rank, Eufame Macalyane, sought the assistance of Agnes Sampson for the relief of pain at the time of birth of her two sons. Agnes Sampson was tried before King James for her heresy, was condemned as a witch, and was burned alive on the Castle Hill of Edinburgh.

It is generally said that the last execution in Scotland was in 1722, but Captain Burt, who visited the country in 1730, speaks of a woman who was burnt as late as 1727. As late as 1736, the divines of the Associated Presbytery passed a resolution declaiming their belief in witchcraft, and deploring the scepticism that was then general.

The Pilgrim Fathers brought to our shores the seeds of the Witchcraft Delusion at a time when it was rapidly fading in England, and again history furnishes us with an example of a people with strong religious instincts who, being freed from their persecutors, became in turn the most violent persecutors of those that did not profess their particular creed. It was particularly due to the preaching of Cotton Mather that a panic of fear was created through the New England Colonies. Mrs. Ann Hibbons was tried before the Great and General Court of Massachusetts, sentenced and hanged on the 19th of June, 1656. "Goody Oliver" was executed as a witch on November 16th, 1688.

There were twenty murders in 1692, and these before a

civil court. The trials took place before the illegal Court of Oyer and Terminer, appointed by Governor Phipps, at the instigation of the Lieutenant-Governor and Chief Justice Stoughton, and Joseph Dudley, formerly governor, and the Chief Judge of the Court which, in 1688, had sent "Goody Oliver" to her death at the gallows.

Cotton Mather defended this practice in his book, "The Wonders of The Invisible World," and Increase Mather, the father of Cotton, was equally as strenuous in the "Witch Hunt." Increase Mather survived this massacre thirty years, and his son, five years longer, but there is hardly a word of regret or sympathy to be found anywhere, even in their private diaries and correspondence. These executions in Massachusetts form one of the darkest pages in the history of America.

It is not surprising that the clergy of the sixteenth and seventeenth centuries supported both in practice and theory the Witchcraft Delusion, but when we find the ablest minds of the laity bursting into print with a vehement defense of this belief, it is difficult for us, in the present day, to conceive of such folly. And yet, today, we have able minds defending a precept of which the Witchcraft Delusion is but a part.

"The defenders of the belief (Witchcraft), who were men of great and distinguished talent, maintained that there was no fact in all history more fully attested, and that to reject it would be to strike at the root of all historical evidence of the miraculous." (*Lecky.*)

The subject was examined in tens of thousands of cases, in almost every country in Europe, by tribunals which included the acutest lawyers and ecclesiastics of the ages, on, the scene and at the time when the alleged acts had taken place, and with the assistance of innumerable sworn witnesses. The judges had no motive whatever to desire the condemnation of the accused, and as conviction would be followed by fearful death, they had the strongest motives to exercise their power with caution and deliberation. The whole force of public opinion was directed constantly and earnestly to the question for many centuries, and although there was some controversy concerning the details of witchcraft, the fact of its existence was long considered undoubted.

For many centuries the ablest men were not merely unwilling to repudiate the superstition, but they often pressed forward earnestly and with the utmost conviction to defend it. Indeed, during the period when witchcraft was most prevalent there were few writers of real eminence who did not, on some occasion, take especial pains to throw the weight of their authority into the scales.

St. Thomas Aquinas was probably the ablest writer of the thirteenth century, and he assures us that diseases and tempests are often the direct act of the Devil; and the Devil can transform men into any shape and transport them through the air.

Gerson, the chancellor of the University of Paris, and, as many think, the author of "The Imitation," is justly regarded as one of the master minds of his age; he too, wrote in defense of this belief. "These men," he wrote, "should be treated with scorn, and indeed, sternly corrected, who ridicule theologians whenever they speak of demons, or attribute to demons any effects, as if these things were entirely fabulous. This error has arisen among some learned men, partly through want of faith, and partly through weakness and imperfection of intellect."

Bodin was unquestionably the most original political philosopher who had arisen since Machiavelli, and he devoted all his learning and acuteness to crushing the rising scepticism on the subject of witches. The truth is that in those ages ability was no guarantee against error; for the single employment of the reason was to develop and expand premises that were furnished by the Church. And this statement is as valid today as it was three hundred years ago.

Bodin was esteemed, by many of his contemporaries, the ablest man who had then arisen in France, and the verdict has been but little qualified by later writers. Amid all the distractions of a dissipated and an intriguing court, and all the labors of a judicial position, he had amassed an amount of learning so vast and so various as to place him in the very first rank of the scholars of his nation. He has also the greater merit of being one of the chief founders of political philosophy and political history, and of having anticipated on these subjects many of the conclusions of our own day. In his judicial capacity he had presided at some trials of witchcraft. He had brought all the resources of his scholarship to bear upon the subject, and he had written a great part of his "Demonomanie des Sorciers" before the appearance of the last work of Wier.

John Wier was a physician of Cleves who had in 1563 published a work which he called, "De Præstigus Dæmonum." He was quite convinced that the world was peopled by crowds of demons, who were constantly working miracles among mankind; and his only object was to reconcile his sense of their ubiquity with his persuasion that some of the phenomena that were deemed supernatural arose from disease.

"Wier," said Bodin, "had armed himself against God. His book was a tissue of 'horrible blasphemies.' For the word of God is very certain that he who suffers a man worthy of death to escape, draws the punishment upon himself, as the prophet said to King Ahab, that he would die for having pardoned a man worthy of death. For no one had ever heard of pardon accorded to sorcerers."

Such were the opinions which were promulgated towards the close of the sixteenth century by one of the most advanced intellects of one of the leading nations of Europe at that time; promulgated, too, with a tone of confidence and of triumph that shows how fully the writer could count upon the religious sympathies of his readers: the "Demonomanie des Sorciers" appeared in 1581.

With a man of the caliber of Bodin writing the above, it is not to be wondered at that the mobs were so active in the "Witch Hunt." For as Lecky cites, "Although the illiterate cannot follow the more intricate speculations of their teachers, they can catch the general tone and character of thought which these speculations produce, and they readily apply them to their own sphere of thought."

In 1587, Montaigne published the first great sceptical work in the French language. The vast mass of authority which those writers loved to array, and by which they shaped the whole course of their reasoning, is calmly and unhesitatingly discarded. The passion for the miraculous, the absorbing sense of diabolical capacities, have all vanished like a dream. The old theological measure of probability has completely disappeared, and is replaced by a shrewd secular common sense. The statements of the witches were pronounced intrinsically incredible. The dreams of a disordered imagination, or the terrors of the rack, would account for many of them; but even when it is impossible to explain the evidence, it is quite unnecessary to believe it. "After all," Montaigne said, "it is setting a high value upon our opinions to roast men alive on account of them."

"It was the merit of Montaigne to rise, by the force of his masculine genius, into the clear world of reality; to judge the opinions of his age, with an intellect that was invigorated but not enslaved by knowledge; and to contemplate the systems of the past, without being dazzled by the reverence that had surrounded them. He was the first great representative of the modern secular and rationalistic spirit. The strong predisposition of Montaigne was to regard witchcraft as the result of natural causes, and therefore, though he did not attempt to explain all the statements which he had heard, he was convinced that no conceivable improbability could be as great as that which would be involved in their reception." (*Lecky.*)

Thirteen years after Montaigne, Charron wrote his famous treatise on Wisdom. In this work he systematized many of the opinions of Montaigne.

Voltaire treated the whole subject with a scornful ridicule and observed that, "Since there had been philosophers in France, witches had become proportionately rare."

In 1681, Joseph Glanvil, a divine who in his day was very famous, took up the defense of the dying belief. "The Sadducismus Triumphatus," which he published, is probably the ablest book ever published in defense of the superstition, and although men of the ability of Henry, More, the famous philosopher Casaubon, the learned Dean of Canterbury,

Boyle and Cudworth, came to his defense, the delusion was fast losing ground. Lecky points out that by this time, "The sense of the improbability of witchcraft became continually stronger, till any anecdote which involved the intervention of the Devil was on that account generally ridiculed. This spirit was exhibited especially among those whose habits of thought were most secular, and whose minds were least governed by authority."

But the belief did not become extinguished immediately. In France, in 1850, the Civil Tribunal of Chartres tried a man and woman named Soubervie for having caused the death of a woman called Bedouret. They believed she was a witch, and declared that the *priest* had told them she was the cause of an illness under which the woman Soubervie was suffering. They accordingly drew Bedouret into a private room, held her down upon some burning straw, and placed a red-hot iron across her mouth. The unhappy woman soon died in extreme agony. The Soubervies confessed, and indeed, exulted in their act. At their trials they obtained the highest possible characters. It was shown that they had been actuated solely by superstition, and it was urged that they only followed the highest ecclesiastical precedent. The jury recommended them to mercy, and they were only sentenced to pay twenty-five francs a year to the husband of the victim, and to be imprisoned for four months. In 1850!!

A great many may remember the "Hex" murder case near Lancaster, Pennsylvania, in 1930! This is scarcely different from an incident which had occurred in 1892 in Wemding, Germany: An hysterical woman was "exorcised" by the Capuchin Father Aurelian, who accused a peasant woman of bewitching him.

The foregoing has shown that witchcraft is not an isolated incident in the history of Christianity, as the ecclesiastics would have us believe, but is a vital part of their religion. Witchcraft bears the same relation to Christianity that an arm bears to the body; neither can be removed without destroying the symmetrical aspect of the whole.

Witchcraft is an integral part of the Christian religion, but its falsity has become so obvious that even the most devout have had to abandon it. Yet the other precepts are still maintained; and in the Bible which is claimed to be infallible, something is forgotten and discarded, something is declared to be ridiculous. And yet they call the Bible infallible. Again, if witchcraft is given up, why not the chief witch of the Bible, the Devil? Yet if this be yielded, then the idea of Atonement, the central doctrine of the Christian Church, must also go.

"Thou shalt not suffer a witch to live." If this be God's word, did God err when He said it? If He erred, He probably did so in many other things; if He did riot Christians must either still maintain the Witchcraft Delusion or deny the Bible

Delusion.

The Witchcraft Delusion is denied and forgotten, and no one thinks of quoting, "Thou shalt not suffer a witch to live." But the Bible Delusion despite all manner of ecclesiastical sophistry still maintains that man was created miraculously some 6000 years ago from the dust of the earth, that woman was made from a bone taken from the side of man, that language came into existence in the course of a single night, that God instituted a horrible massacre of the people by drowning because they did not come up to his expectations. It maintains miracles, virgin births, resurrections from the dead, and a literal heaven and hell.

Again, in the New Testament, Matthew tells how the chief magician of the New Testament, Jesus, exorcised the devils from men and drove them into swine. What could be more explicit? If men were possessed of devils in Jesus' time, what has happened to these devils now? Surely, Jesus could not misinterpret his own words or deeds, if the religionists contend that we are now misinterpreting the Bible? If they state that his recorders were in error, then they admit the error of the entire Bible, for it is illogical for one part to be true and another to be false, when both are components of an infallible statement.

"But they who abondon belief in maleficent demons and in witches as also, for this follows, in beneficent agents, such as angels, find themselves in a serious dilemma. For to this are such committed: If Jesus who came that he might destroy the Devil, and who is reported, among other proofs of his divine ministry, to have cast out demons from the 'possessed human beings,' and in one case, to have permitted a crowd of infernal agents to enter into a herd of swine; if he verily believed that he did these things, and if it be true that the belief is a superstition limited to the ignorant or barbaric mind, then what value can be attached to any statement that Jesus is reported to have made about the spiritual world?" (*Edward Clodd: "Pioneers of Evolution."*)

The old adage that a chain is just as strong as its weakest link is very apt in this case. A belief in witches is part of the Bible; and if the civilized world rejects that concept, it must reject the Bible, for it is no longer infallible, since it is in error.

Disregarding the internal evidence which declares the Bible to be spurious, and the scientific advances which have proven the Bible to be a myth and a fable, if man still insists on "revealed religion" he must admit that sorcery and witchcraft are an integral part of the Bible teaching. He must still either believe in witchcraft or disbelieve all of the Bible. For again, one part cannot be true and another false of an infallible statement.

I thoroughly and emphatically agree with John Wesley who, in 1769, wrote, "The English in general, and indeed most of the men of learning in Europe, have given up all accounts of witches and apparitions as mere old wives' fables. I am sorry for it, and I willingly take this opportunity of entering my solemn protest against this violent compliment which so many that believe in the Bible pay to those who do not believe it. I owe them no such service. I take knowledge that these are at the bottom of the outcry which has been raised, and with such insolence spread through the land, in direct opposition, not only to the Bible, but to the suffrage of the wisest and best of men in all ages and nations. They well know (whether Christians know it or not) *that the giving up of witchcraft is in effect giving up the Bible.*"

Lecky, in that masterful work, "The Rise and Influence of Rationalism in Europe," from which I have so freely quoted, states, "A disbelief in ghosts and witches was one of the most prominent characteristics of Scepticism in the seventeenth century. Yet, for more than fifteen hundred years it was universally believed that the Bible established in the clearest manner, the validity of the crime, and that an amount of evidence, so varied and so ample as to preclude the very possibility of doubt, attested its continuance and its prevalence. . . . In our own day, it may be said with confidence, that it would be altogether impossible for such an amount of evidence to accumulate around a conception which has no substantial basis in fact."

And yet today, in the twentieth century, we do have an amount of "evidence" accumulated around a conception which had no substantial basis of fact. What a perfect analogy presents itself between one precept of revealed religion and religion in its entirety. In the seventeenth century, scepticism confined itself to a disbelief in witchcraft, one particular of revealed religion; in the twentieth century, scepticism expands and reveals the absurdity of all revealed religion. Just as when we read the annals of witchcraft today we sicken with the horror of this insane conception, so will posterity in the none too distant future, perhaps three more centuries, do for *all religion* what three centuries did for witchcraft. Just so will they regard revealed religion in its entirety as we look upon the one factor, the *Witchcraft Delusion*.

Men came gradually to disbelieve in witchcraft because they learned gradually to look upon it as absurd. This new tone of thought appeared first of all in those who were least subject to theological influences, and soon spread through the educated laity, and last of all, took possession of the clergy. So shall it be with all religions.

A belief that was held for 1500 years, in the comparatively insignificant period of 100 years, sinks into oblivion; for the last judicial execution occurred in Switzerland in 1782; and the last law on the subject, the Irish Statute, was repealed in 1821. It is not, therefore, too much of a stretch of the imagination to conceive what the inhabitants of this planet will think of all religion 300 years from now. We have the sterling example of the Witchcraft Delusion before us. Yes, despite the otherwise brilliant men of today who still maintain the Bible Delusion, and the "Hedgers," that group of religious apologists who form those various sects, such as the Unitarians, the Humanists, etc. They are but the middle ground; they are but the intermediate between the delusionists and those that maintain the philosophy that eventually must triumph, the philosophy of atheism. When we think back to that group of capable men headed by Bodin, Gerson, and Joseph Glanvil, who turned their ability and learning to the defense of the Witchcraft Delusion, we find the answer to that ever-present response which the confused of this age give when confronted with the incompatabilities in their religion, namely, "Oh, well, more brilliant men than I believe in this delusion."

Bodin, Gerson, and Glanvil could not bolster up a dying belief; and the Bodins, Gersons, and Glanvils of today cannot long bolster up the dying belief in all religions . . . no matter what their ability or capacities may be. The handwriting is on the wall; the past teaches us what the future may be, but there is still much work to be done.

CHAPTER XIII

RELIGION AND MORALITY

The current religion is indirectly adverse to morals, because it is adverse to the freedom of the intellect. But it is also directly adverse to morals by inventing spurious and bastard virtues.

WINWOOD READE, "Martyrdom of Man."

IT had been formerly asserted by theologians that our moral laws were given to man by a supernatural intuitive process. However, Professor E. A. Westermarck's "Origin and Development of the Moral Ideas," and similar researches, give a comprehensive survey of the moral ideas and practices of all the backward fragments of the human race and conclusively prove the social nature of moral law. The moral laws have evolved much the same as physical man has evolved. There is no indication whatsoever that the moral laws came from any revelation since the sense of moral law was just as strong amongst civilized peoples beyond the range of Christianity, or before the Christian era. Joseph McCabe, commenting

240

on Professor Westermarck's work states, "All the fine theories of the philosophers break down before this vast collection of facts. There is no intuition whatever of an august and eternal law, and the less God is brought into connection with these pitiful blunders and often monstrous perversions of the moral sense, the better. What we see is just man's mind in possession of the idea that his conduct must be regulated by law, and clumsily working out the correct application of that idea as his intelligence grows and his social life becomes more complex. It is not a question of the mind of the savage imperfectly seeing the law. It is a plain case of the ideas of the savage reflecting and changing with his environment and the interest of his priests."

Justice is a fundamental and essential moral law because it is a vital regulation of social life and murder is the greatest crime because it is the greatest social delinquency; and these are inherent in the social nature of moral law. "Moral law slowly dawns in the mind of the human race as a regulation of a man's relation with his fellows in the interest of social life. It is quite independent of religion, since it has entirely different roots in human psychology." (*Joseph McCabe: "Human Origin of Morals."*)

In the mind of primitive man there is no connection between morality and the belief in a God. "Society is the school in which men learn to distinguish between right and wrong. The headmaster is custom and the lessons are the same for all. The first moral judgments were pronounced by public opinion; public indignation and public approval are the prototypes of the moral emotions." (*Edward Westermarck:* "*Origin and Development of the Moral Ideas."*)

Moral ideas and moral energy have their source in social life. It is only in a more advanced society that moral qualities are assumed for the gods. And indeed, it is known that in some primitive tribes, the gods are not necessarily conceived as good, they may have evil qualities also. "If they are, to his mind, good, that is so much the better. But whether they are good or bad they have to be faced as facts. The Gods, in short belong to the region of belief, while morality belongs to that of practice. It is in the nature of morality that it should be implicit in practice long before it is explicit in theory. Morality belongs to the group and is rooted in certain impulses that are a product of the essential conditions of group life. It is as reflection awakens that men are led to speculate upon the nature and origin of the moral feelings. Morality, whether in practice or theory, is thus based upon what is. On the other hand, religion, whether it be true or false, is in the nature of a discovery—one cannot conceive man actually ascribing ethical qualities to his Gods before he becomes sufficiently developed to formulate moral rules for his own guidance, and to create moral laws for his fellowmen. The moralization of the Gods will follow as a matter of course. Man really modifies his Gods in terms of the ideal human being. It is not the Gods who moralize man, it is man who moralizes the Gods." (*Chapman Cohen: "Theism or Atheism."*)

In the formation of the Old Testament, the moralization of Yahveh led to the creation of a god who coincided more with the morality of the later writers, the God Elohim.

"Rather must we say that morality begins in human social relations and passes from them to the relations maintained with the other life and with the Gods. Or, if one prefers to consider ghosts and gods as inseparable elements of the primary organism, then we should say that morality is born in that all-embracing psychical atmosphere. But it does not follow from that fact that the rise and development of morality are conditioned by belief in Gods and in immortality. Merely human relations are sufficient to the production of ethical appreciations. The invisible ghosts and Gods would never have been thought interested in the morality of the tribe, had not the leaders realized the importance of courage, of loyalty, of respect for neighbors' possessions, and the other elementary virtues. It is when the disastrous consequences of their absence became evident that the Gods were made to sanction these virtues. God or no God, immortality or no immortality, the essential morality of man would have been what it is." (*J. H. Leuba: "Belief in God and Immortality."*)

The best that is in man is generated in the experiences of

his daily life. The attributing of moral qualities to the gods was a much later development in the evolution of the moral ideas. At this stage of our development man is fortified by a sense of human fellowship, and in practice, as well as in theory, has long since given up the assumption that he needed superhuman beliefs. He has fully recognized the independence of morality from superhuman beliefs.

James Mill and J. S. Mill taught the greatest happiness of the greatest number as the supreme object of action and the basis of morality. And it was this conception that introduced the new ethical principles of duty to posterity. This conception is a much nobler one than the religious interpretation of morality to consist in mainly defining what man's duty to God is; a morality whose chief selfish inspiration is not the helping of one's fellowmen but the saving of one's own soul. A secular morality teaches that what man thinks, says, and does lives after him and influences for good or ill future generations. This is a higher, nobler, and greater, incentive to righteousness than any life of personal reward or fear of punishment in a future life. There are today a rapidly growing number of eminent moral teachers who condemn the clinging to the belief of personal existence after death as a hindrance to the best life on earth. Professor J. H. Leuba, in his work, "The Belief in God and Immortality," concludes that, "These facts and considerations indicate that the reality of the belief in immortality to civilized nations is much more limited than is commonly supposed;

and that, if we bring into calculation all the consequences of the belief, and not merely its gratifying effects, we may even be brought to conclude that its disappearance from among the most civilized nations would be, on the whole, a gain."

There are few educated men nowadays who would claim that morality cannot exist apart from religion. Theists are desperately attempting to harmonize a primitive theory of things, with a larger knowledge and a more developed moral sense. Morality is fundamentally the expression of those conditions under which associated life is found possible and profitable, and that so far as any quality is declared to be moral its justification and meaning must be found in that direction. "Our alleged essential dependence upon transcendental beliefs is belied by the most common experiences of daily life. Who does not feel the absurdity of the opinion that the lavish care for a sick child by a mother is given because of a belief in God and immortality? Are love of father and mother on the part of children, affection and serviceableness between brothers and sisters, straightforwardness and truthfulness between business men, essentially dependent upon these beliefs? What sort of person would be the father who would announce divine punishment or reward in order to obtain the love and respect of his children? And if there are business men preserved from unrighteousness by the fear of future punishment, they are far more numerous who are deterred by the threat of human law. Most of them would take their chances with heaven a hundred times before they would once with society, or perchance with the imperative voice of humanity heard in the conscience." (*Leuba.*)

The primary motive of moral standards and practices is man's desire to seek happiness and avoid pain. And so it is not strange that morality has become stronger as the power of religion has weakened. "Right through history it has been the social instincts that have acted as a corrective to religious extravagances. And it is worth noting that with the exception of a little gain from the practice of casuistry, religions have contributed nothing towards the building up of a science of ethics. On the contrary, it has been a very potent cause of confusion and obstruction. Fictitious vices and virtues have been created and the real moral problems lost sight of. It gave the world the morality of the prison cell, instead of the tonic of the rational life. And it was indeed fortunate for the race that conduct was not ultimately dependent upon a mass of teachings that had their origin in the brains of savages, and were brought to maturity during the darkest period of European civilization. . . . And we know that the period during which the influence of Christian theism was strongest, was the period when the intellectual life of civilized man was at its lowest, morality at its weakest, and the general outlook hopeless. Religious control gave us heresy hunts, Jew hunts, burning for witchcraft, and magic in place of medicine. It gave us the Inquisition and the *auto da fe*, the fires of Smithfield, and the night of St. Bartholomew. It gave us the war of sects, and it helped powerfully to establish the sect of war. It gave us life without happiness, and death cloaked with terror. The Christian record is before us, and it is such that every Church blames the others for its existence. Quite as certainly we cannot point to a society that has been dominated by Freethinking ideals, but we can point to their existence in all ages, and can show that all progress is due to their presence. We can show that progressive ideals have originated with the least, and have been opposed by the most religious sections of society." (*Cohen.*)

The puerile conception of heaven and the savage conception of hell are still, in modified form, deemed necessary for a religious morality. Why it should be necessary for a supreme intelligence to make all things straight in another world, that he could more convincingly rectify in this one, is a conception which has escaped the reason of a freethinker, but has been very profitable to those on earth that lead their adherents to believe that they hold the keys to our future abodes. Winwood Reade in his "Martyrdom of Man," discussing the moral value of the fears of hell-fire, states, "a metaphysical theory cannot restrain the fury of the passions; as well attempt to bind a lion with a cobweb. Prevention of crime, it is well known, depends not on the severity, but on the certainty of retribution. The supposition that the terrors of hell-fire are essential or even conducive to good morals is contradicted by the facts of history. In the Dark Ages there was not a man or woman from Scotland to Naples, who doubted that sinners were sent to hell. The religion which they had was the same as ours, with this exception, that everyone believed in it. The state of Europe in that pious epoch need not be described. Society is not maintained by the conjectures of theology, but by those moral sentiments, those gregarious virtues which elevated men above the animals, which are now instinctive in our natures and to which intellectual culture is propitious. For, as we become more and more clearly enlightened, we perceive more and more clearly that it was with the whole human population as it was with the primeval clan; the welfare of every individual is dependent on the welfare of the community, and the welfare of the community depends on the welfare of every individual."

The teachings of Christianity towards marriage furnishes a well known example of a reactionary philosophy of morals. The views of St. Paul on marriage are set forth in I Corinthians VII 1-9:

1. Now concerning the things whereof ye wrote unto me: It is good for a man not to touch a woman.

2. Nevertheless, to avoid fornication, let every man have his own wife, and let every woman have her own husband.

3. Let the husband render unto the wife due benevolence; and likewise also the wife unto the husband.

4. The wife hath not power of her own body, but the husband; and likewise also the husband hath not power of his own body, but the wife.

5. Defraud ye not one the other, except it be with consent for a time, that ye may give yourselves to fasting and prayer; and come together again, that Satan tempt you not for your incontinency.

6. But I speak this by permission, and not of commandment.

7. For I would that all men were even as I myself. But every man has his proper gift of God, one after this manner, and another after that.

8. I say therefore to the unmarried and widows, it is good for them to abide even as I.

9. But if they cannot contain, let them marry: for it is better to marry than to burn.

These precepts furnish an example of the harm that can be done when man follows the absurd and unsocial decrees of an ascetic individual written in a barbaric age and maintained as law in a more advanced period. The enlightened physician holds that it is not good for a man not to touch a woman; and one wonders what would have become of our race if all women had carried St. Paul's teaching, "It is good for them if they abide even as I," into practice. Bertrand Russell, in his

"Marriage and Morals," has gone to the root of the matter when he states, "He does not suggest for a moment that there may be any positive good in marriage, or that affection between husband and wife may be a beautiful and desirable thing, nor does he take the slightest interest in the family; fornication holds the center of the stage in his thoughts, and the whole of his sexual ethics is arranged with reference to it. It is just as if one were to maintain that the sole reason for baking bread is to prevent people from stealing cake." But then it is too much to expect of a man living nearly two thousand years ago to have known the psychology of the emotions, but we do know the great harm that his ascetic principles have done. St. Paul took the standpoint that sexual intercourse, even in marriage, is regrettable. This view is utterly contrary to biological facts, and has caused in its adherents a great deal of mental disorder. St. Paul's views were emphasized and exaggerated by the early Church and celibacy was considered holy. Men retired into the desert to wrestle with Satan, and when their abnormal manner of living fired their imagination with erotic visions, mutilated their bodies to cleanse their souls. "There is no place in the moral history of mankind of a deeper or more painful interest than this ascetic epidemic. A hideous, sordid, and emaciated maniac, without knowledge, without patriotism, without natural affections, passing his life in a long routine of useless and atrocious self-torture, and quailing before the ghastly phantoms of his delirious brain, had become the ideal of the nations which had known the writings of Plato and Cicero, and the lives of Socrates and Cato." (*Lecky: "History of European Morals."*)

This concept that the closest of association between man and wife is an obnoxious deed, has strewn its evil influence down through the ages to the present day. The stealth and obscurity placed upon sexual matters has had its roots so firmly fixed in our manner of dealing with this purely normal function, that at this late date medical science is just beginning to eradicate the evils. It is now well recognized by educators and physicians and all clear-thinking individuals that it is extremely harmful for men, women, and children to be kept in artificial ingnorance of the facts relating to sexual affairs. The obscurantism placed upon sexual matters has caused more physical and mental distress than most of our organic diseases. The physician is constantly correcting the abnormal conceptions that exist. The sex act had become something in the nature of a crime which could not be avoided, instead of assuming the manifestation of the consummation of the greatest love and tenderness that can exist between two individuals keenly attuned to the natural desires of a natural act. "The love of man and woman at its best is free and fearless, compounded of body and mind in equal proportions, not dreading to idealize because there is a physical basis, not dreading the physical basis lest it should interfere with the idealization. To fear love is to fear life and those who fear life are already three parts dead." (*Bertrand Russell: "Marriage and Morals."*)

Religion has brutalized the marital relations, and Lecky, dealing with this subject, states, "The tender love which it elicits, the holy and beautiful domestic qualities that follow in its train, were almost absolutely omitted from consideration. The object of the ascetic was to attract men to a life of virginity, and as a necessary consequence marriage was treated as an inferior state. It was regarded as being necessary, indeed, and therefore justifiable, for the propagation of the species, and to free men from great evils; but still as a condition of degradation from which all who aspired to real sanctity could fly. To 'cut down by the axe of Virginity the wood of Marriage' was, in the energetic language of St. Jerome, the end of the saint; and if he consented to praise marriage it was merely because it produced virgins."

Indeed, the entire ascetic attitude was well summed up by St. Jerome when exhorting Heliodorus to desert his family and become a hermit; he expatiated with foul minuteness on every form of natural affection he desired him to violate: "Though your little nephew twine his arms around your neck, though your mother, with dishevelled hair and tearing her robe, asunder, point to the breast with which she suckled you, though your father fall down on the threshold before you, pass over your father's body . . . You say that Scripture orders you to obey parents, but he who loves them more than Christ loses his soul."

It has only been with the advance of secular literature that the degrading, assumption of St. Paul that marriage is to be regarded solely as a more or less legitimate outlet for lust has been discarded, and the act of love as applied to marriage has come to have any meaning. And in this modern day the conception of the relationship of the sex act to marriage is far from being on the high plane where it rightly belongs. Bertrand Russell comments, "Marriage in the orthodox Christian doctrine has two purposes: one, that recognized by St. Paul, the other, the procreation of children. The consequence has been to make sexual morality even more difficult than it was made by St. Paul. Not only is sexual intercourse only legitimate within marriage, but even between husband and wife it becomes a sin unless it is hoped that it will lead to pregnancy. The desire for legitimate offspring is, in fact, according to the Catholic Church, the only motive which can justify sexual intercourse. But this motive always justifies it, no matter what cruelty may accompany it. If the wife hates sexual intercourse, if she is likely to die of another pregnancy, if the child is likely to be diseased or insane, if there is not enough money to prevent the utmost extreme of misery, that does not prevent the man from being justified in insisting on his conjugal rights, provided only that he hopes to beget a child."

What effect has Christianity had upon our moral life, upon crime, drug-addiction, sexual immorality, prostitution, and perversion? These blights upon our moral character existed long before Christianity, and after Christianity. But what effectual check has Christianity contributed?

The agitation concerning increased crime after the recent world conflict has brought this subject to the fore, and aroused a great deal of discussion and consideration of this problem. In its relation to religion, we have but one undeniable fact to bring before the thinking public. An examination of the statistics of penal institutions reveals that practically all criminals are religious. *Absolutely and proportionately smaller numbers of criminals are freethinkers.* Although church members nowhere constitute even half the population outside the prisons, they constitute from eighty to ninety-five per cent of the population inside the prison. This can be verified by reference to any census of any penal institution. As strangely as this may strike a great many readers, just so strange did it appear at one time to the multitude that the earth was round. (It is 500 years since the earth was proven to be round, yet there is a large colony of Christians near Chicago officially maintaining that the earth is as flat and four-cornered as the Bible states.) Neither Christianity nor any religious creed has proved an effectual check on civil crime.

The prostitute has been hounded and abused by ecclesiastics

since Biblical times, yet, it is only true to say that the religionist is not vitally interested in prostitution. Outwardly, he may pour forth a verbal barrage of condemnation, but if he believes he can save her immortal soul, ahunting he goes. He does not attempt to ameliorate the social welfare of this poor, degraded individual, as he thinks; her pitiful condition in the "everlasting present" on this earth interests him not at all, although it is this existence about which he raves, his only interest is in redeeming her soul not her body. If when the religionist tells the prostitute that only those who believe in Christ as God, in His Virgin Birth, and in His Resurrection in the Body, will go to heaven, and she agrees and repents— all is well; the religionist has saved a soul, and the prostitute goes about her business of spreading hideous venereal disease to others whose souls are saved by believing in Christ as a God. Her soul is saved and safe, but the scholar, the poet, the scientist, the benefactor to mankind, all those who make this life bearable and livable, their souls must roast in hell forever if they do not believe in the creed. Divine Justice?

The greatest number of prostitutes are religious, yet prostitution continues to flourish. The ecclesiastic condemns the prostitute as the cause, never stopping to think that the cause must have an effect, and that prostitution is but the effect. The cause is our economic conditions. Prostitution is purely a medico-social problem, and the more the ecclesiastic keeps his hands off the problem the sooner will the condition be remedied to its best. Attempts to repress prostitution without changing the economic organization will always result in failure. Prostitution has always existed and will continue to exist until our economic system has undergone a radical change. So long as girls have to fight with starvation or with beggarly wages, so long as men are deterred from early marriage by inability to support a family, and so long as many married men remain polygamous in their tastes, just so long will prostitution exist. But we have seen that the clergy is never anxious to interfere with the "rights of the few to tyrannize the many," and since prostitution is an economic problem, religion never has, and never will be, of any help in this case. (Aside from the fact that there are many instances of a few centuries ago where the Church in a period of temporary financial distress has owned well paying brothels.)

When we think of morality we are apt to concentrate more on sexual morality than on the more obtuse moral duties. Religion has from time immemorial been held up to our minds as a great force in the production of this morality. That is another myth. In our own country it is a trite phrase that a man has a "Puritan code of ethics," or as "straight laced as a Puritan."

When the Puritan Fathers landed in this country, they began an existence that has revealed to the world for all time the value of a "burning religious zeal." In a sense they showed this zeal in regard to the Witchcraft Delusion.

Coming as they did, to avoid religious persecution in their own native country, they should have established a colony which for meekness and beneficence would have shown the value of a true religious fervor. Instead, the persecuted immediately became the persecutors—again proving the worth of a mind that is imbued with a dominating religious zeal.

Secondly, the principal vocation and recreation of these Fathers was their religion. It is only reasonable to suppose that in such a truly religious atmosphere morality should have reached its zenith of perfection. What actually happened is well illustrated in a very informative and case reporting work by Rupert Hughes, the novelist, "Facts About Puritan Morals":

"Everybody seems to take it for granted that the behavior of the early settlers of New England was far above normal. Nobody seems to take the trouble to verify this assumption. The facts are amazingly opposite. The Puritans admitted incessantly that they were exceedingly bad. The records sustain them. . . . The Puritans wallowed in every known form of wickedness to a disgusting degree. Considering the extremely meagre population of the early colonies, they were appallingly busy in evil. I do not refer to the doctrinal crimes that they artificially construed and dreaded and persecuted with such severity that England had to intervene: the crimes of being a Quaker, a Presbyterian, which they punished with lash, with the gallows, and with exile. I do not refer to their inclusion of lawyers among keepers of disorderly houses, and people of ill-fame. I refer to what every people, savage or civilized, has forbidden by law: murder, arson, adultery, infanticide, drunkenness, theft, rape, sodomy, and bestiality. The standard of sexual morality among the unmarried youth was lower in Puritan England than it is today for both sexes.

"It is important that the truth be known. Is religion, is church membership, a help to virtue? The careless will answer without hesitation, Yes! of course. The statistics, when they are not smothered, cry No!

"If church-going keeps down sin, then the Puritans should have been sinless because they compelled everybody to go to church. They actually regarded absence from church as worse than adultery or theft. They dragged prisoners from jail under guard to church. They whipped old men and women bloodily for staying away. They fined the stay-at-homes and confiscated their goods and their cattle to bankruptcy. When all else failed they used exile. Disobedience of parents was voted a capital offense and so was Sabbath-breaking even to the extent of picking up sticks.

"Yet, as a result of all this religion, the sex life of the Puritan was abnormal. . . . Their sex sins were enormous. Their form of spooning was 'bundling,' an astonishing custom that permitted lovers to lie down in bed together in the dark, under covers. They were supposed to keep all their clothes on, but there must have been some mistake somewhere for the number of illegitimate children and premature children was stupefying. Dunton tells us that there hardly passed a court day in Massachusetts without some convictions for fornication, and although the penalty was fine and whipping, the crime was very frequent.

"Nothing, I repeat, would have surprised the Puritans more than to learn that their descendants accepted them as saints. They wept, wailed, and refused to be comforted. They were terrified and horrified by their own wickedness. The harsh, granite Puritan of our sermons, on statues and frescoes, was unknown in real life. The real Puritan Zealot spent an incredible amount of his time in weeping like a silly old woman. Famous Puritan preachers boast of lying on a floor all night and drenching the carpet with their tears. Their church services according to their own accounts, must have been cyclones of hysteria, with the preacher sobbing and streaming, and the congregation in a state of ululant frenzy, with men and women fainting on all sides.

"The authorities are the best possible, not the reports of travelers or the satires of enemies, but the statements of the Puritans themselves, governors, eminent clergymen, and the official records of the colonies. Hereafter, anybody who refers to the Puritans as people of exemplary life, or morality above the ordinary, is either ignorant or a liar. In our own day, there is an enormous amount of crime and vice among the clergy. Most horrible murders abound, by ministers, of ministers, and for ministers. Published and unpublished adulteries, seductions, rapes, elopements, embezzlements, homosexual entanglements, bigamies, financial turpitudes, are far more numerous than they should be in proportion to the clerical population.

"Governor Bradford breaks out in his heart-broken bewilderment and unwittingly condemns the whole spirit and pretense of Puritanism. The Puritans fled from the wicked old world for purity's sake, they were relentless in prayer, they were absolutely under the control of the church and clergy, and yet, their Governor says that sin flourished more in Plymouth Colony than in vile London!

"If our people are wicked nowadays because they lack religion, what shall be said of the Puritans who were far more wicked, though they lived, moved, and had their being in an atmosphere so surcharged with religion that children and grown persons lay awake all night, sobbing and rolling on the floor in search of secret sins that they could not remember well enough to repent? It is well to remember that there has perhaps never been in history a community in which Christianity had so perfect a laboratory in which to experiment.

"The very purpose of the Colony was announced as the propagation of the Gospel. The Bible was the law book. The Colony lacked all the things on which preachers lay the blame for ungodliness; yet, every infamy known to history, from fiendish torture to luxurious degeneracy flourished amazingly. This ancient and impregnable fact has been ignored. The records have been studiously veiled in a cloud of misty reverence, and concealed under every form of rhetoric known to apologists."

We can only conclude that religion does not seem to act as an effectual check against sexual immorality. Furthermore, high moral principles can be inculcated without any religious background, and have been in spite of religion. A man who is moral because of his reason and his sensibilities, and his comprehension of the necessary social structure of the world is a far better citizen than the man who feebly attempts a moral life because he expects a mythical existence in a delusional heaven or wishes to avoid hell-fire. A secular code of morals based upon the best experiences of communal and national life would place its highest obligation not to a deity but to the welfare of all fellowmen.

CHAPTER XIV

CHRISTIANITY AND WAR

INSTEAD of diminishing the number of wars, ecclesiastical influence has actually and very seriously increased it; we may look in vain for any period since Constantine in which the clergy as a body exerted themselves to repress the military spirit, or to prevent or abridge a particular war with an energy at all comparable to that which they displayed in stimulating the fanaticism of the Crusades, in producing the atrocious massacres of the Albigenses, in embittering the religious contests that followed the Reformation." (*Lecky.*)

Any institution that can sanction war is the most immoral institution that the mind of man can imagine. That an institution which claims to have under its guidance the moral activity of this earth, has instituted and condoned war is a known historical fact. That the Church has blessed the banners of opposing factions, and has gloried in the butchering of innocent heretics, no manner of present disregard for the facts and apology can refute and redeem. The religious and civil wars, the massacre of the Albigenses and other sects, the

Massacre of St. Bartholomew, are still alive in the memories of historians and still rankle. The Crusades were a bloody blot in the none too peaceful times of the Middle Ages. Christianity hurled itself at Mohammedanism in expedition after expedition for nearly three centuries. Millions of men perished in battle, hunger, and disease, and every atrocity the imagination can conceive of disgraced the warriors of the cross. When one crusade failed, a papal bull instigated the next. Taxes were imposed to defray the expenses, and Europe was so drained of men and money that it was threatened with social bankruptcy and annihilation.

The Inquisition between 1481 and 1808 had punished 340,000 persons, and of these, nearly 32,000 had been burnt. This was the result of the declaration that "The Inquisition is an urgent necessity in view of the unbelief of the present age." The Church forgot to mention the vast amount of wealth that accrued to her by these means. But we need not turn to the dead ages for material, for the present still firmly holds its war memories.

"Armenians massacred by Turks and Kurds; Christians slaughtered by Mohammedans is a horror as hideous in the name of religion as in the name of war. The persecution of Jews by Christians in the name of Christ is diabolical. The atrocities inflicted on Christian Belgium by Christian Germany stains the Teuton's hand as red as the Turk's, but with a difference.

The Teuton outraged his own 'holy women,' despoiled and murdered his own 'sisters in Christ,' while the Mohammedan hordes perpetrated their nameless infamies on those whom they believed to be the imps of Satan. Mercifully, call these things the logical crimes of a state of war! Then we must admit that savagery still is more powerful than religion, and we must concede that no religion so far has achieved the success that one might reasonably expect of a divine institution." (*Bell: "Woman from Bondage to Freedom."*)

The World War proved the utter worthlessness of Christianity as a civilizing force. The nations engaged were not fighting non-Christians; Germany, Austria, Russia, England, Belgium, Servia, Italy, and the United States are all Christian nations. They all worship the same God, they are all brothers in Christ, but that did not prevent their cutting each other's throats on the battlefield. Their common religious belief did not render the war less bitter nor less bloodthirsty.

Is it not a fact that if the Christian nations of the world would only live at peace together, war would be impossible? Neither Mohammedan nations nor Japan could threaten. When the Christian speaks of the brotherhood of man, he means a brotherhood of *believers* only. What kind of brotherhood did Christians bestow on Jews or heretics in the Middle Ages? Was it the brotherhood of man that Christianity bestowed on the conquered Mexican and Peruvian nations, and on the

Indians of our own country? If Christianity had expended as much energy in teaching its adherents the fundamentals of a sane social life, as it did to prepare mankind for a mythical life in Heaven, civilization would be today greatly in advance of where it is.

Does any one believe that Jew, Mohammedan, Catholic, and Protestant can long live in peace together? Common social needs bring mankind together but religion drives them apart. There can never be a lasting peace until the myth of God is dispelled forever from the minds of men. Then and then only, can the adjustment between economic and political forces lead to a permanent peace.

CHAPTER XV

CHRISTIANITY AND SLAVERY

Nothing during the American struggle against the slave system did more to wean religious and God-fearing men and women from the old interpretation of Scripture than the use of it to justify slavery.

ANDREW DICKSON WHITE.

THE Christian Church has had the audacity, in modern times, to proclaim that it had abolished slavery and the slave trade. It is difficult to understand how any "righteous" man could make that contention remembering that it was not until the middle of the nineteenth century that slavery became illegal in Christian countries, with one exception, Abyssinia, the oldest of the Christian countries, which still maintains slavery. In our own country, a nation had to be embroiled in a civil war before slavery could be abolished. Abolished by Christianity in the nineteenth century, when Christianity has been dominant in most civilized countries since the third century, and when the traffic in human flesh flourished right through those centuries in which Christianity was most powerful!

A reference to the facts show that this claim is as spurious as many others which the ecclesiastics have boldly affirmed throughout the ages. For not only is this contrary to the truth, but it is an undeniable fact that it was only by the aid and sanction of the theological forces that slavery was able to degrade our civilization as long as it did.

On referring to that legend which has been the source of most of our suffering and inhumanity, the Bible, a direct sanction for slavery is given in the Old Testament. Leviticus XXV gives explicit instructions as to where and from whom slaves should be bought, and sanctions the repulsive feature of separation of the slave from his family. Leviticus XXVII gives the "price" of human beings.

The Koran, which the Christians look upon as a ridiculous smattering of utterances of a spurious prophet, sets a superior example to the Christian "Divine Revelations."

"God hath ordained that your brothers should be your slaves, therefore, let him whom God hath ordained to be the slave of his brother, his brother must give him of the clothes wherewith he clotheth himself, and not order him to do anything beyond his power . . . A man who illtreats his slave will not enter paradise. . . . Whoever is the cause of separation between mother and child by selling and giving, God will separate him from his friends on the day of resurrection."

The New Testament follows the Old Testament, and there is nowhere to be found in its contents anything to suggest the elimination of this practice. Jesus did not condemn this practice, but accepted slavery as he accepted most institutions about him, and all superstitions. The teachings of Paul on the question of slavery are clear and explicit. Pope Leo, in his letter of 1888 to the Bishop of Brazil, remarks:

"When amid the slave multitude whom she has numbered among her children, some led astray by some hope of liberty, have had recourse to violence and sedition, the Church has always condemned these unlawful efforts, and through her ministers has applied the remedy of patience. . . ."

St. Peter was addressing himself especially to the slaves when he wrote, "For this is thankworthy, if for conscience towards God a man endures sorrows, suffering wrongfully."

The Church certainly saw nothing wrong with slavery when she preached patience to her slaves. It did not condemn slavery, but condemned the slaves for revolting. This in 1888!

In the "Encyclopedia of Religion and Ethics" is found: "There is no explicit condemnation in the teaching of our Lord . . . It remains true that the abolitionist could point to no one text in the Gospels in defense of his position, while those who defended slavery could appeal at any rate to the letter of Scripture."

It is true that slavery existed under Pagan civilization, but there it represented a phase of social development, while Christian slavery stood for a deliberate retrogression in social life. It was Seneca who said, "Live gently and kindly with your slave, and admit him to conversation with you, to council with you, and to share in your meals."

Think of what would have occurred if one of our philosophers had admonished a slave-holding Christian in the above manner.

"We are apt to think of the ancient slave as being identical with the miserable and degraded being that disgraced Christian countries less than a century ago. This, however, is far from the truth. The Roman slave did not, of necessity, lack education. Slaves were to be found who were doctors, writers, poets, philosophers, and moralists. Plautus, Phædrus, Terence, Epictetus, were slaves. Slaves were the intimates of men of all stations of life, even the emperor. Certainly, it never dawned on the Roman mind to prohibit education to the slave. That was left for the Christian world, and almost within our own time." (For a good account of the close association of Christianity with slavery see, *"Christianity, Slavery, and Labor," Chapman Cohen.*)

In Rome, the slave kept his individuality, and outwardly there was no distinction in color and clothing; there was very little sound barrier between the slave and the freeman. The slave attended the same games as the freeman, participated in the affairs of the municipality, and attended the same college. The ancients kept the bodies of their slaves in bondage, but they placed no restraint upon the mind and no check upon his education. It has even been said that the slave class of antiquity really corresponded to our free laboring class. It is also well known that a well-conducted slave, by his own earnings, was able to purchase his freedom in the course of a few years.

There can be no comparison, therefore, between Pagan and Christian slavery, except to the detriment of the latter. The Christian slave trade represents one of the most frightful and systematic brutalities the world has ever known. The contrast between the Pagan and Christian slavery is even more marked when the dependence of the Christian slave upon the good nature of his master is considered. Compare this with the decrees of the Roman emperors:

"Masters were prohibited sending their slaves into the arena without a judicial sentence. Claudius punished as a murderer any master who killed his slave. Nero appointed judges to hear the complaints of slaves as to ill-treatment or insufficient feeding. Domitian forbade the mutilation of slaves; Hadrian forbade the selling of slaves to gladiators, destroyed private prisons for them, and ordered that they who were proved to have ill-treated their slaves be forced to sell them. Caracalla forbade the selling of children into slavery."

"All that need be added to this is that the later Christian slavery represented a distinct retrogression, deliberately revived from motives of sheer cupidity, and accompanied by more revolting features than the slavery of ancient times." (*Chapman Cohen*.)

In the "History of Ethics Within Organized Christianity" is recorded, "The Church, as such, never contemplated doing away with slavery as such, even though Stoicism had denounced it as 'Contra Mundum.' Nowhere does the early Church condemn slavery as an institution. Kindness to the slave is frequently recommended, but this was done quite as forcibly, and upon a much broader ground by the pagan writers. It would be indeed nearer the truth to say that the Christians who wrote in favor of the mitigation of the lot of the slave were far more indebted to pagans than to Christian influence."

The Church itself owned many slaves, advised its adherents to will their slaves to her, and was the last to liberate the slaves which she owned. Yet, the apologists for the Church would have us believe that she was instrumental in the destruction of slavery, when it is a fact that there is nowhere a clear condemnation of slavery on the part of the Church.

H. C. Lea in his "Studies of the Church History" says, "The Church held many slaves, and while their treatment was in general sufficiently humane to cause the number to grow by voluntary accretions, yet it had no scruple to assert vigorously their claim to ownership. When the Papal Church granted a slave to a monastery, the dread anathema, involving eternal perdition, was pronounced against anyone daring to interfere with the gift; and those who were appointed to take charge of the lands and farms of the Church, were especially instructed that it was part of their duty to pursue and recapture fugitive bondsmen."

It must not be assumed that the Catholic Church was the only ecclesiastical body to condone slavery, or that it was only the traffic in black slaves that flourished a few hundred years ago.

"In the seventeenth century, thousands of Irish men, women and children, were seized by the order or under the license of the English government, and sold as slaves for use in the West Indies. In the Calendar of State Papers, under various dates, between 1653-1656, the following entries occur: 'For a license to Sir John Clot-worthy to transport to America 500 natural Irishmen.' A slave dealer, named Schlick, is granted a license to take 400 children from Ireland for New England, and Virginia. Later, 100 Irish girls and a like number of youths are sold to the planters in Jamaica.

"Had the Church been against slavery it would have branded it as a wrong, and have set the example of liberating its own slaves. It did neither. Nay, the Church not only held slaves itself, not only protected others who held slaves, but it thundered against all who should despoil its property by selling or liberating slaves belonging to the Church. The whole history of the Christian Church shows that it has never felt itself called upon to fight any sound institution, no matter what its character, so long as it favored the Church. Slavery and serfdom, war, piracy, child labor, have all been in turn sanctioned." (*Chapman Cohen: "Christianity, Slavery, and Labor."*)

In Abyssinia, the influence of Christianity has been dominant for a longer period of time than anywhere else in the world. The population of Abyssinia is at least ten million, and of this population not less than one-fifth, probably more, are slaves. In 1929, Lady Kathleen Simon published her book entitled, "Slavery," dealing with the slave trade of the world. In this work it is pointed out that slave-owning is an integral part of the religion of the country, and that opposition to the abolition of slavery comes principally from the priesthood which considers itself the guardian of the Mosaic law, and regards slavery as an institution ordered by Jehovah.

Slave raids are constant in this country, and are accompanied by the greatest brutality and cruelty. Vast areas are depopulated by these raids and even at this date, gangs of slaves may be seen by travelers, with the dead and dying bodies of those that have fallen strewn along the roadside. "The slave trade in Abyssinia is open, its horrors are well known, and it is supported by the Christian Church of the country. Such is slavery in the most Christian country in the world today, the country which has the longest Christian history of any nation in the world. Its existence helps us to realize the value of the statement that the power of Christianity in the world destroyed the slave trade. Slavery flourishes in the oldest of Christian countries in the world, backed up by the Church, the Old Bible, and the New Testament. It has all the horrors, all the brutalities, all the degradations of the slave trade at its worst. Such is Christian Abyssinia, and such, but for the saving grace of secular civilization, would be the rest of the world." (*Chapman Cohen.*)

The slave system that arose in Christian times, created by and continued by Christians in the most Christian of countries, provides the final and unanswerable indictment of the Christian Church.

Slavery was unknown to the Africans until it was introduced by the Christian Portuguese. In 1517 the Spaniards began to ship negro slaves to Hispaniola, Cuba, Jamaica, and Porto Rica. John Hawkins was the first Englishman of note to engage in the traffic, and Queen Elizabeth loaned this virtuous and pious gentleman the ship *Jesus*. English companies were licensed to engage in this trade and during the reign of William and Mary it was thrown open to all.

Between 1680 and 1700, it has been said that 140,000 Negroes were imported by the English-African Company, and about 160,000 more by private traders. Between 1700 and 1786, as many as 610,000 were transported to Jamaica alone. In the hundred years ending 1776, the English carried into the Spanish, French, and English Colonies three million slaves.

The cruelty experienced by these human cargoes on their transportation defies description. The chaining, the branding, the mutilation, the close quarters, the deaths by suffocation and disease, are a sterling example of man's inhumanity to man when his conscience is relieved by finding support of his inhumane actions sanctioned in that most holy of holies, the Bible. Exclusive of the slaves who died before leaving Africa, not more than fifty out of a hundred lived to work on the plantations. Ingram's "History of Slavery" calculates that although between 1690 and 1820 no less than 800,000 Negroes had been imported to Jamaica, yet, at the latter date, only 340,000 were on the island.

Slavery in America received the same sanction by the religionists which it received on the continent. George Whitefield, the great Methodist preacher, was an earnest supporter of slavery. When the importation of slaves finally ceased the states began the new industry of breeding slaves; the leading state for this breeding, and the one which contained the largest number of stud farms, was Virginia. Lord Macaulay, in a speech delivered before the House of Commons on February 26, 1845, said: "The slave states of the Union are of two classes, the breeding states, where the human beast of burden increases, and multiplies, and becomes strong for labor; and the sugar and cotton states to which these beasts of burden are sent to be worked to death. Bad enough it is that civilized man should sail to an uncivilized quarter of the world where slavery existed, should buy wretched barbarians, and should carry them away to labor in a distant land; bad enough! But that a civilized man, a baptized man, a man proud of being a citizen of a free state, a man frequenting a Christian Church, should breed slaves for exportation, and if the whole horrible truth must be told, should even beget slaves for exportation, should see children, sometimes his own children, gambolling from infancy, should watch their growth, should become familiar with their faces, and should sell them for $400 or $500 a head, and send them to lead in a remote country a life which is a lingering death, a life about which the best thing that can be said is that it is sure to be short; this does, I own, excite a horror exceeding even the horror excited by that slave trade which is the curse of the African coast. And mark, I am speaking of a trade as regular as the trade in pigs between Dublin and Liverpool, or as the trade in coals between the Tyne and the Thames."

It has been estimated that the members and ministers

of the Orthodox churches in the South owned no less than 660,000 slaves.

Thomas Paine, in 1775, when he wrote his article on "Justice and Humanity," was the first to demand emancipation in a lucid manner. The campaign for liberation of the slaves was therefore inaugurated by a freethinker, and triumphantly closed by another freethinker, Abraham Lincoln. In this manner did the Church abolish slavery. With characteristic disregard for the truth, the religionists have laid claim to Lincoln, which claim has been amply refuted; but we are still awaiting the Church's claim to Paine as one of her devotees.

"And, truly, the case against Christianity is plain and damning. Never, during the whole of its history has it spoken in a clear voice against slavery; always, as we have seen, its chief supporters have been pronounced believers. They have cited religious teaching in its defence, they have used all the power of the Church for its maintenance. Naturally, in a world in which the vast majority are professing Christians, believers are to be found on the side of humanity and justice. But to that the reply is plain. Men are human before they are Christians; both history and experience point to the constant lesson of the many cases in which the claims of a developing humanity override those of an inculcated religious teaching.

"But the damning fact against Christianity is, not that it found slavery here when it arrived, and accepted it as a settled institution, not even that it is plainly taught in its 'sacred' books, but, that it deliberately created a new form of slavery, and for hundreds of years invested it with a brutality greater than that which existed centuries before. A religion which could tolerate this slavery, argue for it, and fight for it, cannot by any stretch of reasoning be credited with an influence in forwarding emancipation. Christianity no more abolished slavery than it abolished witchcraft, the belief in demonism, or punishment for heresy. It was the growing moral and social sense of mankind that compelled Christians and Christianity to give up these and other things." (*C. Cohen: "Christianity, Slavery, and Labor."*)

CHAPTER XVI

CHRISTIANITY AND LABOR

The mortgage which the peasant has on heavenly property guarantees the mortgage of the bourgeois on the farms.

MARX.

The same Christ, the same Buddha, the same Isaiah, can stand at once for capitalism and communism, for liberty and slavery for peace and war, for whatever opposed or clashing ideals you will. For the life and the power of a church is in the persistent identity of its symbols and properties. Meanings change anyhow but things endure. The rock upon which a church is founded is not the word of God; the rock upon which a church is founded is the wealth of men.

HORACE M. KALLEN, "Why Religion?"

DURING the Middle Ages the heads of the Church exercised

279

all the rights of a feudal lord, and were even more tenacious of their privileges. The serfs were prohibited from migrating from one part of the country to another. The daughter of a serf could not marry without the consent of the lord, who frequently demanded payment for permission; or, worse still, the in famous "Right of the First Night." The serf was bonded in a hundred different ways, and it is significant of the esteem in which the Church was held that in every peasant revolt which occurred, there was always a direct attack on the Church.

Professor Thorold Rogers, writing of the twelfth century, gives the following picture of the poorer classes:

"The houses of these villagers were mean and dirty. Brickmaking was a lost art, stone was found only in a few places. The wood fire was on a hob of clay. Chimneys were unknown, except in castles and manor houses, and the smoke escaped through the door or whatever other aperture it could, reach. The floor of the homestead was filthy enough, but the surroundings were filthier still. Close by the door stood the mixen, a collection of every abomination—streams from which, in rainy weather, fertilized the lower meadows, generally the lord's pasture, and polluted the stream. The house of the peasant cottager was poorer still. Most of them were probably built of posts wattled and plastered with clay or mud, with an upper storey of poles reached by a ladder."

"What the lord took he held by right of force; what the Church had it held by force of cunning. And as, in the long run, the cunning of the Church was more powerful than the force of the robber-lord, the priesthood grew in riches until its wealth became a threat to the whole of the community. In England, in the thirteenth century, the clergy numbered one in fifty-two of the population, and the possessions of the Church included a third of the land of England. No opportunity was lost by the Church to drain money from the people whether they were rich or poor. The trade done in candles, and sales of indulgences brought in large sums of money, and there were continuous disputes between the clergy and the king and the Pope as to the divisions of the spoil. The picture of the Church watching over the poor, sheltering them from wrong, tending them in sickness, and relieving them in their poverty will not do. It is totally without historic foundation. When the poor revolted, and apart from the great revolts, there were many small and local outbreaks, the anger of the poor was directed as much against the Church as it was against the nobles." (*C. Cohen: "Christianity, Slavery, and Labor."*)

When the downtrodden masses of Spain, Mexico, and Russia revolted against the tyranny which had held them in the slough of medieval degradation, they likewise, in recent times, proved that they realized that their submission was as much caused by the Church, allied as it is with the state, as by the government itself.

The Church did attend the sick, but its trade was in the miracle cures and prayers, and so they very much resembled men hawking their own goods, and attending to their own business. And there is the plain, historic fact, that in defense of its miracle cures it did what it could to obstruct the growth of both medical and sanitary science. It did give alms but these constituted but a small part of what it had previously taken.

Through all the changes of the sixteenth, seventeenth, and eighteenth centuries, it is impossible to detect anxiety on the part of the Churches, Roman Catholic or Protestant, to better the status of, or improve the condition of, the working classes. Whatever improvements may have come about, and they were few enough, came independently of Christianity, organized or unorganized. Controversies about religious matters might, and did, grow more acute; controversies about bettering the position of the working classes only began with the breaking down of Christianity. And when, as in Germany, there occurred a peasants' revolt, and the peasants appealed to Luther for assistance, he wrote, after exhorting the peasants to resignation, to the nobles:

"A rebel is outlawed of God and Kaiser, therefore who can and will first slaughter such a man does right well, since upon such a common rebel every man is alike the judge and executioner. Therefore, who can shall openly or secretly smite, slaughter and stab, and hold that there is nothing more poisonous, more harmful, more devilish than a rebellious man."

And in pre-revolutionary France, the Church saw unmoved a state of affairs almost unimaginable, so far as the masses of the people were concerned, in their misery and demoralization. And this at a time when half the land of France, in addition to palaces, chateaux, and other forms of wealth were possessed by the nobility and clergy, and were practically free from taxation.

A contemporary observer writes, "Certain savage-looking beings, male and female, are seen in the country, black, livid, and sunburnt, and belonging to the soil which they dig and grub with invincible stubbornness. They stand erect, they display human lineaments, and seem capable of articulation. They are, in fact, men. They retire at night into their dens, where they live on black bread, water and roots. They spare other human beings the trouble of sowing."

In pre-revolutionary France, the clergy, counting monks and nuns, numbered, in 1762, over 400,000, with total possessions estimated at two thousand million pounds, producing an annual revenue of about one hundred and forty millions. The clergy were free from taxation and the higher members of the order possessed all the rights and privileges of the feudal nobility. To the end the Church in France, as in our day, in pre-revolutionary Russia, remained the champion of privilege and misgovernment.

In England, during the latter half of the eighteenth century and the beginning of the nineteenth century, developed the English manufacturing system. Woman- and child-labor were common in both mines and factories. The regular working hours were from 5 A.M to 8 P.M., with six full days' labor per week. One investigator remarks: "It is a very common practice with the great populous parishes in London to bind children in large numbers to the proprietors of cotton-mills in Lancashire and Yorkshire, at a distance of 200 miles. The children are sent off by waggon loads at a time, and are as much lost for ever to their parents as if they were shipped off for the West Indies. The parishes that bind them, by procuring a settlement for the children at the end of forty days, get rid of them for ever; and the poor children have not a human being in the world to whom they can look up for redress against the wrongs they may be exposed to from these wholesale dealers in them, whose object it is to get everything they can possibly wring from their excessive labor and fatigue."

In the mines conditions were still worse, and a report in 1842 states: "Children are taken at the earliest ages, if only to be used as living and waving candlesticks, or to keep rats from a dinner, and it is in pits of the worst character, too, in which most female children are employed. It would appear from the practical returns obtained by the commissioner, that about one-third of the persons employed in coal mines are under eighteen years of age, and that much more than one-third of this proportion are under thirteen years of age." In certain mines there was no distinction of sex so far as underground labor was concerned. The men worked entirely naked and were assisted by females of all ages, from girls of six years to women of twenty-one, who were quite naked down to the waist.

But if oppression was rife, education at a low ebb, and misery prevalent, the religion of the people was receiving attention. The period was, in fact, one of revival in religion. The Wesleyan revival was in full swing, and Evangelical Christianity was making great advances. Between 1799 and 1804 there were founded, "The British and Foreign Bible Society," "The London Missionary Society," and "The Mission To The Jews."

When the Education Bill of 1819 came before the House of Lords, out of eighteen Bishops who voted on the measure, fifteen voted against it! Thus the religionists were most active during the period when a condition approximating white slavery existed. And why should this not have been so, when the Church is not interested in the social and economic status of its adherents during their existence on this planet, but is avowedly concerned with deluding its devotees into a mythical belief in a life hereafter? The greatest number of slaves and the greatest degradation of workers is to be found in those times and places where religious superstition is most powerful.

In our own country, as well as in England, the labor movement has developed not merely outside the range of organized Christianity, but in the teeth of the bitterest opposition to it. Christianity, since it came into power, has always preached to the poor in defense of the privileges and possessions of the rich.

In a recent publication by Jerome Davis, which is entitled "Labor Speaks for Itself on Religion," the author has compiled the opinions of labor leaders in the United States, Canada, Great Britain, Russia, Germany, Czechoslovakia, Mexico, China, Austria, Australia, Belgium, and Japan. It is a terrific indictment by labor against organized religion. The author tells us, "Here is labor speaking for itself, and in the by and large it feels that the Church has not understood or helped it to secure justice. The majority believe that the Church has a capitalistic bias. It is a class institution for the upper and middle classes." This is putting the matter rather mildly when one considers their grievances expressed in their own words. Again Jerome Davis asks, "Is it possible that our Church leaders are to some extent blinded by current conventional standards? Are they so busy sharing the wealth of the prosperous with others in spiritual quests that they fail to see some areas of desperate social need? Do they to some degree unconsciously exchange the gift of prophecy for yearly budgets and business boards?"

James H. Maurer, the president of the Pennsylvania Federation of Labor, speaks for labor and the title of his subject is, "Has the Church Betrayed Labor?" Mr. Maurer's opinion follows: "A worker living from hand to mouth, and lucky if he is not hopelessly in debt besides, working at trip-hammer speed when he has work, with no security against enforced idleness, sickness, and old age, can hardly be expected to become deeply interested in, or a very enthusiastic listener to sermons about Lot's disobedient wife, who because she looked back was turned into a pillar of salt. He is far more concerned about his own overworked and perhaps underfed wife who, due to the strain of trying to raise his family on a meager income that permits of no rest or proper medical care, is slowly but surely turning into a corpse. To go to a church and listen to a sermon about the sub-limeness of being humble and meek, that no matter how desperate the struggle to live may be one should be contented and not envy the more fortunate, because God in His infinite wisdom has ordained that there shall be rich and poor and that no matter how heavy one's burdens on this earth, one should bear them meekly and look for reward in the world to come and remember that God loves the poor—such sermons naturally sound pleasing to the ears of the wealthy listeners, and the usual reward is a shower of gold and hearty congratulations by the sleek and well-fed members of the congregation. But to an intelligent worker such sermons sound like capitalistic propaganda, upon which he is constantly being fed by every labor-exploiting concern in the country, and quite naturally he tries to avoid getting an extra dose of the same kind of buncombe on Sunday. . . .

"In Churches, men have listened for nearly two thousand years to lessons and sermons about 'the brotherhood of man,' 'the forging of swords of war into plowshares of peace,' 'man is his brother's helper,' 'peace on earth, good will toward men,' 'thou shalt not kill,' We are taught to say the Lord's Prayer, and ask for heaven on earth, and yet, at every war opportunity, with a very few noble exceptions, the Church, at the command of the war lords, has scrapped its peace sentiments and turned its back to the Prince of Peace and Heaven on Earth and has shouted itself hoarse for hell on earth. And then the spokesmen of the churches of each nation at war have had the impudence to pray to a just God and ask Him to play favorites, to use His infinite power on their side and join in the mad slaughter of His own beloved children. And those slaughtered are the workers, and their folks at home naturally wonder why the one big international peace organization on earth, the Church, at the crack of the war demon's whip, deserts its principles of 'Thou shalt not kill,' and 'Peace on earth,' and helps to stampede its followers in the very opposite direction."

Mr. Maurer points out that labor's struggle to have a Federal

Child Labor amendment to the Constitution ratified by the various state legislatures, and to have such legislation enacted as the Workmen's Compensation Laws, Mothers' Pensions, and Old Age Pensions, received no support from the clergy. He concludes by citing this occurrence:

"For a good illustration of what the Church is sometimes guilty of let us take a glimpse at what happened in Detroit, during the month of October, 1926, when the American Federation of Labor was holding its annual convention there. Nearly every church in Detroit sent invitations to prominent labor officials to speak in their churches before Bible classes, Sunday schools, and Young Men's Christian Associations. Most of the invitations were accepted by the labor officials, including President Green of the A. F. of L. As soon as the big employers learned about the program they not only frowned upon the idea of allowing their sacred temples to be contaminated with representatives of the working class, but put both feet down as hard as they could on the proposition. Did the clergymen stand firm when men with dollars talked? To their everlasting shame they did not. Ninety-five percent of them bowed to the will of Mammon and the representatives of labor were barred from the sacred temples erected in the name of God and the lowly Nazarene, proving conclusively to the minds of the average citizen who controls the churches and whom they serve. Small wonder that many workers have a poor opinion of the Church, and that so many pews are empty."

J. B. S. Hardman, the editor of *The Advance*, the official journal of the Amalgamated Clothing Workers, gives us his opinion regarding the religion of labor. "It lulls the social underdog with a sham consolation for the oppression and exploitation which are his lot, and furnishes the exploiter and oppressor with graceful distraction and absolution from his daily practice and meanness. This is the actual basis of Church activity to-day. The religion of labor is godless, for it seeks to restore the divinity of man."

James P. Thompson, the national organizer of the Industrial Workers of the World, heads his article for Jerome Davis, "Religion is the Negation of the Truth," and in his militant manner proclaims "This organization designed to praise God and help him run the universe is known as the Church. The established Church has always been on the side of the rich and powerful. Its robed representatives, pretending to be Godlike and favorites of God, having special influence with Him, have ever functioned as the moral police agents of the ruling classes. At one time or another, they have asked God to bless nearly everything, from the slave driver's lash to murderous wars. Thus they strive to extend the blessings of God to the infamies of men.

"To-day, under Capitalism, they teach the working class the doctrine of humility: tell them that if they get a slap on one cheek to turn the other, and, 'blessed are the poor.' They tell us to bear the cross and wear the crown, that we will get back in the next world what is stolen from us in this. In other words, they try to chloroform us with stories of heaven while the robbers plunder the world. For this support the ruling classes donate liberally to the Church. The organized robbers and organized beggars support each other."

James P. Noonan, vice-president of the American Federation of Labor, asks a pertinent question, "Labor observes an increasing tendency on the part of the Church to regulate what man may eat, drink, or smoke, where and how he shall spend his Sundays, the character and kind of amusements he may participate in, and various other activities, many of which seem more or less trivial; all of which leads the average worker to ponder rather seriously just why it is that the Church can vigorously advocate and promote legislation seeking to curtail his liberty to enjoy, in his own way, the limited number of leisure hours at his disposal, and yet turn a deaf ear to the cry of tortured men, women, and children for relief from the curse of low wages, long hours, and scores of other industrial conditions and abuses which inevitably pave the way for numberless cases of moral turpitude."

James S. Woodsworth, a former minister, speaking for the Canadian Labor Party, exclaims: "The Church—a class institution—what does the Church do to help me and those like me? The Church supported by the wealthy, yes, 'He who pays the piper calls the tune.' The well-groomed parson, with his soft tones prophesying smooth things, well, I'm glad I'm not in his shoes!"

James Simpson, secretary of the Canadian Labor Party, makes this statement: "I found that the conditions which called for radical change if the social and economic security of the people was going to be established did not concern the Church. As an institution it was concerned in establishing an outlook upon life that would induce men to do the right, but, if the right was not done, there was very little distinction drawn between the wrong-doer and the right-doer. This lack of distinction did not apply so much to what were re-regarded as moral indiscretions as it did to the larger failures to recognize man's relationship to man in the industrial and commercial activities of life. Labor thinks the Church is insincere. It is an exceptional case for a minister to take a stand on the side of the workers, even when the issue between the employers and employees is a clear case of the former trying to enforce conditions upon the latter which are unfair and inhuman."

A. Fenner Brockway, the political secretary of the Independent Labor Party in England, writes in this manner: "The hymns of the Church are obsolete; the sermons are very rarely worth listening to; the forms of worship are unrelated to life; and such inspiration as comes from the devotion and beauty of some church services and buildings can be found ever more intimately and fully in the silences and beauty of nature."

George Lansbury is another Englishman speaking for British Labor, and he tells us that, "Ordinary working people in Britain think very little about Churches, or about religion. Years ago I was asked, 'Why don't people accept religion? Why don't the masses go to Church?' I said then, as I say now, 'They, the masses, believe we Christians do not believe what we say we believe."

Lenin, Trotzky, Lunacharsky, and Yaroslavsky, are the speakers for Russian Labor in Soviet Russia. Their attitude toward Church and Religion is well known. . . .

Arthur Crispien, president of the German Social Democratic Party, gives us his opinion. "Men should not look upon this earth as a vale of tears and fly from rude realities to a world of phantasms; they should embrace the beauties of the world, and realize and fulfill their social rights and duties. Our work lies in this world. As to the other, each is at liberty to decide according to his needs."

Karl Mennicke, another former minister, points out the attitude of German Labor. "For modern labor the feeling that human life is first of all a matter of eternal life, and only secondarily a matter of this world, has been entirely lost. The high-strung eschatologic mood, or expectation of Jesus, has no sounding board in the masses of the proletariat of to-day. The Christian epoch in history is obviously on its way to extinction. The eschatological mood of Christianity has been a handicap, and still is, for the Christian community has difficulty finding an organic relationship to the creative problems of social life."

Emanuel Radl speaks of labor and the Church in Czechoslovakia. "In general the churches play a far lesser part in our public life than in the United States. People are accustomed to speak of the churches as exploded institutions that are factors only among the uneducated classes. The churches are not measuring up in understanding and helping the poor."

Robert Haberman, representing the Mexican Labor Party, gives a clear-cut summation of the tyranny that the clergy of that country yoked upon the masses and the retardation that it has produced. It furnishes striking and conclusive evidence of the harm that is done when the Church and State are still integrally intertwined. There is no better example of the efforts of a reactionary clergy to keep the masses in poverty and ignorance than is this study of the church in modern Mexico. Mr. Haberman gives an account of the church activities in old Mexico and coming to the present, "By the year 1854, the Church had gained possession of about two-thirds of all the lands of Mexico, almost every bank, and every large business. The rest of the country was mortgaged to the Church. Then came the revolution of 1854, led by Benito Juarez. It culminated in the Constitution of 1857, which secularized the schools and confiscated Church property. All the churches were nationalized, many of them were turned into schools, hospitals, and orphan asylums. Civil marriages were made obligatory. Pope Pius IX immediately issued a mandate against the Constitution and called upon all Catholics of Mexico to disobey it. Ever since then, the clergy has been fighting to regain its lost temporal power and wealth. It has been responsible for civil wars and for foreign intervention." Under the rule of Diaz, the constitution was disregarded and the Church was permitted to regain most of its lost privileges. "The Church bells rang out at sunrise to call the peons out, with nothing more to eat than some tortillas and chili, to work ail day long in the burning fields, until sunset when the Church bells rang again to send them home to their mud huts. During their work they were beaten. On Sundays they were lashed and sent bleeding to Mass. After Church they had to do Faenas (free work) for the Church, in the name of some saint or other—either to build a new church or do some special work for the priests. It is no wonder then, that after the revolution against Diaz, in many places, as soon as the peons were told they were free, their first act was to climb up the church steeples and smash the bells. After that, they rushed inside the churches and destroyed the statues and paintings of the saints. During the whole period of havoc and exploitation, *not once* was the voice of the Church heard in behalf of the downtrodden. Illiteracy amounted to eighty-six percent. But the Church helped the further enslavement of the workers. There was not a church ceremony, birth, marriage, or death, that did not cost money. The worker had to borrow for each; and the more he borrowed, the more closely he riveted upon himself the chains of peonage. . . . The present conflict started in February, 1926, when Archbishop Jose Mora del Rio, head of the Church in Mexico, issued a statement in the press declaring war against the Constitution."

Gideon Chen, speaking for Chinese Labor asserts: "The Christian Church in China, brought up in a Western greenhouse, with all its achievements and shortcomings, does not speak a language intelligible to the labor world."

Karl Kautsky, the Austrian representative of labor, takes the attitude that, "The less Labor as a whole has to do with Church questions and the less it is interested in the churches, the more successful will be its strife for emancipation."

Otto Bauer, another representative of Austrian labor, makes the assertion: "Capitalism forces the worker into the class struggle. In this class struggle he comes across the clergy and finds it the champion of his class adversary. The worker transfers his hate from the clergyman to religion itself, in whose name this clergyman is defending the social order of the middle classes. In Austria the bourgeois parties take advantage of the belief of hundreds of thousands of proletarians in a Lord in Heaven to keep them in subjection to their earthly masters."

Ernest H. Barker, the general secretary of the Australian Labor Party, holds forth in an article entitled, "The Church is Weighed and Found Wanting." He is quite emphatic in his statements. "The attitude of the Labor Movement in Australia to the Church is one of supreme indifference. There is little or no point of contact between the two and apparently neither considers the other in its activities and plan of campaign. . . . The Church preaches the brotherhood of man. What brotherhood can exist between the wealthy receiver of interest, profit, and rent and the struggling worker who sees his wife dragged down by poverty and overwork, and his children stunted and dwarfed physically and intellectually—between the underworked and overfed commercial or industrial magnate and the underfed, overworked denizen of the slums? . . . The Church is put on trial in the minds of men. They ask, 'What did the Church do when we sought a living wage, shorter hours of work, safer working conditions, abolition of Sunday work, abolition of child labor?' The answer is an almost entirely negative one. The few instances when church officials have helped are so conspicuous as to emphasize the general aloofness. . . . In how many of the advanced ideas of our time has the Church taken the lead? Is it not renowned for being a long way in the rear rather than in the vanguard of progressive thought and action? It resents any challenge to its ideas, doctrines, or authority."

Emile Vandervelde, the leader of the Belgian Labor Party, discusses the personal religious convictions of the Labor leaders in France and Belgium. "Today as yesterday the immense majority are atheists, old-fashioned materialists, or at least agnostics, to whom it would never occur to profess any creed, no matter how liberal it might be."

Toyohiko Kogawa, the secretary of the Japan Labor Federation, says: "Labor considers the Church too otherworldly. It thinks it has no concern with the interests of labor; and that the Church has lost her aim in this world and is looking up only into heaven. And labor forgets where to go, loses its sense of direction. So labor stops thinking about religion, and religion stops thinking about industry. The Church has no principle of economics, and labor has no religious aspiration."

The opinions of these men who are daily in contact with the problem of social justice the world over surely furnish a tremendous amount of information regarding both the unconcern of religion upon the furtherance of social justice and its actual negative and harmful influence. The devout Sherwood Eddy, a sincere and noble exponent of social justice, is forced to exclaim: "But I saw that there would be much more opposition from professing Christians if I preached a gospel of social justice, than ever there had been from so called 'heathen' nations in calling them to turn from their idols. Indeed, Mammon is a much more potent idol, it is more cruel, smeared with more human blood, than Kali of Siva. They sacrifice goats to Kali and we shudder; we sacrifice men to Mammon and justify our 'rights.' In simple fact, though they are not worthy of mention, I have met with more opposition and misrepresentation, ten times over, in 'Christian' America, than I ever met in fifteen years in India, or in repeated visits to China, Turkey, or Russia." (*Sherwood Eddy: "Religion and Social Justice."*)

Religious philosophy is slave philosophy; it teaches of a God who is personally interested in the individual and who will reward present misery with future bliss. The demoralizing effect of this infamous fraud is apparent everywhere. If a worker is constantly assailed with this nonsense from the pulpit, the result is the production in him of a mental as well as a physical slavery; it aggravates his mental inertia, and the force of repetition achieving its effects, he soon resigns himself to his present miserable state drugged with the delusion of a better life in the hereafter. He believes that his destiny is predetermined by God and that he will be rewarded in heaven for his sufferings on earth.

What a marvelous opiate the ecclesiastics have been

injecting into the minds of the masses! It is not to be wondered at, therefore, that capital has aided throughout the ages and has stood by religion. The irony of the situation lies in the fact that the slave will fight so valiantly for his tyrannical master, that the unscrupulous few who derive all the benefits, can, like a malignant parasite, suck the life-blood of its victims while their still living prey submits without-a struggle! The worker, inebriated with his religious delusion, calmly allows his very substance to be the means through which his parasitic employer grows fat.

"That was the net result of Christianity, and of the activity of the Christian Church in spreading abroad a spirit of kindliness, humanity and brotherhood! The coquetry of Christianity with Labor within the last generation or two is only what one would expect. But it is clear that the one constant function of Christianity has been to encourage loyalty to existing institutions, no matter what their character so long as they were not unfriendly to the Church. Slavery and the oppression of labor continued while Christianity was at its strongest and wealthiest; its own wealth derived from the oppression it encouraged. Slavery died out when social and economic conditions rendered its continuance more and more difficult. And the conditions of labor improved when men ceased to talk of a 'Providential Order,' of 'God's Decree,' and dismissed the evangelical narcotic served out by the Church, and began to realize that social conditions were the products of understandable and modifiable natural forces." (*C. Cohen:* *"Christianity, Slavery and Labor."*)

CHAPTER XVII

RELIGION AND WOMAN

She was the first in the transgression therefore keep her in subjection.

———————

Fierce is the dragon and cunning the asp; but woman has the malice of both.

ST. GREGORY OF NAZIANZUM.

Thou art the devil's gate, the betrayer of the tree, the first deserter of the Divine Law.

TERTULLIAN.

What does it matter whether it be in the person of mother or sister; we have to beware Eve in every woman.

How much better two men could live and converse together than a man and a woman.

ST. AUGUSTINE.

No gown worse becomes a woman than the desire to be wise.

LUTHER.

———

The Bible and the Church have been the greatest stumbling blocks in the way of women's emancipation.

ELIZABETH CADY STANTON.

IT is noticed in most calculations of churchgoers that women have remained attached to the churches in a far higher proportion than men. The proportion of women in the churches is vastly greater than their proportion in the general population. Most of the men who still passively attend their churches do so under the pressure of professional interest or social or domestic influence.

The degree of religiosity has always been associated with the free play of the emotions and woman being more imaginative and emotional than man, it seems clear that this strong emotional factor in woman accounts, at least partly, for the greater proportion of women as churchgoers. And this, be it noted, lies not in any inherent inferiority in the mental make-up of woman, but rather in the environmental influences that until very recently shaped woman's education in such a manner that it was little adapted to strengthening her reason, but rather calculated to enhance her emotionalism.

Ecclesiastic historians have a notorious habit of viewing pre-Christian times for the single biased purpose of only stating the aspects of that civilization which they deemed inferior to that exerted by Christianity. Researches have established fairly well the position of women in the Egyptian community of 4000 years ago. It is no exaggeration to state that she was free and more honored in Egypt 4000 years ago, than she was in any country of the earth until only recently. Scholars assure us that, at a period which the Bible claims the Earth was just coming into being, the Egyptian matron was mistress of her home, she inherited equally with her brothers, and had full control of her property. She could go where she liked and speak to whom she pleased. She could bring actions in the courts and even plead in the courts. The traditional advice to the husband was, "Make glad her heart during the time that thou hast."

Contrast this position of woman in the community and society in general with the statement given in Mrs. E. Cady Stanton's "History of Woman's Suffrage," in which she speaks of the status of the female of the species in Boston about the year 1850. "Women could not hold any property, either earned or inherited. If unmarried, she was obliged to place it in the hands of a trustee, to whose will she was subject. If she contemplated marriage, and desired to call her property her own, she was forced by law to make a contract with her intended husband by which she gave up all title or claim to it. A woman, either married or unmarried, could hold no office or trust or power. She was not a person. She was not recognized as a citizen. She was not a factor in the human family. She was not a unit, but a zero in the sum of civilization. . . . The status of a married woman was little better than that of a domestic servant. By the English Common Law her husband was her lord and master. He had the sole custody of her person and of her minor children. He could punish her 'with a stick no bigger than his thumb' and she could not complain against him. . . . The common law of the State [Massachusetts] held man and wife to be one person, but that person was the husband. He could by will deprive her of every part of his property, and also of what had been her own before marriage. He was the owner of all her real estate and earnings. The wife could make no contract and no will, nor, without her husband's consent, dispose of the legal interest of her real estate. . . . She did not own a rag of her clothing. She had no personal rights and could hardly call her soul her own. Her husband could steal her children, rob her of her clothing, neglect to support the family: she had no legal redress. If a wife earned money by her own labor, the husband could claim the pay as his share of the proceeds." With such a contrast in mind, it is indeed difficult to see where the truth of the assertion lies when it is stated that the status of woman was indeed pitiful until Christianity exerted its influence for her betterment. And it is again curious to note that after a period of nearly 2000 years of Christian influence it was left for a sceptic such as Mrs. Stanton and her sceptical co-workers to bring about an amelioration of the degrading position of woman in Christian society.

The degrading picture of womankind as depicted in the Old Testament is well known to anyone who has glanced through this storehouse of mythology. It would be well for the multitude of devout female adherents of all creeds to take the time, just a little of the time they give to the plight of the poor, benighted heathen and read some of the passages in the Old Testament dealing with their lot. The entire history of woman under the administration of these "heaven-made" laws is a record of her serviture and humility.

In the 24th chapter of Deuteronomy we find the right of divorce given to the husband. "Let him write her a bill of divorcement and give it in her hand and send her out of his house." The discarded wife must acquiesce to "divine justice." But if the wife is displeased, is there any justice? Under no clause of the Divorce Law could the wife have a divorce on her part. None but the husband could put her asunder from him.

In the 22d chapter of Deuteronomy is enacted the law for "Test of Virginity," which states that, "If any man take a wife, and is disappointed in her, and reports, 'I found her not a maid,' then, her father and mother shall bring forth the tokens of the damsel's virginity unto the elders of the city in the gate." The gynecological elders then go into a "peeping Tom's" conference and "If virginity be not found for the damsel: Then they shall bring out the damsel to the door of her father's house, and the men of the city shall stone her with stones that she die." Most probably the male partner in her "crime" was the first to cast the largest stone.

The law laid down in the 12th chapter of Leviticus may have been intended for hygienic purposes but it is cruel and degrading to women because it assumes that the parturient woman who has borne a female child is twice as impure as one who has borne a male child.

The "law of jealousies" as described in the 5th chapter of Numbers is a good example of the mentality of the writers of this "divine revelation." God in His infinite wisdom had caused to be written for Him, that to test whether a woman has laid carnally with another man, the priest shall, "take holy water in an earthen vessel, and of the dust that is on the floor of the tabernacle the priest shall take and put it in the water . . . the bitter water that causeth the curse, and shall cause the woman to drink the water." The divine revelation then continues with, "if she be defiled, her belly shall swell and her thigh shall rot."

But after all, God did not know that in the dust of the Tabernacle sprawled the germs of Dysentery, Cholera, and Tuberculosis, and a few other such mild infections. Or did the Divine Father know that even a self-respecting germ could not inhabit the filthy floor of the Tabernacle?

Consequently, it is not to be wondered at that in the "good old days of the old-fashioned woman," the acme of hospitality was the giving of wife or daughter to a visitor for the night. It was not religion that put an end to this barbarous custom; it was the advance of civilization; not the religious force, but the place rational thinking assumed in the life of people.

The following is a description of a religious riot which took place in Alexandria during the early days of the Church: "Among the many victims of these unhappy tumults was

Hypatia, a maiden not more distinguished for her beauty than for her learning and her virtues. Her father was Theon, the illustrious mathematician who had early initiated his daughter in the mysteries of philosophy. The classic groves of Athens and the schools of Alexandria equally applauded her attainments and listened to the pure music of her lips. She respectfully declined the tender attentions of lovers, but, raised to the chair of Gamaliel, suffered youth and age, without preference or favor, to sit indiscriminately at her feet. Her fame and increasing popularity ultimately excited the jealousy of St. Cyril, at that time the Bishop of Alexandria, and her friendship for his antagonist, Orestes, the prefect of the city, entailed on her devoted head the crushing weight of his enmity. In her way through the city, her chariot was surrounded by his creatures, headed by a crafty and savage fanatic named Peter the Reader, and the, young and innocent woman was dragged to the ground, stripped of her garments, paraded naked through the streets, and then torn limb from limb on the steps of the Cathedral. The still warm flesh was scraped from her bones with oyster-shells, and the bleeding fragments thrown into a furnace, so that not an atom of the beautiful virgin should escape destruction." The cruelty of man when spurred on by the mania of religious zeal!

In more historic times there are numerous instances of the tyranny exercised over women by the feudal system. Feudalism, composed as it was of military ideas and ecclesiastical traditions, exercised the well known "rights of seigniory." These "rights" comprised a jurisdiction which is now unprintable, and had even the power to deprive woman of life itself.

A history of the licentiousness of the monks and the early popes would fill a great number of volumes; and indeed, many are the volumes which have been devoted to this subject. It will suffice to point out only a few representative incidents. In 1259, Alexander IV tried to disrupt the shameful union between concubines and the clergy. Henry III, Bishop of Liege, was such a fatherly sort of individual that he had sixty-five "natural children!" William, Bishop of Padreborn, in 1410, although successful in reducing such powerful enemies as the Archbishop of Cologne, and the Count of Cloves by fire and sword, was powerless against the dissolute morals of his own monks, who were chiefly engaged in the corruption of women. Indeed, the Swiss clergy in 1230, frankly stated that they "were flesh and blood, unequal to the task of living like angels." The Council of Cologne, in 1307, tried in vain to give the nuns a chance to live virtuous lives; to protect them from priestly seduction. Conrad, Bishop of Wurzburg, in 1521, accused his priests of habitual "gluttony, drunkenness, gambling, quarrelling, and lust." Erasmus warned his clergy against concubinage. The Abbot of St. Pilazo de Antealtarin was proved by competent witnesses to have no less than seventy concubines. The old and wealthy Abbey of St. Albans was little more than a den of prostitutes, with whom the monks lived openly and avowedly. The Duke of Nuremburg, in 1522, was concerned with the clerical immunity of monks who night and day preyed upon the virtue of the wives and daughters of the laity.

The Church openly carried on a sale of indulgences in lust to ecclesiastics which finally took the form of a tax. The Bishop of Utrecht in 1347 issued an order prohibiting the admittance of men to nunneries. In Spain, conditions became so intolerable that the communities forced their priests to select concubines so that the wives and daughters would be safe from the ravages of the clergy.

"The torture, the maiming, and the murder of Elgira by Dunstan illustrates further, amongst thousands and thousands of similar bloody deeds, the diabolical brutality of superstition perpetuated in the name of Christianity upon women in the earlier centuries of our epoch. Indeed, religious superstition always has contrived to rob, to pester, to deceive, and to degrade women." (*Bell: "Women from Bondage to Freedom."*)

During the Middle Ages, the ages in which the Church was in complete domination of all forms of endeavor, the status of woman was no better than the general conditions of the time. This Age of Faith is characterized by "the violence and knavery that covered the whole country, the plagues and famines that decimated towns and villages every few years, the flood of spurious and indecent relics, the degradation of the clergy and monks, the slavery of the serfs, the daily brutalities of the ordeal and the torture, the course and bloody pastimes, the insecurity of life, the triumphant ravages of disease, the check of scientific inquiry and a hundred other features of medieval life." (*Joseph McCabe: "Religion of Woman."*)

The Church was chiefly responsible for the terrible persecutions inflicted on women on the ground of witchcraft and this must be taken into calculation when one considers what woman owes to religion. The Reformation reduced woman to the position of a mere breeder of children. During the sway of Puritanism woman was a poor, benighted being, a human toad under the harrow of a pious imbecility.

The pioneers in the Modern Woman Movement in this country were, of course, Mrs. Stanton, Mrs. Gage, and Miss Susan B. Anthony. In their "History of Woman Suffrage" they comment on the vicious opposition which the early workers encountered in New York. "Throughout this protracted and disgraceful assault on American womanhood the clergy baptised every new insult and act of injustice in the name of the Christian religion, and uniformly asked God's blessing on proceedings that would have put to shame, an assembly of Hottentots."

And while the clergy either remained silent or heaped abuse on this early movement, such freethinkers as Robert Owen, Jeremy Bentham, George Jacob Holyoake, and John Stuart

Mill in England entered the fray wholeheartedly in behalf of the emancipation of woman. In France it was Michelet and George Sand that came to their aid. In Germany it was Max Sterner, Büchner, Marx, Engels, and Liebknecht. In Scandinavia it was Ibsen and Björnson.

The battle was begun by freethinkers in defiance of the clergy and it was only when the inevitable conquest of this movement was manifest that any considerable number of clergy came to the aid of this progressive movement. The righting of the wrongs imposed on womankind therefore had been started not only without the aid of the churches but in face of their determined opposition. It was not the clergy that discovered the injustice that had been done to women throughout the centuries, and when it was finally pointed out to them by sceptics, it was the rare ecclesiastic that could see it so and attempt to right the wrong.

R. H. Bell, in tracing this struggle of woman in her publication, "Woman from Bondage to Freedom," has this pertinent remark to make. "If there are any personal rights in this world over which Church and State should have no control, it is the sexual right of a woman to say, 'Yes' or 'No.' These and similar rights are so deeply imbedded in natural morality that no clearheaded, clean-hearted person would wish to controvert them. . . . Enforced motherhood, through marriage or otherwise, is a mixed form of slavery, voluntary motherhood is the glory of a free soul."

In the age-long struggle for freedom, woman's most rigorous antagonist has always been the Church.

CHAPTER XVIII

THE PHILOSOPHERS AND THE GREAT ILLUSION

But the powers of man, so far as experience and analogy can guide us, are unlimited; nor are we possessed of any evidence which authorizes us to assign even an imaginary boundary at which the human intellect will, of necessity, be brought to a stand.

BUCKLE.

THERE has been an effort made in certain religious publications to imply that there is a dearth of thought and thinkers beyond the pale of theism. The subsequent examination of the theological beliefs of great minds will show that there has never been a lack of brilliant thinkers who have not sought truth apart from the dominant faith of their age. It was Socrates, I believe, who first asked if it was not a base superstition that mere numbers will give wisdom. Granting this truth, it certainly cannot be claimed that the philosophers of any time constituted a majority of any population, nor that

315

the philosopher, as such, was not greatly in advance of the mental status of the populace of his particular age. It would seem appropriate to briefly comment on the opinions of the philosophers, both ancient and modern, concerning their views on "man's giant shadow, hailed divine."

In former ages, philosophy was the handmaiden of theology. From the time of Socrates and Plato, and throughout the medieval ages, the foremost task of the philosopher seemed to be to attempt the proof of the existence and nature of God, and the immortality of the soul. The leading thinkers of the seventeenth century, Hobbes, Descartes, Spinoza, Leibnitz, and Malebranche, liberated philosophy from its bondage to theology. The criticism of Kant of the philosophical foundations of belief destroyed the "theological proofs," and modern thinkers now spend little time on the question of the existence and nature of God and the soul.

Modern philosophy has been completely secularized, and it is a rare occasion to find a philosopher dwelling on the problems of God and immortality. This question in philosophy, as in all other branches of thought, is utterly irrelevant and at present there is less insistence on God and more on the world, man, morals, and the conditions of social life.

It cannot be denied that we are under a heavy obligation intellectually to the Greek philosophers. And it may be that the fruitful efforts of those minds were largely due to their unhampered intellectual freedom. They had no "holy books" and few authorities to check their free speculation and hence these Greek thinkers furnish the first instance of intellectual freedom, from which arose their intelligent criticism and speculation. "They discovered skepticism in the higher and proper significance of the word, and this was their supreme contribution to human thought." (*James Harvey Robinson: "The Mind In The Making."*)

We know the teachings of Socrates only through his disciple Plato, as Socrates wrote nothing himself. From this source we gather that Socrates firmly upheld the right and necessity of free thought. He was mainly a moralist and reformer, and attempted to prove the existence of God by finding evidence of design in nature. He rejected the crude religious ideas of his nation, was opposed to anthropomorphism, but considered it his duty to conform publicly to this belief. In his old age, he was charged wtih rejecting the gods of the state, and was sentenced to death.

The philosophy of Plato has given rise to diverse interpretations and there are those who, on reading the Dialogues, believe that it is not amiss to state that in certain utterances there is ground to hold that Plato argued for the pragmatic value of a belief in God and personal immortality; that he does not stress the truth of the matter, but argues mainly for the benefit which the State derives from the belief;

that such theistic beliefs cannot be demonstrated, and may well be but a craving and a hope, yet it will be of no harm to believe. He inferred the existence of God from what he considered the intelligence and design manifested in natural objects. Mainly, however, Plato's theism was founded upon his doctrine of a universe of ideas, and as no one today holds that ideas are self-existing realities, the foundation of his theism is destroyed. James Harvey Robinson, in his "Mind in The Making," discusses the influence of Plato, and remarks, "Plato made terms with the welter of things, but sought relief in the conception of supernal models, eternal in the heavens, after which all things were imperfectly fashioned. He confessed that he could not bear to accept a world which was like a leaky pot or a man running at the nose. In short, he ascribed the highest form of existence to ideals and abstractions. This was a new and sophisticated republication of savage animism. It invited lesser minds than his to indulge in all sorts of noble vagueness and impertinent jargon which continue to curse our popular discussions of human affairs. He consecrated one of the chief foibles of the human mind, and elevated it to a religion."

The philosophy of Aristotle is commonly known to be the reverse of Plato's. Plato started with universals, the very existence of which was a matter of faith, and from these he descended to particulars. Aristotle, on the other hand, argued from particulars to universals, and this inductive method was the true beginning of science. The accumulated knowledge of his age did not furnish him facts enough upon which to build and he had to resort to speculation. It does not detract from the stupendous achievement of this man that the clergy of the Middle Ages, in control of the few isolated centers of learning, looked upon the philosophy of Aristotle as final and considered his works as semi-sacred, and in their immersion in un-reason and unreality, exalted as immutable and infallible the absurdities in the speculations of a mind limited to the knowledge of centuries before theirs.

In the attempt to explain plant and animal life, Aristotle formulated the theory that a special form of animating principle was involved. The "élan vital" of Bergson and the theory of Joad are modern reiterations of this conception. Aristotle is not quite consistent when he attempts to give us his theistic beliefs. At times God is, for him, a mysterious spirit that never does anything and has not any desire or will. Elsewhere, he conceives God as pure energy; a prime mover unmoved. Certain modern physicists still cling to this Aristotelian god. This conception of a deity was far from the beliefs of his age, and it is not strange that Aristotle was charged with impiety and with having taught that prayer and sacrifice were of no avail. He fled from Athens and shortly afterwards died in exile.

These three supreme Greek thinkers, Socrates, Plato, and Aristotle, have not contributed a single argument for the existence of a supreme being which is now not discredited. Socrates relied on the now outmoded argument from design; and only in a greatly modified form are the arguments of Plato and Aristotle accepted by modern theists. Holding such heretical views in an age when history was a frail fabric of legends, and the scientific explanation of nature in its extreme infancy, what would their views be today?

In the consideration of the Greek thinkers of lesser importance one finds that they were continually storming against the religious conceptions of the populace. The philosophers were ever unpopular with the credulous. "Damon and Anaxagoras were banished; Aspasia was impeached for blasphemy and the tears of Pericles alone saved her; Socrates was put to death; Plato was obliged to reserve pure reason for a chosen few, and to adulterate it with revelation for the generality of his disciples; Aristotle fled from Athens for his life, and became the tutor of Alexander." (*Winwood Reade: "The Martyrdom of Man."*)

Anaxagoras, the friend and master of Pericles, Euripides, and Socrates, was accused by the superstitious Athenians of atheism and impiety to the gods. He was condemned to death and barely escaped this fate through the influence of Pericles; which resulted in the accusation of atheism against Pericles. Euripides was accused of heresy, and Aeschylus was condemned to be stoned to death for blasphemy and was saved from this fate by his brother Aminias. The philosophy of Parmenides was distinctly-pantheistic, and Pythagoras, who attempted to purify the religion of the Greeks and free it from its absurdities and superstitions, was exiled for his scepticism.

Democritus, a materialist and atheist of 2500 years ago, formulated a mechanical view of phenomena in accordance with which everything that happens is due to physical impacts. "Such a materialist was a great liberation from superstition; and had it survived in its integrity, the path of European wisdom would have been vastly different from what it was. What the path would have been, we are beginning to see to-day, for since the nineteenth century we have been treading it more or less consistently but by no means so gallantly and courageously as Democritus." (*G. Boas: "The Adventures of Human Thought."*)

Democritus and the Epicureans strove to deliver men from their two chief apprehensions: the fear of the gods, and the fear of death; and in so doing rejected the religious beliefs and substituted a rational and scientific conception of the universe.

It was Xenophanes, the Voltaire of Greece, who brought to the atttention of his countrymen the discovery that man created the gods in his own image. He attacked the conceptions of the Greek deities with these words, "Mortals deem that the gods are begotten as they are, and have clothes like theirs, and voice and form . . . Yes, and if oxen and horses or lions had hands, and could paint with their hands, and produce works of art as men do, horses would paint the forms of the gods like horses, and oxen like oxen, and make their bodies in the image of their several kinds . . . The Ethiopians make their gods black and snub-nosed; the Thracians say theirs have blue eyes and red hair."

Considering Greek philosophy in its entirety, we see that it was naturalistic rather than supernaturalistic, and rationalistic rather than mystical. These gifted men saw no clear indication for the existence of a supreme being; very few of them speak of the deity in the role of Providence and fewer still believed in personal immortality.

Professor Boas, in contrasting Asiatic mythology with Greek philosophy, remarks: "The Asiatic myths assumed the existence of beings beyond the world, not subject to mundane laws, who made and controlled the course of events. There was no reason why they should have made a world. They seemed to be living as divine a life without it as with it. The question was one which persisted in Asiatic thought, and when Christianity became dominant in Europe, much of its theologians' time was spent in answering it. The only plausible answer then was that God made the world because He felt like it. For no reason could be given sufficiently compelling to sway the will of the Omnipotent. But such an answer was unsatisfactory to the

Greek. In his philosophy all this is changed. No god steps out of the machine to initiate cosmic history. The First Cause is a physical substance, some material thing, which operates by the laws of its own nature. Its every movement is theoretically open to the scrutiny of reason. And hence, a scientific rather than a religious answer can be given to every question."

At the beginning of the Christian era, the cultured Romans were stoics or epicureans. The poet Lucretius was an epicurean who regarded the belief in the gods as a product of the terrors of primitive man and recommended that the mind should be emancipated from the fear of the gods and argued against the immortality of the soul. Seneca, Epictetus, and Marcus Aurelius were stoics. Cicero insinuates that the gods are only poetical creations, that the popular doctrine of punishment in a world to come is only an idle fable, and is uncertain whether the soul is immortal. Seneca wrote against the religion of his country, and the philosophy of cultured Romans of the time of the physician Galen tended towards atheism.

The prime factor of Greek philosophy was the insistence on intelligence and knowledge, and by these means it reached its pinnacle of reasoning. The blight that exterminated all scientific progress, with the fall of the Roman Empire, carried with it the neglect of the Greek thinkers. Similar to the retrogression of scientific thought, traced in former chapters, is the corresponding retrogression in philosophic thought.

In place of the free inquiry of the Greeks we see arising the theology of Clement of Alexandria, Origen, St. Augustine, and finally that of St. Thomas Aquinas. At the time of St. Augustine most of the cultural Greek writings had disappeared in western Europe. The greatest store of Greek thought was in the hands of the Arab scholars and led to a marked scepticism, as we see manifested in the writings of the Spanish Moors.

It is significant that during the "age of faith" in Europe no philosopher of merit arose, and the only philosophy permitted was the puerile Scholastic-Aristotelic. This scholastic philosophy, hemmed in between metaphysics and theology, sought to reconcile Plato, Plotinus, and Aristotle with the needs of orthodoxy, and split hairs over subtle essences and entities. Francis Bacon impeaches, in this manner, the medieval philosophers: "Having sharp and strong wits, and abundance of leisure, and small variety of reading, but their wits being shut up in the cells of a few authors, as their persons were shut up in the cells of monasteries and colleges, and knowing little history, either of nature or time, did out of no great quantity of matter and infinite agitation of wit spin out unto us those laborious webs of learning which are extant in their books."

The sole preoccupation of medieval philosophy seemed to be conjectures as to what would happen to man after death, and the entire system of thought was based on authority. The medieval philosopher turned in disdain from the arduous path of investigation of actual phenomena and confidently believed that he could find truth by easy reliance upon revelation and the elaboration of dogmas. A few brave minds rebelled against this unnatural imprisonment of the intellect, with the usual consequences. Peter Abelard was condemned for his scepticism at a council at Sens in 1140; the philosophy of John Scotus Erigena was condemned for its pantheistic ideas by a council at Sens in 1225; and the pantheistic views of Bruno had much to do with his martyrdom in the year 1600.

Montaigne, the pioneer of modern scepticism, gave voice to his repugnance for dogmas in his brilliant Essays, in which he stated that all religious opinions are the result of custom; and that he doubted if, out of the immense number of religious opinions, there were any means of ascertaining which were accurate. Bacon, Hobbes, Locke, and Descartes were the inaugurators of a school of thought which is characterized by its practical spirit; and while these men professed theistic beliefs, their systems of thought had done much, when applied and amplified by their followers, to undermine that belief. These men furnished the source of a later agnosticism.

Thomas Hobbes agreed with Bacon and Galileo that all knowledge starts from experience, and, carrying out the inductive method of Bacon, he produced his "Leviathan" in 1651. It was promptly attacked by the clergy of every country in Europe. Hobbes says of the immortality of the soul, "It is a belief grounded upon other men's sayings that they knew it supernaturally; or that they knew those who knew them, that knew others that knew it supernaturally."

Locke concerned himself with a philosophic inquiry into the nature of the mind itself, and was looked upon as a destroyer of the faith. Descartes based his philosophy on the rejection of authority in favor of human reason for which his works were honored by being placed on the Index in 1663. Hume, with the publication of the highly heretical "Treatise on Human Nature," threw consternation into the ranks of the theists. His theory of knowledge played havoc with the old arguments for belief in God and immortality of the soul. His works were widely read and were instrumental in leading to the philosophical agnosticism of the nineteenth century.

Spinoza's religious views seemed in his time little short of atheism and brought him the hostility of both Jews and Christians, to which was added the excommunication from the synagogue. In his philosophy God and nature are equivalent terms and it is pantheistic only in the sense that if man is to have a god at all, nature must be that god, and whatever man considers godlike must be found in nature. Spinoza recognizes no supernatural realm and denies the survival of personal memory. Professor G. Boas, in his "Adventures of Human Thought," discusses the attitude of public opinion of the time of Spinoza. "He was the arch-atheist, the materialist, the subverter of all that was held most dear by the reigning powers. It was only after the French Revolution that he came into his own when certain Germans, captivated by Neo-Platonism, emphasized the pantheistic element in him. But by then Christianity had ceased to be a dominant intellectual force and had become what it is today, a folk belief." In the "Tractus Theologico-Politicus," Spinoza states: "When people declare, as all are ready to do, that the Bible is the Word of God teaching men true blessedness and the way of salvation, they evidently do not mean what they say, for the masses take no pains at all to live according to Scripture, and we see most people endeavoring to hawk about their own commentaries as the word of God, and giving their best efforts, under the guise of religion, to compelling others to think as they do. We generally see, I say, theologians anxious to learn how to wring their inventions and sayings out of the sacred text, and to fortify them with divine authority."

In France, Pierre Bayle cleverly satirized the absurdity of dogma, and La Mettrie, an army physician, was exiled for the publication of his "Man a Machine." He insisted that if atheism were generally accepted society would be happier. His views were taken up and expanded by such atheists as Helvetius, d'Holbach, d'Alembert, and Diderot, who taught that morality should be founded on sociology and not on theology. The publication of their Encyclopædia incurred the fierce opposition of the Church. Of Voltaire's anti-clericism little need be said, except to recall our debt to his victory over ecclesiasticism and superstition. His assertion that "a fanaticism composed of superstition and ignorance has been the sickness of all the centuries," still holds too great an extent of truth. His denial of miracles, the supernatural efficacy of prayer, and the immortality of the soul earned for him the undying enmity of the clergy. Condorcet, another deist, was the successor of Voltaire in the Encyclopædic warfare.

The "Critique of Pure Reason" of Kant demolished the ontological and the cosmological arguments for the existence of God and showed the weakness in the teleological argument. He demonstrated that all the current arguments for God and immortality; the entire basis of rational proof of religious beliefs; were invalid. The, theists protested vehemently, and showed their superiority by calling their dogs "Immanuel Kant." In his "Critique of Practical Reason," however, he went on to restore the credit of religion through the moral sense, the "Categorical Imperative," and, as certain commentators have stated, after having excluded God from the cosmos, he attempted to find Him again in ethics. Holding that the moral sense is innate and not derived from experience, he reduced the truth of religion to moral faith. Kant believed that he found a divine command in Ms own conscience; but the science of ethics now gives a natural account of moral laws and sentiments. The study of the evolution of our moral ideas has, today, destroyed Kant's theory of an innate and absolute moral sense.

When Franklin showed the nature of lightning, the voice of God was displaced from that of thunder. The sciences of ethics and psychology, like modern Franklins, show plainly that conscience is no more the voice of God than is thunder. Schopenhauer, commenting on Kantian theology, offers the suggestion that Kant was really a sceptic, but became frightened when he contemplated what he thought would happen to public morals if belief were to be denied to the masses. Nietzsche speaks of Kant: "With the aid of his concept of 'Practical Reason,' he produced a special kind of reason, for use on occasions when reason cannot function: namely, when the sublime command, 'Thou shalt,' resounds." In his old age Kant became more bold, and perhaps voiced his true views, for we find that in "Religion Within the Limits of Pure Reason," he is actively antagonistic to ecclesiasticism, so much so that, for publishing this work, he was censured by the Prussian king, who wrote, "Our highest person has been greatly displeased to observe how you misuse your philosophy to undermine and destroy many of the most important and fundamental doctrines of the Holy Scriptures and of Christianity." Indeed, many a man approaching Kant with a firm theistic belief finds his belief somewhat shaken by Kantian logic.

Schopenhauer's "Will" has nothing in common with the God-idea as commonly held, and he was bitterly anti-theistic.

In a dialogue entitled "Religion," he places these words in the mouth of his character Philalethes: "A certain amount of general ignorance is the condition of all religions, the element in which alone they can exist. And as soon as astronomy, natural science, geology, history, the knowledge of countries and peoples, have spread their light broadcast, and philosophy finally is permitted to say a word, every faith founded on miracles and revelation must disappear; and philosophy takes its place."

Hegel's deification of thought or reason left no room for personal immortality, and his query, "Do you expect a tip for having nursed your ailing mother, and refrained from poisoning your brother?" is well known. A vague conception of a deity whose existence can be proved, if it can be proved at all, only by the abstruse arguments of a Hegel is not a god of practical service to the theists.

Schelling was pantheistic, and Feuerbach played havoc with the philosophic evidence for God and immortality and treated all religions as a dream and an illusion.

Herbert Spencer, James Mill, J. S. Mill, and Huxley popularized the agnostic standpoint. Spencer in his "First Principles" argues in this manner: "Those who cannot conceive of a self-existent Universe, and therefore assume a creator as the source of the Universe, take for granted that they can conceive a self-existent creator. The mystery which they recognize in this great fact surrounding them on every side, they transfer to an alleged source of this great fact, and then suppose that they have solved the mystery. But they delude themselves. Self-existence is inconceivable; and this holds true whatever be the nature of the object of which it is predicated. Whoever agrees that the atheistic hypothesis is untenable because it involves the impossible idea of self-existence, must perforce admit that the theistic hypothesis is untenable if it contains the same impossible idea. . . . If religion and science are to be reconciled, the basis of reconciliation must be this deepest, widest, and most certain of all facts, that the Power which the Universe manifests to us is inscrutable."

Nietzsche, the great liberator of modern thought, vigorously opposed religious morality, the influence of Christianity, and all religious beliefs. "When the natural consequences of an action," he wrote, "are no longer looked upon as natural, but are considered to be produced by the phantasms of superstition, by 'God,' 'Ghosts,' and 'Souls,' and appear as 'moral' consequences, as rewards, punishments, guidance and revelation, then the whole basis of knowledge is destroyed; and the greatest possible crime against humanity has been committed."

William James, claimed as a supporter of religion, argues that our inner experience makes us cognizant of a spiritual world. The advance of psychological research does not deal kindly with this contention, and such works as Leuba's "Psychology of Religious Mysticism" give a rational explanation of the mystic state. Moreover, James did not give his support to monotheism. "That vast literature of proofs of God's existence," he stated, "drawn from the order of nature, which a century ago seemed so overwhelmingly convincing, today does little more than gather dust in the libraries, for the simple reason that our generation has ceased to believe in the kind of God it argued for. Whatever sort of God may be, we know today that he is nevermore that mere external inventor of 'contrivances' intended to make manifest his 'glory' in which our great-grandfathers took such satisfaction."

James claimed to be a pluralist in the sense that there are several or many spiritual beings above us, and his writings lead one to believe that he was not convinced that man, as a distinct personality, survives the grave.

Royce rejected all the current arguments for God and immortality and argues for the mysticism of internal experience. Eucken offers no support to theologians; and Bergson does not seem to express a clear belief in a personal god or personal immortality.

Coming to the more popular of contemporary philosophers one finds that, just as the Greek philosophers reasoned outside the pale of the then held beliefs which were theistic, so do these modern philosophers reach conclusions that are outside the pale of organized religion of today. George Santayana is a materialist and sceptic who, in his "Reason in Religion," reveals his scepticism and frowns upon personal immortality. "It is pathetic," he comments, "to observe how lowly are the motives that religion, even the highest, attributes to the deity, and from what a hard-pressed and bitter existence they have been drawn. To be given the best morsel, to be remembered, to be praised, to be obeyed blindly and punctiliously, these have been thought points of honor with the gods, for which they would dispense favors and punishments on the most exhorbitant scale. . . . The idea that religion contains a literal, not a symbolic, representation of truth and life is simply an impossible idea. Whoever entertains it has not come within the region of profitable philosophizing on that subject."

Bertrand Russell, considered by some the keenest philosophical mind of the present age, is an agnostic who maintains "The objections to religion are of two sorts, intellectual and moral. The intellectual objection is that there is no reason to suppose any religion true; the moral objection is that religious precepts date from a time when men were more cruel than they are now, and therefore tend to perpetuate inhumanities which the moral conscience of the age would otherwise outgrow."

The Italian philosopher Benedetto Croce is an atheist who states that philosophy removes from religion all reason for existing. C. E. M. Joad is a young English philosopher who repeatedly predicts the disappearance in the near future of the present forms of theistic beliefs. M. C. Otto holds to "An affirmative faith in the non-existence of God." William P. Montague discards all organized religions for a "Promethean Religion." John Dewey is a naturalistic philosopher who will have nothing to do with supernatural causation and insists that all things be explained by their place and function in the environment. His philosophy is permeated with the secular ideal of control of the external world.

What consolation does organized religion receive from the views of such modern philosophers as Russell, Alexander, Joad, Croce, Santayana, Dewey, Otto, Montague, Sellars, and the Randalls? The views of an intellectual incompetent, such as Bryan was, are spread widecast, but few know the extent of the scepticism of Edison, Luther Burbank, Albert Einstein, Paul Ehrlich, Ernst Haeckel, Robert Koch, Fridjof Nansen, and Swante Arrhenius. What consolation can the theists derive from the religious views of Shelley, Swinburne, Meredith, Buchanan, Keats, George Eliot, Thomas Hardy, Mark Twain, and Anatole France?

In the not far distant past deism and pantheism served as a polite subterfuge for atheism. There is a growing tendency in this present age to dress one's atheistic belief in an evening suit, and for the sake of social approbation call such a belief

334

"religious humanism." A quotation from the Associated Press, appearing recently in one of our magazines, states the need for this "new religion" as being the inadequacy of the religious forms and ideas of our fathers, and the new creed to be:

"Religious humanists regard the universe as self-existing and not created.

"Religion must formulate its hopes and plans in the light of the scientific spirit and method.

"The distinction between the sacred and secular can no longer be maintained.

"Religious humanism considers the complete realization of human personality to be the end of a man's life, and seeks its development and fulfilment in the here and now.

"In place of the old attitudes involved in worship and prayer, the humanist finds his religious emotions exprest in a heightened sense of personal life and in a cooperative effort to promote social well-being.

"There will be no uniquely religious emotions and attitudes of the kind hitherto associated with belief in the supernatural. Man will learn to face the crises of life in terms of his knowledge of their naturalness and probability. Reasonable and manly attitudes will be fostered by education and supported custom.

"We assume that humanism will take the path of social

and mental hygiene, and discourage sentimental and unreal hopes and wishful thinking.

"The goal of humanism is a free and universal society in which the people voluntarily and intelligently cooperate for the common good.

"The time has come for widespread recognition of the radical changes, in religious thoughts throughout the modern world. Science and economic change have disrupted the old beliefs.

"Religions the world over are under the necessity of coming to terms with new conditions created by a vastly increased knowledge and experience."

Professors John Dewey, E. A. Burtt, and Roy Wood Sellars are among the signers of this statement. It is an excellent and comprehensive statement, but one is left wondering why the name "religious humanism"? It is difficult to become enthusiastic when one realizes that these men take to themselves the thunder of the atheists of the past, and under the misnomer, "religious," place before the public what all atheists of the past ages have been preaching.

It is most gratifying to perceive that such distinguished men as signed this statement are frank enough to admit the extent of the religious revolution, and determined enough to take a hand in the clearing away of the débris that clutters the crumbling of all religious creeds. Yet it is only fair to point out that this statement contains nothing that would not be recognized by those intrepid atheists of the past, and little more than they urged in their time. I refer to those brilliant French atheists La Mettrie, Helvetius, d'Holbach, d'Alembert, and Diderot.

CHAPTER XIX

THE DOOM OF RELIGION; THE NECESSITY OF ATHEISM

One should recall the charge of atheism directed against the keenest thinkers of antiquity and the greatest of its moral reformers. But what was personal and incidental in the past, depending largely upon the genius and inspiration of seers and leaders, has now become a social movement, as wide as science.

JAMES T. SHOTWELL.

The drift from God is a movement of events, a propulsion of vital experience, not a parade of words to be diverted by other words.

MAX CARL OTTO.

IN the Babylonian and Assyrian mythologies we have the chief deities as Ishtar, Tammuz, Baal, and Astarte. In the Phrygian religion we have the Goddess Cybele and her husband Attis. Among the Greeks we have the Goddess Aphrodite and the God Adonis. The Persians had their Mithra. Adonis and Attis flourished in Syria. In the Egyptian religion was found the Goddess Isis and the God Osiris. The Semites have their Jehovah, the Mohammedans their Allah, and the Christians the Goddess Mary, the God the Father, and a son Jesus.

Christianity has divided itself into, Catholicism and Protestantism; and when Protestantism gave the right of interpretation of the Bible to each individual, there were evolved such forms of Protestantism as Christian Science, Holy Rollerism, Seventh Day Adventism, Swedenborgianism, and the cults of the Doukhobors, the Shakers, the Mennonites, the Dunkards and the Salvation Army.

In the early days of the Church were seen the wrangling of sects, the incomprehensible jargon of Arians, Nestorians, Eutychians, Monotheists, Monophysites, Mariolatrists, etc. Today we behold the incomprehensible jargon of the first-mentioned sects.

Christ, born of an immaculate virgin, died for mankind, arose from the dead, and ascended into Heaven.

Buddha, who lived over 500 years before Jesus, was born of the Virgin Maya, which is the same as Mary. Maya conceived by the Holy Ghost, and thus Buddha was of the nature of God and man combined. Buddha was born on December 25, his birth was announced in the heavens by a star, and angels sang. He stood upon his feet and spoke at the moment of his birth; at five months of age he sat unsupported in the air; and at the moment of his conversion he was attacked by a legion of demons. He was visited by wise men, he was baptized, transfigured, performed miracles, rose from the dead, and on his ascension through the air to heaven, he left his footprint on a mountain in Ceylon.

The Hindu Savior, Krishna, was born of a virgin 600 years before Christ. A star shone at his birth which took place in a cave. He was adored by cowherds who recognized his greatness, he performed miracles, was crucified, and is to come to judge the earth.

Christ died for mankind,—so did Buddha and Krishna. Adonis, Osiris, Horus, and Tammuz, all virgin-born gods, were saviors and suffered death. Christ rose from the dead, so have Krishna and Buddha arisen from the dead and ascended into Heaven. So did Lao Kium, Zoroaster, and Mithra.

A star shone in the sky at the births of Krishna, Rama Yu, Lao Tsze, Moses, Quetzalcoatl, Ormuzd, Rama, Buddha, and others. Christ was born of a virgin, so was Krishna and Buddha. Lao Tsze was also born of a virgin. Horus in Egypt was born of the Virgin Isis. Isis, with the child Horus on her knee, was worshiped centuries before the Christian era, and was appealed to under the names of "Our Lady," "Queen of

Heaven," "Star of Heaven," "Star of the Sea," "Mother of God," and so forth. Hercules, Bacchus, and Perseus were gods born by mortal mothers. Zeus, father of the gods, visited Semele in the form of a thunderstorm and she gave birth, on the 25th of December, to the great savior and deliverer, Dionysis.

Mithra was born of a virgin, in a cave, on the 25th of December. He was buried in a tomb from which he rose again. He was called savior and mediator and sometimes figured as a lamb. Osiris was also said to be born about the 25th of December; he suffered, died, and was resurrected. Hercules was miraculously conceived from a divine father and was everywhere invoked as savior. Minerva had a more remarkable birth than Eve; she sprang full-armed from the brow of Jupiter. He did this remarkable feat without even losing a rib.

The Chinese Tien, the holy one, died to save the world. In Mexico, Quetzalcoatl, the savior, was the son of Chimalman, the Virgin Queen of Heaven. He was tempted, fasted forty days, was done to death, and his second coming was eagerly looked for by the natives. The Teutonic Goddess Hertha, was a virgin, and the sacred groves of Germany contained her image with a child in her arms. The Scandinavian Goddess Frigga was a virgin who bore a son, Balder, healer and savior of mankind.

When one considers the similarity of these ancient pagan legends and beliefs with Christian traditions if one believes

341

with Justin Martyr, then indeed the Devil must have been a very busy person to have caused these pagans to imitate for such long ages and in such widespread localities the Christian mysteries. Indeed, Edward Carpenter comments, "One has only, instead of the word 'Jesus' to read Dionysis or Krishna or Hercules or Osiris or Attis, and instead of 'Mary' to insert Semele or Devaki or Alcmene or Neith or Nona, and for Pontius Pilate to use the name of any terrestrial tyrant who comes into the corresponding story, and lo! the creed fits in all particulars into the rites and worship of a pagan God."

A legend stated that Plato, born of Perictione, a pure virgin, suffered an immaculate conception through the influences of Apollo (B. C. 426). The God declared to Ariston, to whom she was about to be married, the parentage of the child.

St. Dominic, born A.D. 1170, was said to be the offspring of an immaculate conception. He was free from original sin and was regarded as the adopted son of the Virgin Mary.

St. Francis, the compeer of St. Dominic, was born A.D. 1182. A prophetess foretold his birth; he was born in a stable; angels sang forth peace and good will into the air, and one, in the guise of Simeon, bore him to baptism.

The Egyptian trinities are well known: thus, from Amun by Maut proceeds Khonso; from Osiris by Isis proceeds Horus; from Neph by Saté proceeds Anouké. The Egyptians had propounded the dogma that there had been divine incarnations, the fall of man, and redemption.

In India, centuries before Christianity, we find the Hindu trinity; Brahma, Vishnu, and Siva. In the Institutes of Manu, a code of civil law as well as religious law, written about the ninth century before Christ, is found a description of creation, the nature of God, and rules for the duty of man in every station of life from the moment of birth to death.

Professor James T. Shotwell when speaking of paganism reminds us, "Who of us can appreciate antique paganism? The Gods of Greece or Rome are for us hardly more than the mutilated statues of them in our own museums; pitiable, helpless objects before the scrutiny and comments of a passing crowd. Venus is an armless figure from the Louvre; Dionysos does not mean to us divine possession, the gift of tongues, or immortality; Attis brings no salvation. But to antiquity the 'pagan' cults were no mockery. They were as real as Polynesian heathenism or Christianity to-day." (*James T. Shotwell: "The Religious Revolution of To-day."*)

It is seen, therefore, that from time immemorial, man does not discover his gods, *but invents them.* He invents them in the light of his experience and endows them with capacities that indicate the stage of man's mental development.

Religion is not the product of civilized man. Man inherits his god just as he inherits his physical qualities. The idea of a supernatural being creating and governing this earth is a phantom born in the mind of the savage. If it had not been born in the early stages of man's mental development, it surely would not come into existence now. History proves that as the mind of man expands, it does not discover new gods, but that it discards them. It is not strange, therefore, that there has not been advanced a new major religious belief in the last 1300 years. All modern religious conceptions, no matter how disguised, find their origin in the fear-stricken ignorance of the primitive savage.

A Christian will admit that the gods of others are man-made, and that their creed is similar to the worship of the savage. He looks at their gods with the vision of a civilized being; but when he looks at his own god, he forgets his civilization, he relapses centuries of time, and *his* mental viewpoint is that of the savage.

Christianity, with its primitive concepts, can make its adherents firm in the belief of great monstrosities. When its adherents believed that the Bible sanctioned the destruction of heretics and witches, they were certainly doing things from a Christian standpoint. It was this standpoint that justified an embittered denunciation of evolution at one time and then recanting, adopted it as a part of the Bible teaching. When the Spaniards blotted out an entire civilization in South America, when Catholics butchered Protestants, or Protestants butchered Catholics, they were all justified from the Christian standpoint.

Man has been living on this planet some 500,000 years. Jesus appeared less than 2000 years ago to save mankind. What of those countless millions of men that died before Christ came to save the world from damnation? If the Christian creed, that except a man believes in the Lord Jesus Christ he cannot be saved, is maintained, then it must be that those millions of human beings who lived before Christ and had no chance to believe, are in hell-fire.

It is probable that one of the factors that turned primitive man's attention away from his cruel and short, earthly existence to the thought of a more lengthy and less cruel existence in a hereafter, was the extreme uncertainty and short duration of his own life. And this primitive trend of thought that turns man's mind from the here and now to a contemplation of a mythical hereafter persists to this day, produces the same slavish resignation. This false release from the actualities constitute a mental aberration which we see in the hysterical and weak-minded. When such an individual is confronted by problems that tax his mental strength, if that individual has not strength of mind to reason and to persevere so that he overcomes his environmental difficulties, he will seek an avenue of escape in a fanciful existence which the physician recognizes in hysteria and certain forms of mental disease. So, throughout the ages, man has sought release from the realities of his existence into a fanciful and pleasantly delusional flight into a hereafter. "There is no salvation in that sickly obscurantism which attempts to evade realities by confusing itself about them. Safety lies only in clarity and the struggle for the light. No subliminal nor fringe of consciousness can rank in the intellectual life beside the burning focal center where the rays of knowledge converge. The hope must be in following reason, not in thwarting it. To turn back from it is not mysticism, it is superstition. No; we must be prepared to see the higher criticism destroy the historicity of the most sacred texts of the Bible, psychology analyze the phenomena of conversion on the basis of adolescent passion, anthropology explain the genesis of the very-idea of God. An where *we* can understand, it is a moral crime to cherish the un-understood. (*James T. Shotwell: "The Religious Revolution of Today."*) Religious beliefs are clearly mental aberations from which it is high time that the progress of knowledge should lead to a logical cure. Man is steadily overcoming and conquering his environment; the uncertainty of life and cruelty are much diminished as compared with the past ages, but man has not as yet fully utilized the means of an emancipating measure from his mental enslavement and fear of his environment.

Chapman Cohen, in his "Theism or Atheism," clearly states: "We know that man does not discover God, he invents him, and an invention is properly discarded when a better instrument is forthcoming. To-day, the hypothesis of God stands in just the same relation to the better life of to-day as the fire drill of the savage does to the modern method of obtaining a light. The belief in God may continue awhile in virtue of the lack of intelligence of some, of the carelessness of others, and of the conservative character of the mass. But no amount of apologizing can make up for the absence of genuine knowledge, nor can the flow of the finest eloquence do aught but clothe in regal raiment the body of a corpse."

Religion arose as a means of explanation of natural phenomena at a time when no other explanation of the origin of natural phenomena had been ascertained. God is always what Spinoza called it, "the asylum of ignorance." When causes are unknown, God is brought forward; when causes are known, God retires into the background. In an age of ignorance, God is active; in an age of science, he is impotent. History attests this fact.

"The single and outstanding characteristic of the conception of God at all times, and under all conditions is that it is the equivalent of ignorance. In primitive times it is ignorance of the character of the natural forces that leads to the assumption of the existence of Gods, and in this respect the God idea has remained true to itself throughout. Even to-day, whenever the principle of God is invoked, a very slight examination is enough to show that the only reason for this being done is our ignorance of the subject before us." (*Chapman Cohen*.)

The belief in God is least questioned where civilization is lowest; it is called into the most serious question where civilization is most advanced. It is clear that had primitive man known what we know today about nature, the gods would never have been born.

"The suspicious feature must be pointed out that the belief in God owes its existence, not to the trained and educated observation of civilized times, but to the uncritical reflection of the primitive mind. It has its origin there, and it would indeed be remarkable, if, while in almost every other direction the primitive mind showed itself to be hopelessly wrong, in its interpretation of the world in this particular respect, it has proved itself to be altogether right." (*Chapman Cohen.*)

All intelligent men admit that human welfare depends upon our knowledge and our ability to harness the forces of nature. "I myself," writes Llewelyn Powys, "do not doubt that the good fortune of the human race depends more on science than on religion. In all directions the bigotry of the churches obstructs amelioration . . . as long as the majority of men rely upon supernatural interference, supernatural guidance, from a human point of view all is likely to be confusion. . . . Trusting in God rather than in man it is in the nature of these blind worshippers to oppose every advance of human knowledge. It was they who condemned Galileo, who resisted Darwin and who to-day deride the doctrines of Freud." Science has given us an account of the operation of the universe *sans* God, and investigation has also given us a clear conception of the evolution of all religious beliefs from the crude conceptions of the savage to the but little altered form of the modern conception.

"If we are to regard the God idea as an evolution which began in the ignorance of primitive man, it would seem clear that no matter how refined or developed the idea may become, it can rest on no other or sounder basis than which is presented to us in the psychology of primitive man. Each stage of theistic belief grows out of the proceeding stage, and if it can be shown that the beginning of this evolution arose in a huge blunder, I quite fail to see how any subsequent development can convert this unmistakable blunder into a demonstrable truth." (*Chapman Cohen.*)

Men of today are trying to force themselves to believe that there must be something true in that which had been believed by so many great and pious men of old. But it is in vain; intellect has outgrown faith. They are aware of the fallacy of their opinions, yet angry that another should remind them of it. And these men who today are secretly sceptics, are loudest in their public denunciation of others who publicly announce their scepticism. In ancient Greece, when the philosophers came into prominence, Zeus was superseded by the air, and Poseidon by the water; in modern times, all hitherto supernatural events are being explained by physical laws. Plato regarded it as a patriotic duty to accept the public faith although he full well knew the absurdities of that faith. Today, there are many Platos that hold to the same conviction. The freethinkers hold to the view of Xenophanes who denounced the public faith as an ancient blunder which had been converted by time into a national imposture. All religion is a delusion which transfers the motives and thoughts of men to those who are not men. No ecclesiastic has as yet offered a satisfactory answer as to why there has been a marvelous disappearance of the working of miracles, and why human actions alone are now to be seen in this world of ours.

We are witnessing today what happened in the Roman empire during the decline of polytheism. Draper states: "Between that period during which a nation has been governed by its imagination, and that in which it submits to reason, there is a melancholy interval. The constitution of man is such that, for a long time after he has discovered the incorrectness of the ideas prevailing around him, he shrinks from openly emancipating himself from their dominion, and, constrained by the force of circumstances, he becomes a hypocrite, publicly applauding what his private judgment condemns. Where a nation is making this passage, so universal do these practices become that it may be truly said hypocrisy is organized. It is possible that whole communities might be found living in this deplorable state."

And, indeed, in our own country we are witnessing an example of this very thing. Religion has led to widespread hypocrisy. Our religious influences have created a race of men mentally docile and obedient to the dictates of tyrannical ecclesiasticism. It has created a fear of truth, and our minds are still brutish and puerile in our methods of reasoning. Credulity has led to stultification, and stultification of the mind is the bitter fruit which we have been reaping for thousands of years.

There are probably hundreds of thousands of men and women in these United States that give lip-service to their creed, but deep in the recesses of their minds a small voice cries to them and shames them, for as soon as they reason, they become sceptics. How can we know the actual number of earthlings that are sceptics? It is impossible in our present state of development. Religious persecution today is just as active as it was during the Middle Ages. Surely, a man is not burned at the stake for his scepticism in this age; but is he not done to death? If the grocer, the butcher, the doctor, the lawyer, the scholar, the business man, were to boldly announce his scepticism, what would happen to him? The answer is well known to all. Immediately, each of his religious customers would take it upon himself to act as a personal inquisition. The sceptic would be shunned socially, he would be ignored, his wares would be sought after elsewhere, and he would suffer. His wife, his family, his children, would suffer with him, for our economic scheme makes the would-be sceptic dependent upon the whims of the majority believers. He is forced to hold his tongue, or else is tortured. Are not the wants of his family, the hunger, and ostracism torture? Thus thousands are forced into hypocrisy. Many others, although they have outgrown all fear of the god of orthodoxy, the fear of the god of social pressure remains.

There are embodied in all creeds three human impulses: fear, conceit, and hatred; and religion has given an air of respectability to these passions. Religion is a malignant disease born of fear, a cancer which has been eating into the vitals of everything that is worth while in our civilization; and by its growth obstructing those advances which make for a more healthful life.

Morally and intellectually, socially and historically, religion has been shown to be a pernicious influence. Some of these influences falling into these classifications have been considered in previous chapters.

The modern Christian, in his amusing ignorance, asserts that Christianity is now mild and rationalistic, ignoring the fact that all its so-called mildness and rationalism is due to the teaching of men who in their own day were persecuted by all orthodox Christians.

"Historically, churches have-stood on the side of the powers that be. They have defended slavery or have held their tongues about it. They have maintained serfdom and kept serfs. They have opposed every movement undertaken for the liberation of the masses of men; the ideals of liberty, equality and fraternity are the creations of the camps of their enemies, of the rationalists of the eighteenth century, and the liberals and socialists of the nineteenth century. They have defended and condoned the industrial exploitation of children. They have fought bitterly the enfranchisement of women. They have justified unjust war. They have fought with book and bill and candle and fagot every new great step in the advancement of science from gravitation to evolution. Wardens, ever since Constantine gave the schools of antiquity into the keeping of the Christian bishops, of the education of the people, they have fought with all their power the establishment of free public schools and the spread of literacy and knowledge among the people." (*Horace M. Kallen: "Why Religion."*)

If Christianity has made any progress in the assimilation of doctrines that are less barbarous than heretofore, they have been effected in spite of the most vigorous resistance, and solely as a result of the onslaught of freethinkers.

Throughout the ages, when a thinking man had questioned the how and why of any secular problem, so long as that problem had no direct or indirect bearing upon religion, or upon any branch of knowledge that was assumed to be infallibly foretold in the Bible, that man was unmolested. The problems falling into the above classification were extremely small due to the strongly defended theological lunacy that asserted itself in the declaration that all knowledge both spiritual and material was contained in the Bible as interpreted by the Church.

Man, however, when he broached his religious doubts, was regarded as the most sinful of beings, and it was forbidden him to question and yield to the conclusions that his mind evolved.

Think of the irony and tragedy of this self-enslavement of the human mind! There is one characteristic that man prides himself as having apart from all lower animals, his ability to reason and to think. Is it his superior musculature and brute strength that has placed man upon his present pinnacle of advanced civilization, or is it his mental development, his mind, that has taught him to harness the forces of nature? Has not his mind so coordinated his movements that he has enslaved those forces of nature to be his aid? And yet, if mind is one thing that has enabled man to pull himself out of the morass of brute life, why has it been that man himself has been so persistently decrying and degrading the efforts of that mind?

The answer is, that religion has provided the shackles and securely and jealously enslaved the mind. With the aid of his religious beliefs man has been ensnared into a mental prison in which he has been an all too willing captive. Surely it is easier to believe than to think.

Napoleon, himself a sceptic, was cognizant of this slave philosophy. "What is it," he is reported to have asked, "that makes the poor man think it is quite natural that there are fires in my castle when he is dying of cold? That I have ten coats in my wardrobe while he goes naked? That at each of my meals enough is served to feed his family for a week? It is simply religion, which tells him that in another life I shall be only his equal, and that he actually has more chance of being happy than I. Yes, we must see to it that the doors of the churches are open to all, and that it does not cost the poor man much to have prayers said on his tomb."

How well the ecclesiastical psychologists have grasped this fact, and how well they have fashioned a strong chain for the mind out of this weakness of human minds!

Church and government have been well aware of this psychology, and have fought constantly the spread of Freethought literature to the masses. Professor Bury, in his "History of Freedom of Thought," speaking of England, tells us, "If we take the cases in which the civil authorities have intervened to repress the publication of unorthodox opinions during the last two centuries, we find that the object has always been to prevent the spread of free thought among the masses."

Think but a moment how well the above is borne out by

the attitude of the Church in the stand that it took during the Middle Ages, when she prohibited the reading of the Bible by any person except her clergy. When she prohibited the printing of all books except those that she approved of; books that minutely agreed in all details with the phantastic fables of her Bible were the only ones allowed to be printed.

The Church also strenuously objected to the printing of Bibles in the languages of the masses. That most efficient shackle to the mind, that precept that there was no knowledge, whether material or spiritual, that was not contained in the Bible, how strenuously the Church upheld that doctrine!

And in our own day, the ridiculous assumption that "mysteries" (a special form of ignorance) are the special province of the Church. Considering these few examples as well as all ecclesiastical endeavor, no rational mind can escape the fact that that primeval curse, religion, has had for its object, down through the centuries, the sadistic desire to enslave and trample on the mind of man. It has been a defensive measure on the part of the Church, for she well recognizes that once the mind is free, it will free itself of the shackles of religion also.

Nor is this all. I execrate the enslavement of the mind of our young children by the ecclesiastics. Is anything so pitiful to behold as the firm grasp that the Church places on the mind of the youngest of children? Children at play, children of four and five years of age, will be heard to mention with fearful tones various religious rites, such as baptism and confirmation, and to perform in their manner these rites with their dolls. Fear! Fear! instilled into the minds of the impressionable children! Think of the degradation that the ecclesiastics practice when they insist that from the time a child is out of its infancy its instruction shall be placed in their hands. They take the most precious possession of man, his mind, and mould it to their desire. The mind of a child is plastic, it is like a moist piece of clay and they mould it and form it to their desire. Warped and poured into the ecclesiastic mould of fear, the mind of the child becomes set and fixed with the years. Then it is too late for rational thinking, as far as religious matters go, the mind of the adult is firmly set in the form that the ecclesiastic has fashioned for him in his youth. It is impossible for the adult so taught to reason clearly and rationally concerning his religion; the mould is too strong, the clay has set, reason cannot penetrate into that hardened form. That is why it is almost impossible for the adult who has been exposed to this mental moulding from his infancy to break away from the fears and superstitions learned on his mother's knee.

If Christianity, Hebrewism, Mohammedanism, or any other creed is true, its truth must be more apparent at the age of twenty-five than it is at the age of five. Why does the ecclesiastic not leave off his advances until the child reaches a mature age, an age when he can reason? Then, if theism is

357

true, he can accept it with a reasoning mind, not a blindly faithful mind. The theist realizes, however, that belief is at one pole, reason at the other. Belief, creed, religion, are ideations of the primitive mind and the mind of the child; reason is the product of mature thought. Schopenhauer remarked that, "The power of relligious dogma when inculcated early is such as to stifle conscience, compassion, and finally every feeling of humanity."

It is an undeniable fact that if the clergy would but leave their tainted hands off the minds of our children until they would have reached a mature age, there would be no religious instinct. Religious instinct is a myth. Give me but two generations of men who have not been subjected to this religious influence in childhood, and there will be a race of atheists.

The ecclesiastic has from earliest times taken the standpoint that the masses of people are of crude susceptibility and clumsy intelligence, "sordid in their pursuits and sunk in drudgery; and religion provides the only means of proclaiming and making them feel the high import of life." (*Schopenhauer.*) Thus the theist is led to the conclusion that the end justifies the means.

Theism is a hypothesis which, among other things, attempts an explanation of the universe. The theist recognizes a creator who created the universe and is responsible for its operation. The atheist clearly perceives that the assumption of a creator does not advance him in the slightest degree towards the solution of the mysterious problem of the universe. The oft-repeated question still admits of no answer, "Who created the creator"?

It is an absurd answer to reply that the creator created himself, yet, even if this is granted, may not the universe have created itself? If the theist puts forward the statement that God has always existed, the atheist may well reply that if God has always existed, why can he not say that the universe has always existed? The atheist is not concerned with the creation of the universe; to him it presents a problem which is beyond the comprehension of his present mental capacities. He comprehends the fact of its being, and that is as far as he or any rational mind can go. Atheism confines itself to a refutation of theism, and avoids the theistic fallacy of assuming without any proofs or reasonable arguments to substantiate the assumption of an intelligent, omnipotent, omniscient, anthropomorphic, and anthropocentric creator. The theistic assumption has but retarded the advance of practical knowledge, and prepared the soil for superstition and the countless terrors of religious beliefs.

Atheism, as far as a rational explanation of the universe is covered, although it does not offer an explanation of the "ultimate," or "the riddle of the universe," does insist that any view held be one that shall be based on truth and conformity to reality. It further maintains that if a view be propagated it should be held in the same position that any scientific proposition is held. It must be open to verification; if it be verified as any scientific theory is verified, it will be accepted in part, or in toto, and be proven to be true or displaced by a closer approximation to the truth. To certain types of men there may be a negative attitude expressed in this credo, which leaves the mind unsatisfied. This is but an emotional bias and has nothing to do whatsoever with the attainment of truth. A delusion may be more comforting than the truth, but that does not necessitate the conclusion that a delusion may be of more ultimate benefit than a constant striving for the truth. It has often been said that atheism, in that negative aspect, places a question mark upon our problems. However, while a question mark may indicate a negative value, it may also prove to be a mental provocative. A period placed at the end of a problem denotes that it has been definitely solved. In connection with the origin of the universe, no period can be placed at the end of that problem, and since we are awaiting the solution, it is much more to the interest of further advances to place the question mark there, than to consider the matter solved. Surely, sufficient instances have been enumerated in this discussion to show the stultification and retardation that ensues when an institution maintains an insistence that a problem be held to conform in any of its explanatory aspects to a preconceived infallible statement, or considers a problem not to exist, or closes its eyes to the inconsistencies in an explanation which is being maintained by mental persuasion and force. When the Bible was considered as containing the answer to all our problems we have seen what the result was. If atheism places a question mark upon the problem of the universe, it does so in a constructive manner; for that mark points to the direction in which a logical solution may be possible. Such is the mental attitude of the scientist. He places an interrogation point upon his problems and that mark is the impetus, the mental stimulus, that leads him on to take infinite pains in his labors and, as time passes, each question mark is replaced by knowledge; it is knowledge and knowledge alone, reason not faith, that furnishes the period.

It was Haeckel who asserted that, "The most dangerous of the three great enemies of reason and knowledge is not malice, but ignorance, or perhaps, indolence." The question mark as applied to a problem that is recognizably not solved is a signpost, to the knowledge that time must bring. The spurious period placed at the end of a probelm is the death warrant for that problem and there it must lie devitalized by ignorance and indolence.

It has often been affirmed that what we see in this universe is phenomena, and all explanations but interpret the manifestations of these phenomena. What is in back of and beyond these phenomena may never be known, and if it be known, would be of no further use to us. It is equally as true that if we but see phenomena and our mental capacities deny us a conception of the reality beyond phenomena, yet, we have a growing knowledge of the laws that govern these phenomena. And it is a comprehensive knowledge of these invariable laws that govern the universe that are of universal value. These laws have been ascertained by the questioning mental attitude, and not by a futile reliance on faith.

Human knowledge has expanded immensely in the last fifty years, and this by the purely scientific method, the materialistic method, and the questioning attitude. The value of these findings when they can be converted into practical applications in industry are well known to all.

We have added nothing to our store of knowledge except by the exercise of our mentality and reason. The application of the scientific method to the workings of the mind has made more progress in explaining the mind in the brief period of fifty years than philosophical deductions had made in the past two thousand years. Every new fact that has been discovered has fitted into the mechanistic scheme of the universe, and not one new fact has been disclosed that suggested anything beyond nature. The theistic interpretation of the universe has been completely discredited by the scientific investigations. Science has brought to the confines of invariable laws multitudes of problems that had hitherto been supposed to point to "spiritual" interference. Theology has been driven out of the open spaces of reason and still persists in clinging to the twilight zone of the present unknown, only to be driven from its precarious position constantly by our increasing knowledge and with increasing rapidity from shadow to shadow.

There has been an increasing tendency shown by physicists to consider that matter and energy are interchangeable, and that the one ultimate reality is energy. If this be so, we are still dealing with an ultimate that is a material reality. The Nobel prize in medicine for the year 1932 was awarded to two British investigators, Sir Charles Scott Sherrington, professor of physiology at Oxford University, and Dr. Edgar Douglas Adrian, professor of physiology at Cambridge University. Their researches seem to have settled definitely a problem that has long been a bone for contention. Nerve energy has been shown conclusively to be of an electric type of energy. The old question of whether mind was part of the material world has been shown by these experiments to be answered in the affirmative. There is no duality, mind and matter are one, and mind is but a special property of highly specialized matter.

It is with a great deal of regret that the freethinker contemplates the attitude of such scientists as Jeans, Eddington, Millikan, and the philosopher Professor Whitehead. Their hesitation to divorce themselves completely from all conceptions of a supernatural force leads to a great deal of confusion. An acquaintance with the writings of Einstein brings one the certainty that he is as much in accordance with the attitude of freethought as is the most militant atheist. The "cosmic sense" and "totality of existence" of Einstein is as far removed from the conception of a Yahveh as is the mentality of an Australian black man from that of Einstein's mental grasp. Similarly with the cosmic consciousness expressed in the writings of Jeans, Eddington, and Whitehead. With characteristic disregard for the truth certain modern theologians have grasped this cringing attitude of the above-mentioned men and have stressed their viewpoints by a dishonest interpretation that these men actually give a scientific certitude to their own theologic creeds and dogmas. Nothing can be further from the truth. The freethinker would have each theologian who tells his adherents that these men lend credence to their beliefs to consider the following: if the above-named men would be asked if they believed in a deity who actively interposed his will and influence in the lives of men, as is commonly expressed in the term "Providence," if they ascribed to the belief in personal immorality, if they themselves believed in the existence of a "soul," if they ascribed to the statement that "prayer" influenced the opinion of an all-powerful being to intercede for them in their problems and grief, if they believed that the Bible was a book dictated by God, or that a god caused to be written for him his "revelations"; that heaven and hell exist in the meaning that theologians assure their adherents that they do; that sin and morality is what theologians still hold it to be; that there has been a "fall" and therefore the necessity for a "redemption" of man; and that creed and dogma are necessary factors in the worship of a deity,—what would their answers be? Eddington, Jeans, Einstein, and Whitehead would answer these questions exactly as would the most militant atheists.

The mental attitude of these men can best be explained when one considers certain similarities between theological asceticism and scientific asceticism. And it is the duty of the freethinker clearly to point out why this confusion has arisen. During the ages of faith, the world beheld a swarm of men and women who retired from the grim realities of a world which at that time was made abhorrent to all sensitive men by the most exacting insistence of theologians that "faith" was the all necessary ingredient of life, and that closed its eyes completely to the degrading actualities of life that this insistence led to. Multitudes of men retired to the desert and to the protective walls of monasteries. There, by constant privations, fastings, continual prayer, flagellation, and introspection, they spent their lives. These ascetic individuals by these means were enabled to enter what may be called a "theologic trance" and their subsequent hallucinations, illusions, and delusions gave to them what they deemed to be a transcendental insight into the construction of the universe and what was expected between "fallen" and debased man and his omnipotent creator.

These men keenly apprehended what some today, in a gentler age, have called "cosmic consciousness."

I do not mean to imply that these before-mentioned scientists have applied such a rigor to their lives. What is meant to be stated is that these men by their research and comprehension of the vastness of the universe stand in awe and fear before this brain-benumbing aspect. Modern astrophysics, to one who attempts to comprehend its vastness, imposes on the mind but a faint comprehension of the vastness of the universe in space, time, and size; but imposes a deep conviction of the infinitesimal meaning of our planet Earth, both as to size and its relation to the millions of related heavenly bodies. The evolution of man on our planet in this broad conception of space and time is most infinitesimal. It has been just a few hours ago in this widened conception of time that Halley's comet was excommunicated from the skies by Pope Calixitus III, who looked upon this comet as one of unheard-of magnitude and from the tail of which was flung down upon the earth, disease, pestilence, and war.

Most certainly the minds of Jeans and Eddington carry in their recesses a vast amount of knowledge that was not common to men living in 1456, the year in which the above-mentioned comet caused such consternation. Much as one admires the superiority of the minds of these present-day physicists, yet one cannot help but think that if our present rate of progress meets no serious obstacle, then in another five hundred years, the attitude of awe of Jeans and Eddington towards the vastness of our universe will be held in some similar position to which Jeans and Eddington now hold the misguided conception of Halley's comet in the year 1456. The mind of man is just beginning to emerge from its swaddling clothes and we cannot assume to judge what its broadest capabilities may be. Certain great modern minds, therefore, when they contemplate this vastness of astrophysics are apt to dwell a bit too literally on the "music of the heavenly spheres," and under the influence of these celestial harmonies fall into the trance of scientific asceticism. Men who can no longer seriously hold to a belief in an anthropomorphic god, the soul and immortality are apt to allow themselves when in this mood to emotionalize their knowledge; and these same men are the ones who would in their scientific endeavors be the first to eliminate all emotions from their reasoning efforts in their laboratories. One seems justified, therefore, in stating that this conception of "cosmic consciousness" is but another instance of the mere illusions of a craving heart.

Discussing the question as to whether science and religion conflict, the physicist Professor Bazzoni, of the University of Pennsylvania, in a recent work "Energy and Matter," makes the following pointed comment: "Some scientists resort to metaphysics and make contact with a kind of mysticism which may be taken for a religious belief at precisely that point where ignorance prevents further progress along sound scientific lines. The primitive medicine man appealed to the gods to explain the precipitation of rain and the phase changes of the moon, and some modern scientists appeal to metaphysics and mysticism to explain the limits of the infinite and the nature of electricity."

He further cautions theologians against placing undue emphasis on the opinions of scientists when they express their minds on religious topics, and he remarks: "They (the laity) should realize that in the spiritual field the opinion of an eminent scientist has exactly the same weight as the opinion of any other cultivated and thoughtful individual."

When the scientist examines with the impartial mind of the laboratory the science of the origin of religious beliefs and delves into the complicated intricacies of religious history, he becomes as convinced as any other thoughtful individual that the facts of science and history are deadly to religion. Moreover, as man contemplates the construction and forces at work in the universe he still must exclaim, "end, beginning, or purpose, it knows not of."

The theologians are devoting a great deal of their time to the writings of physicists who venture into the field of theology. It may be that in this manner they can divert attention from the drastic findings concerning all religious beliefs that the anthropologists and psychologists are patiently accumulating.

"Many physicists and biologists like Pupin, Millikan, Oliver Lodge, J. Arthur Thomson, and Henry Fairfield Osborn, have recently blossomed forth as liberal theologians. They are still emotionally attached to the older religious faith. They are aware that modern physics and biology have abandoned doctrines that once were hostile to religious claims. They, therefore, proclaim that there is no further conflict between religion and science. In so doing, however, they show themselves abysmally ignorant of all that anthropology and psychology have done to study religion and religious man scientifically. They show their ignorance of the philosophy that has built upon such data. They do not realize that the present-day conflict between religious faith and science is no longer with a scientific explanation of the world, but with a scientific explanation of religion." (*J. H. Randall and J. H. Randall, Jr.: "Religion and the Modern World."*)

The cultured Greeks and Romans had their omnipotent gods and these have long ago died a death of ridicule. At a time when beauty and sculpture were at their height the religion of these ancient artists was absurd. Similarly, with some of our modern scientists, their religion has not kept pace with their intellect. Their emotions have overbalanced their reason in this field. Professor H. Levy, of the University of London, tersely remarks: "The assertion of contemporary scientists, who state that the universe is a fickle collection of indeterminate happenings, and a great thought in the Mind

369

of its Architect, a Pure Mathematician, serves merely to divert the activity of the scientific brain from its concentration on the contradictions and confusions of the all too real outward world to a state of passive and unreal contemplation." (*Professor H. Levy: "The Universe of Science."*)

Among the theologians, some at least have learned the futility of waxing indignant at each new scientific hypothesis that encroached, as they thought, within their domain. A great many liberal theologians have as yet not learned the extreme danger to their theology in grasping at some concept of science that for the present moment does not appear to be detrimental to their theology, or, as they think, seems to bolster up their particular creed. "The enthusiasm aroused in certain theological circles by recent developments in mathematical physics," states Dr. M. C. Otto, "seems to me to indicate just one thing, that these theologians felt themselves to be in so desperate a state that a floating straw assumed the appearance of a verdure-clad island. I am of the opinion that all persons who would work for a more decent and happy existence for themselves and for their fellows must turn their backs upon religion just to the extent that religious leadership seeks spiritual renewal in these hallucinations of despair." (*Drs. Wieman, Macintosh, and Otto: "Is There a God?"*)

It is only proper to point out that what certain emancipated minds are trying to reconstruct as a basis of religious belief is not what is held by the masses as their conception of religion. In a recent clear and frank statement of the religious revolution, John Herman Randall and John Herman Randall, Jr., state: "Such beliefs, even so fundamental a one as belief in God, must Stand their chances with the philosophic interpretation men give their experience. . . . The really revolutionary effect of the scientific faith, so far as religion is concerned, has been not its new view of the world, but its new view of religion. Reinterpretations of religious belief have been unimportant compared with reinterpretations of religion itself. For those who have come to share the scientific world-view, even more for those who have absorbed the spirit of scientific inquiry, it has been impossible to view religion as a divine revelation entrusted to man. It has even been impossible to see it as a relation between man and a cosmic deity. Religion has rather appeared a human enterprise, an organization of human life, an experience, a social bond, and an inspiration." (*J. H. Randall and J. H. Randall, Jr.: "Religion and the Modern World."*) To the man who literally entreats his deity, "Our Father, who art in Heaven, grant us our daily bread," the above reinterpretation of what is meant by religion can have no meaning. To the cultivated mind that comprehends what is meant, the above interpretation is what he conceives of as his social secular activities for the betterment of his fellowmen. A living philosophy of life is a much better name for this attitude than is the misnomer "religion," and avoids a great deal of confusion.

Some of our "scientists on a holiday," as they have been facetiously called when they stepped into a field in which they had not become well acquainted with the ground, have proceeded to lend assurance that God *is* by subtracting so drastically from what is generally attributed to the conception of God, that there is nothing much left to what they conceive as what God *means*. They have stripped the conception of what has been heretofore regarded as fundamental, namely, the conception that God is a superhuman personality or mind.

In Mr. Whitehead's philosophy, God is spoken of as, "God is not concrete, but He is the ground for concrete actuality." I believe such confusion of language may have been in the mind of Dr. M. C. Otto when he remarked: "Some persons endeavor more than ever to make necessary distinctions to keep meanings as clear as possible; and to have an eye on the tendency of language to become its own object. Other persons repudiate these obligations. They act as if it were a virtue to love darkness rather than light if your intentions are good. Under their manipulations conceptions are dimmed or replaced by vague intimations. One boundary line after another is obliterated until the whole substance of things swims in mists."

History has illustrated that the greatest source of evil on

this planet has arisen from the fact that physical phenomena for which our limited mental capacities were not able to formulate a logical solution, were ascribed to preternatural causes.

From this original stem arose religion and the Church, the two greatest obstacles which have been a burden to mankind for 2000 years and a barrier to all progress which has made life endurable and desirable.

The lower man is in the scale of civilization, the more does he call in the supernatural to explain all the happenings and experiences of his life. When he had been beset by an intellectual failure he had been thrown back to religion. Lacking the courage and mental capacity to proceed further against obstacles he succumbed to the drug of religious explanations. The need was not for a narcotic, but for a stimulant.

The mental stimulant was provided for man in the form of science. Science is but organized knowledge, and it is this knowledge that has elevated man to the position where he is now, his own god. When difficulties confront him in this age, he blames them upon his own ignorance and incompetence. And, when he sets about to overcome these difficulties, he does not rely on divine revelation or supernatural aid or on miracles; he relies on his reason. He knows that when a problem eludes his mental capacity, it is not the supernatural which eludes him but some natural force, some law which he has not been able to grasp as yet. There is no resignation in this attitude; only resolute, peaceful patience. The problem that he cannot solve at present will yield to his reason eventually. The ecclesiastic is well aware that science is his natural and implacable enemy. He knows that every time the bounds of exact knowledge are widened, the domain of religion is narrowed.

Man's knowledge of the universe is still incomplete, but it is certainly more complete than it was fifty years ago; and when we consider what that knowledge was a few thousand years ago, it is no breach of logic to state that all natural processes, in the course of time, will be brought into the confines of invariable laws.

Sir Arthur Keith clearly states: "The ancient seeker, to explain the kingdom of life, with man as its Regent, had to call in the miracle of creation. The modern seeker finds that although life has the appearance of the miraculous, yet all its manifestations can be studied and measured, and that there is a machinery at work in every living thing which shapes, evolves, and creates. His inquiries have led him to replace the miracle of creation by the laws of evolution.

"Whichever department of the realm of Nature the man of science has chosen for investigation, the result has always been the same; the supernatural has given place to the natural, superstition is succeeded by reason. The world has never had such armies of truth seekers as it now has. Those equipped with ladders of science have so often scaled the walls which surround cities of ignorance that they march forward in the sure faith that none of Nature's battlements are impregnable."

In the last analysis, if we reach a point in thinking where we cannot proceed further, a fathomless landmark, must we revert to the theological error of "thinking," and assume it must be of supernatural character? Because the unknown in the past has been assigned to the supernatural is no indication for us also, in the present age, to relegate the unknown to divine cause. It is unseemly that minds that have emancipated themselves should go just so far—as far as *their own reason* can explain the unknown—and when their limited reason can go no further to revert back to the primitive stage where solution is considered impossible to man save it be "revealed to him by God." If man's mind is free, if no coercion of any kind is placed on its exercise, it will expand and unravel what at present is still fathomless. Give man endless centuries and ample opportunities and he will unravel the miracles of development and growth just as he has done other miracles which at first seemed impossible of rational solution.

For how much longer will man be a slave to his inferiority complex with regard to his own rational capacities? If faith is vital to man, why not relate it to that which at least holds a promise of solution? Man's mind has not as yet arrived at the point which might give even the slightest indication of its ultimate exhaustion. We cannot assume the knowledge of what man's fullest capacities are. All things must unravel themselves with the progress of his mind, those things that he cannot explain now, he must not assign to a superhuman force; man must use his reasoning faculties to investigate and search for the truth so that these unknown may become part of the known.

Again to quote Sir Arthur Keith: "Only eighty years have come and gone since the anatomist obtained his first glimpse of the structural complexity of the human brain; it will take him eight thousand years and more to find out the exact part played by every departmental unit of this colossal system of government which carries on the mental life of a human being. *We have no reason to think there is anything supernatural in its manifestation.* As our knowledge of the brain accumulates, the names and terms we now use will give place to others which have a more precise meaning. In our present state of ignorance we have to use familiar and loose terms to explain the workings of the brain—such words as "soul," "spirit," "heart," "superstition," and "prejudice." These manifestations of the mind will be dissected and made understandable."

Science has as yet not fully explained the origin of life on earth, but there is reason to believe that it will do so in the future. The laws governing the production of life itself are under investigation in the laboratories and it is highly probable that this law will be unraveled at some future date. It will be interesting for our posterity to witness the confusion of the ecclesiastics and their attempted confirmation of this fact in the Bible; their finding of some obscure phrase that will be interpreted by them as a prediction of the fact in the Bible.

The theists have maintained, as we have seen, many false beliefs that have cost the lives of innumerable men and suffering incalculable; beliefs which they themselves have subsequently recognized as false but relinquished only by the onslaught of rising secular knowledge. It was the ecclesiastic who pointed to the God-dictated phrase, "Thou shalt not suffer a witch to live," and the various precepts that have been enumerated in the preceding chapters. Surely sufficient evidence has been noted to convince a thinking being that reason is a better guide than theism. Belief is the antithesis of reason; reason is rationality; religious belief is clearly mental abnormality.

If a religionist is asked what he thinks of a secular institution which vigorously condemns and persecutes inquiry, experiment, and truth, he will reply with the logical answer. When it is pointed out to him that religion has done and still is doing this, he will hem and haw until he manufactures some illogical answer. It has been stated that the more we think, the less we believe; and that the less we think, the more we believe. The Christian will analyze the creed of the Mohammedan and find it ridiculous; the Mohammedan analyzes the creed of the

Christian and in turn finds it ridiculous. That is thinking. But does the Mohammedan or the Christian analyze as critically each his own belief? Will he endeavor to analyze it at all? That is believing. The ecclesiastic concerns himself not with truth or knowledge; it is creed which is his shrine. He definitely is at war with knowledge and he wants to learn only such things as fit in with his preconceived notions and prejudices. When the minds of men are from infancy perverted with these ideals, how can mankind build a virile race?

It is often asserted that the alleged universality of the belief in God is an argument for its truth. But what of the fact that men had everywhere come to the conclusion that the earth was flat, and yet a wider and truer knowledge proved that universal belief to be false! In the discussion of witchcraft, it has been shown that a delusion may be as widespread as a truth. During the tenth and eleventh centuries, the Spanish Moors had recognized the sphericity of the earth and were teaching geography from globes in their common schools. Rome, during the same ages, was asserting in all its absurdity the flatness of the earth. It was not until almost five hundred years later that Rome was forced to see its absurdity and then only when the enlightened world mocked at its error.

In this twentieth century, certain enlightened men are teaching the absurdity and harmfulness of a belief in a deity. Must it take five hundred years for all mankind to come to a similar conclusion? May it not well be that in a few centuries our posterity will view belief in a deity in the same light that we in this age view the Church's insistence that the earth was flat?

The God idea has been one of the most divisive and anti-social notions cherished by mankind. In fact it has been asserted that the idea of God has been the enemy of man. It has driven multitudes of men and women into the unnatural asceticisms and wasted lives of the convent and abbey. It has taxed the economic resources of every nation. Every church, no matter of what creed, is a pathetic monument of God-ridden humanity which has been built by the pennies sweated by the poor, and wrested from them by fraudulent promises of reward, appeals to fear, and the pathetic human tendency to sacrifice.

The theologians have in their arguments resorted to philosophy. The consequence of this transference of the idea of God to the sphere of philosophy is the curious position that the god in which people believe is not the god whose existence is made the product of an experimental argument, and the god of the argument is not the god of belief.

"It is a nice question," remarks Walter Lippmann, "whether the use of God's name is not misleading when it is applied by modernists to ideas so remote from the God men have worshipped. Plainly the modernist churchman does not believe in the God of Genesis who walked in the garden in the cool of the evening and called for Adam and his wife who had hidden themselves behind a tree; nor in the God of Exodus who appeared to Moses and Aaron and seventy of the Elders of Israel, standing with his feet upon a paved walk as if it were a sapphire stone; nor even in the God of the fifty-third chapter of Isaiah who in his compassion for the sheep who had gone astray, having turned everyone to his own way, laid on the Man of Sorrows the iniquity of us all." (*Walter Lippmann: "A Preface to Morals."*)

It is one kind of god that is being set up in argument, and it is really another god that is being depended upon and believed. The philosophical conception of a deity, that may be in control of phenomena is an impersonal physical law, and has nothing to do with the conception of a personal deity to whom people pray for active intervention in their troubles. Religious belief is a monstrous apparition; the philosophy of atheism is a solid structure laboriously founded on solid rock.

The philosophy of atheism had temporarily failed in previous ages, since the knowledge of those ages did not furnish facts enough upon which to build. At the present, although our knowledge is far from complete and the surface has only been scratched, yet sufficient facts have been unearthed to reveal that there is no supernatural and the greatest hope of advancement lies in the philosophy of atheism. A philosophy that builds upon a foundation of purely secular thought, that leaves the idea of God completely discarded as a useless and false relic of bygone days, is the essence of atheism. "Atheism is more than the speculative philosophy of a few, that it is in sober truth the logical outcome of mental growth. So far as any phase of human life can be called inevitable, atheism may lay claim to being inescapable. All mental growth can be seen leading to it, just as we can see one stage of social development giving a logical starting point for another stage, and which could have been foretold had our knowledge of all the forces in operation been precise enough. Atheism is, so to speak, implicit in the growth of knowledge, its complete expression is the consummation of a process that began with the first questionings of religion. And the completion of the process means the death of super-naturalisms in all forms. Circumstances may obstruct its universal acceptance as a reasoned mental attitude, but that merely delays, it does not destroy the certainty of its final triumph." (*C. Cohen.*)

The philosophy of atheism leads man to a critical, analytical, and logical examination of his environment, and it is this that has lead to all of our advances. Religion creates a stunted standard of reasoning. The pathetic cry of St. Augustine, "But if I was shapen in iniquity, and in sin did my mother conceive me, where I pray thee, O my God, where, Lord, or when was I, thy servant innocent?" typifies the major concern of the

the narrow, egotistical mystic. From the time that the ideas of the later Greek philosophers had been forgotten until the present time, man has floundered in a sea of supernaturalism. It is high time that man faced his realities with fortitude in his own mentality, and when he does this, there will be produced a race of men who will seek for truth, for truth's sake, a race of supermen who will lead the world intellectually.

It is to Russia that all eyes will turn in the next few generations. At the present, she is going through the throes of childbirth. She is immature, and as a child she staggers. The abuse and ridicule heaped upon her now is but the repetition of that given by all frightened societies of past ages, when they contemplated new ideas which their immature minds could not fathom. But Russia will emerge in the not too distant future, and the infant will shortly reach maturity; and that maturity may set a standard for those timid and frightened societies that at present look with dilated eyes upon her daring.

The age is approaching when the god idea in its entirety will be classed with the gods of the Egyptians and Babylonians, when surplices and sacramental plate will be exhibited in museums; when nurses will relate to children the legends of the Christian mythology, as they now tell them fairy tales. The gods of monotheism will join the gods of polytheism and Yahveh and his associates will occupy in the minds of men the position now held by the gods of Olympus. To our ancestors Jupiter and Yahveh will have the same significance. "In a little time the cathedrals and churches will have taken upon themselves the proud, poetical glamour of abandoned temples. Men and women will enter them with reverent indulgence as they now in meditative mood visit the few remaining pantheons of the pagan worship." (*Llewelyn Powys: "An Hour On Christianity."*)

The age is aproaching when the current idea of the hereafter will be accounted a strange and selfish idea, just as we smile at the savage chief who believes that his station will be continued in the world beneath the ground, and that he will there be attended by his concubines and slaves. The age is fast approaching when love, not fear, will unite the human race. In that age, the *ideal*, not the *idol*, will be truth, and the one faith, not religion, but a sincere and lofty conception of the dignity and resourcefulness of the human mind; and an overwhelming desire to aid in the progress of all mankind, the extinction of disease, the perfection of genius, the perfection of love, and, therefore, the abolition of war, the exploration of the infinite, and the conquest of creation.

Such an age can never come to be during the mal-jurisdiction of a theistic philosophy. It can only come into being when the vast majority of men are by the force of advancing knowledge made aware of the truth of the atheistic philosophy.

An English observer, C. E. M. Joad, remarks: "The churches, no doubt, will continue to function for a time, but they will be attended increasingly, and in the end exclusively, by ignorant men, women, and children. Already, a stranger attending an average church of England service would almost be justified in assuming that the churches, like theatre matinées, were kept up for the benefit of women and children. So far as present indications go, it seems not unlikely that science will deliver the coup de grace to organized Christianity within the next hundred years."

We have caught a glimpse of what theism has done, and what the philosophy of atheism might have done, and will yet achieve. Has man profited by having remained in his mental infancy so long? Atheism is an emancipating system of thought that frees the mind from myths, fables, and childish fancies. There can be no inquisition, no witchcraft delusion, no religious wars, no persecutions of one sect by another, no impediment to science and progress, no stultification of the mind, as a result of its teachings.

The philosophy of atheism teaches man to stand on his own feet, instills confidence in his reasoning powers, and forces him to conquer his environment. It teaches him not to subject himself and debase himself before mythical superhuman powers, for his reason is his power. The march from faith to reason is the march on which dwells the future hope of a really civilized mankind.

Atheism teaches man to endeavor constantly to better his own condition and that of all of his fellowmen, to make his children wiser and happier; it supplies the powerful urge to add something new to the knowledge of mankind. And all this, not in the vain hope of being rewarded in another world, but from a pure sense of duty as a citizen of nature, as a patriot of the planet on which he dwells. This is no cold and cheerless philosophy; it is an elevating and ennobling ideal which may console him in his afflictions and teach him how to live and how to die. It is a self-reliant philosophy that makes a man intellectually free, and this mental emancipation allows him to face the world without fear of ghosts and gods. It relates solely to facts, while theism resorts to opinions that are grounded only upon emotionalism. Joseph Lewis has well noted that, "Atheism does not believe that man's mission on earth is to love and glorify God, but it does believe in living this life so that when you pass on, the world will be better for your having lived."

The history of the past ages informs us what the world was like with God. The progress of secular knowledge and science have given us measures by which we could produce a better society than has ever existed under the obstructionism of the Gods.

"The knowledge exists by which universal happiness can be

secured, the chief obstacle to its utilization for that purpose is the teaching of religion. Religion prevents our children from having a rational education; religion prevents us from removing the fundamental causes of war; religion prevents us from teaching the ethics of scientific cooperation in place of the old fierce doctrines of sin and punishment. It is possible that mankind is on the threshold of a golden age, but if so, it will be necessary to slay the dragon that guards the door, and this dragon is religion." (*Bertrand Russell.*)

It is interesting to contemplate the changes that may occur in our civilization in the next few centuries. On the one hand we have that long period of sterile time, 15,000 years, for the stage of neolithic man, and on the other the vast material progress of the past three hundred years. We may not be able to discern with clarity in what direction changes will occur, but in one aspect we can discern a well-marked tendency. That is the inevitable conquest of the philosophy of atheism. And with this conquest can be clearly seen that it would give to this earth a much sounder foundation upon which to build our progress, and that long-delayed freedom, the emancipation of the mind from all myths and fables. The inevitableness of atheism has been well summed up by Chapman Cohen:

"Looking at the whole course of Human History, and noting how the vilest and most ruinous practices have been ever associated with religion, and have ever relied upon religion for support, the cause for speculation is, not what will happen to the world when religion dies out, but how human society has managed to flourish while the belief in the Gods ruled. . . .

"Substantially, we have by searching found out God. We know the origin and history of one of the greatest delusions that ever possessed the human mind. God has been found out; analytically and synthetically we understand the God-idea as previous generations could not understand it. It has been explained, and the logical consequence of the explanation is Atheism."

Man is fast attaining a mastery of his environment, and his religious creeds are becoming as irrational to him as the witchcraft delusion. Religion with its burden of fear ties him to the dead ages. But knowledge not only supplies him with power, but also furnishes him with courage, and that courage will aid him in freeing himself from that fear—religion. Religion is doomed to occupy the same place in history as the institution of slavery. Lies and imposture, no matter how powerfully sustained, can be dispelled by knowledge. The Church will destroy itself with its own poison. Knowledge and courage spell the doom of religion.

CHAPTER XX

CONTEMPORARY OPINION

The Vanguard

Let us make no mistake—great minds are skeptical. . . . The strength and the freedom which arise from exceptional power of thought express themselves in skepticism. . . . A mind which aspires to great things and is determined to achieve them is of necessity skeptical.

NIETZSCHE.

BERTRAND RUSSELL

MY own view on religion is that of Lucretius. I regard it as a disease born of fear and as a source of untold misery to the human race. I cannot, however, deny that it has made *some* contributions to civilization. It helped in early days to fix the calendar, and it caused Egyptian priests to chronicle eclipses with such care that in time they became able to predict them. These two services I am prepared to acknowledge, but I do not know of any others.

MAX CARL OTTO

It is my conviction that the happiest and noblest life attainable by men and women is jeopardized by reliance upon a superhuman, cosmic being for guidance and help. I know, of course, that God has been defined in various terms. I do not choose among them. For it seems to me indisputable that those who turn to God, however God be defined, do so because, consciously or unconsciously, they seek there the satisfaction of wants, the worth of living, and security for what they passionately prize, which they have not found and despair of finding in the human venture as they know it. Reliance upon God for what life does not afford, has, in my opinion, harmful consequences. It diverts attention from the specific conditions upon which a better or a worse life depends; it leads men to regard themselves as spectators of a course of events which they in reality help to determine; it makes the highest human excellence consist in acquiescence in the supposed will of a being that is defined as not human, a being that is above the driving force of impulse, that does not experience vacillating moods or conflicting desires, that is never harassed by doubts or misled by ignorance. . . . Theism is in essence repressive, prohibitory, ascetic. The outcome of its influence is that expertness in practical living and expertness in evaluating life, instead of uniting to take advantage of a common opportunity, are set against each other. This is the profound dualism which remains to be mastered. It can be mastered by the concentration upon human needs and powers.

JOHN DEWEY

The method we term "scientific" forms for the modern man (and a man is not modern merely because he lives in 1931) the sole, dependable means of disclosing the realities of existence. It is the sole authentic mode of revelation. This possession of a new method, to the use of which no limits can be put, signifies a new idea of the nature and possibilities of experience. It imports a new morale of confidence, control, and security.

C. E. M. JOAD

All through the century (nineteenth), whenever and wherever there is a movement for change and betterment, the clergy are found opposing it. In this they are merely carrying on the tradition of their order. When one looks back over history, one realizes that there is scarcely any discovery which science has made for human advancement and happiness which churchmen and theologians have not violently opposed. Not content with burning each other, they burnt the men who discovered the earth's motion, burnt the men who made the first tentative beginnings of physics and chemistry, burnt the men who laid the foundations of our medical knowledge. . . . Bad as has been the church's record in the past, it is not greatly improved in the present. . . . For two thousand years teachers and preachers have striven, by inculcating the principles and precepts of Christianity, to mould men's character and to improve their conduct; yet we still have our prisons, our judges, and our wars, and it remains today, as it has done for two thousand years past, an arguable question whether men are better or worse than they were before Christianity was introduced.

WILLIAM PEPPERELL MONTAGUE

If we will for a moment imagine the Bible to have come suddenly to our attention today, unencumbered by a tradition of divine authority, and with no more sacredness than a newly discovered writing of ancient China or Egypt, we can see quite readily that it would occur to nobody who took the work merely on its merits either to accept it as scientifically and historically true, or to twist its statements into a far-fetched allegory of the truth.

Religion will be *outmoded;* and its tidings of escape to

another and better world will ring cold in the ears of those who love this. The new worldliness that religion must face is based on the faith that there is not only no *place* for heaven, but no *need* for it. Humanity, adolescent at last, has tasted the first fruits of the victory of secular intelligence over nature, and dreams grandly of far greater victories to come.

IRWIN EDMAN

The hope of the world certainly lies in intelligence. Certainly, there is no hope anywhere else. I cannot look to anything so remotely definable as God for aid, nor do I ever regret not being able to do so.

WALTER LIPPMANN

Many reasons have been adduced to explain why people do not go to church as much as they once did. Surely the most important reason is that they are not so certain that they are going to meet God when they go to church. If they had that certainty they would go. If they really believed that they were being watched by a Supreme Being who is more powerful than all the kings of the earth put together, if they really believed that not only their actions but their secret thoughts were known and would be remembered by the creator, and ultimate judge of the universe, there would be no complaint whatever about church attendance. The most worldly would be in the front pews, and preachers would not have to resort so often to their rather desperate expedients to attract an audience. If the conviction were there that the creed professed was invincibly true, the modern congregation would not come to church, as they usually do today, to hear the preacher and to listen to the music. They would come to worship God.

H. L. MENCKEN

Alone among the great nations of history we have got rid of religion as a serious scourge, and by the simple process of reducing it to a petty nuisance. For men become civilized, not in proportion to their willingness to believe, but in proportion to their readiness to doubt. The more stupid the man, the larger his stock of adamantine assurances, the heavier his load of faith. When Copernicus proved that the earth revolved around the sun, he did not simply prove that the earth revolved around the sun, he also proved that the so-called revelation of God, as contained in the Old Testament, was rubbish. The first fact was relatively trivial: it made no difference to the average man then, as it makes no difference to him today. But, the second fact was of stupendous importance, for it disposed at one stroke of a mass of bogus facts that had been choking the intelligence and retarding the progress of humanity for a millennium and a half. . . .

I believe that religion, generally speaking, has been a curse to mankind; that its modest and greatly overestimated services on the ethical side have been more than overborne by the damage it has done to clear and honest thinking.

HORACE M. KALLEN

It is a significant trait of history that the times and nations most distinguished for piety are also most distinguished for backwardness. Czarist Russia, and contemporary Spain are near examples, but illustrations may be drawn from any part of the world; the Southern States of the United States of America, for instance. Everywhere the scope and intensity of belief in the supernatural seem to be directly proportional to the misery and weakness of the believer (one compensates for the other). Freedom of speech and of press and discussion which means generally restraint of all interference in the amicable threshing out of conflicting opinions, means, with respect to religious beliefs, refraining from talking, writing or discussing candidly at all. In every society belief in the supernatural is privileged belief, and there accrue to it all the advantages and disadvantages of privilege. . . . But mystics and religionists are not silent. On the contrary, they become, having passed through a religious experience, voluble.

ALBERT EINSTEIN

I do not believe we can have any freedom at all in the

philosophical sense, for we act not only under external compulsion, but also by inner necessity. . . . I cannot imagine a God who rewards and punishes the objects of his creation, whose purposes are modelled after our own, a God, in short, who is but a reflection of human frailty. Neither can I believe that the individual survives the death of his body, although feeble souls harbor such thoughts through fear or ridiculous egotism. It is enough for me to contemplate the mystery of conscious life perpetuating itself through all eternity, to reflect upon the marvelous structure of the universe which we can dimly perceive, and to try humbly to comprehend even an infinitesimal part of the intelligence manifested in nature.

LUTHER BURBANK

Our lives as we live them are passed on to others, whether in physical or mental forms tinging all future lives forever. This should be enough for one who lives for truth and service to his fellow passengers on the way. No avenging Jewish God, no satanic devil, no fiery hell is of any interest to him. The scientist is a lover of truth for the very love of truth itself, wherever it may lead. Every normal human being has ideals, one or many, to look up to, to reach up to, to grow up to. Religion refers to the sentiments and feelings; science refers to the demonstrated everyday laws of nature. Feelings are all right, if one does not get drunk on them. Prayer may be elevating if combined with works, and they who labor with head, hands, or feet have faith and are generally quite sure of an immediate and favorable reply.

Those who take refuge behind theological barbed wire fences, quite often wish they could have more freedom of thought, but fear the change to the great ocean of scientific truth as they would a cold bath plunge.

SIR ARTHUR KEITH

Certainly the creative power which is at work bears no resemblance to the personal God postulated by the Hebrews, and the modern man of science cannot fit Him into the scheme of the world as he knows it. He has to try to reconceive God, and when he has done so, nothing but an unsatisfying abstraction is left. It is unsatisfying because even the greatest men of science, although they possess the intellects of giants, have still the hearts of children. And children cling to that which is endowed with a human shape and has been given the warmth of living flesh.

H. LEVY

A structure of absolute moral and religious beliefs erected initially as beyond criticism, imposed upon a changing society from above rather than emerging from below, has no affinity with science, whatever personal solace and comfort it may provide, for it assumes that the facts of life, including the material facts of the world, can be compassed within a rigidly prescribed framework. It has taken several centuries of history for the scientific movement to be emancipated from just these cramping human assumptions. The writings of many scientists show, alas, that the emancipation has not yet been completed.

J. B. S. HALDANE

We know very little about what may be called the geography of the invisible world. The religions, if I may continue the metaphor, have covered the vacant spaces of its map with imaginary monsters; the philosophies have ruled them with equally imaginary parallels of latitude. But both have affirmed, in opposition to the so-called practical man, that the meaning of the visible world is to be found in the invisible. That has been the secret of their success. They have failed when they tried either to describe the details of the visible world or to dictate the details of conduct in it. The churches are half empty today because their creeds are full of obsolete science, and their ethical codes are suited to a social organization far simpler than that of today.

HOWARD W. HAGGARD, M. D.

When in the fifth century the Roman Empire fell at the

hands of the barbarians, rational medicine ceased altogether in Europe. Although the Christian religion survived, the Christian theology of that time denied liberty of conscience and taught superstitions and dogma. It was bitterly hostile to the scientific spirit. All knowledge necessary to man's salvation, physical as well as spiritual, was to be found in the Bible as the Church interpreted the Bible. Since the teachings of the Church were supposed to be sufficient for all needs, there was no excuse for observations and experimental investigations. The inquisitive spirit was wholly suppressed, the rigorous methods of Greek logic were for many centuries lost from European civilization, and intelligent thought was replaced by revelation, speculation, tradition, and subservience to the written word of the Bible, to the writings of saints, and later, in medical matters, to the work of Galen. The theological beliefs of the time became the controlling influence in Western civilization.

HARRY ELMER BARNES

There has never been any religious crisis of this kind before, and any attempt at exact comparisons with the past are here bound to be misleading and distorting. Even the extreme assailant of pagan religions, like Lucretius, had no basis for the critical attitude as the contemporary sceptic. The bitter attack of Lucretius upon supernatural religion was based mainly upon assumptions and intuitions, as incapable of proof at the time as were the most extreme pietistic views of his age. Today the situation has been profoundly altered. Contemporary science, especially astrophysics, renders the whole set of assumptions underlying the anthropomorphic and geocentric supernaturalism of the past absolutely archaic and preposterous. Our scientific knowledge has undermined the most precious tales in the holy books of all peoples. The development of biblical criticism has discredited the dogma of direct revelation and unique nature of the Hebrew Bible. Textual scholarship has been equally devastating to the sacred scriptures which form the literary basis of the other world religions. It avails one nothing to deny these things, for they are actually undeniable. We must face the implied intellectual revolution honestly and see what is to be done about it.

GEORGE JEAN NATHAN

To be thoroughly religious, one must, I believe, be sorely disappointed. One's faith in God increases as one's faith in the world decreases. The happier the man, the farther he is from God.

RUPERT HUGHES

It is important that the truth be known. Is religion, is church membership a help to virtue? The careless will answer without hesitation, "Yes!" Of course. The statistics, when they are not smothered, cry, "No!"

HU SHIH

On the basis of biological, sociological, and historical knowledge, we should recognize that the individual self is subject to death and decay, but the sum total of individual achievement, for better or for worse, lives on in the immortality of the Larger Self; that to live for the sake of the species and posterity is religion of the highest kind; and that those religions which seek a future life either in Heaven or in the Pure Land, are selfish religions.

DR. FRANKWOOD E. WILLIAMS

In these difficult times we are told that we should go to the temple, that we should get in touch with God. We do not need the temple. We do not need to get in touch with "God." We need to get in touch with each other.

WILLIAM FLOYD

This Bible bears every evidence of being a book like every other book, conceived by man, written by man, altered by man, translated by man, printed by man, but—and this is where it differs from every other book—the Bible is swallowed by man. And it has disagreed with him; man has not digested it properly through lack of sufficient dissection of its parts. It has been taken with a spiritual sauce that has disguised its real flavor. Anything in the Bible, no matter how raw, is taken as God's food. It is used to demonstrate problems of diet which do not provide a balanced ration; it is accepted by the gullible though contradicted by the revelations of Geology, Astronomy, Anthropology, Zoology, and Biology. Taken as prescribed by the doctors of divinity, the Bible is a poisonous book.

LLEWELYN POWYS

The idea of an incarnation of God is absurd: why should the human race think itself so superior to bees, ants, and elephants as to be put in this unique relation to its maker? Christians are like a council of frogs in a marsh or a synod of worms on a dung hill croaking and squeaking, "For our sakes was the world created."

THEODORE DREISER

And why again, composed though we may be of this, that, and the other proton, electron, etc., etc., why should we not in some way be able to sense why we are as we are—assembled as we are of the same ultimate atoms and doing as we do? Why? Good God—surely in the face of all this sense of aliveness and motion, and this and that, there should be some intimation of

WHY? But no—none.

UPTON SINCLAIR

It is a fact, the significance of which cannot be exaggerated, that the measure of the civilization which any nation has attained is the extent to which it has curtailed the power of institutionalized religion. There are a score of great religions in the world, each with scores or hundreds of sects, each with its priestly orders, its complicated creed and ritual, its heavens and hells. Each has its thousands or millions or hundreds of millions of "true believers"; each damns all the others, with more or less heartiness, and each is a mighty fortress of Graft.

The Middle Guard

It is terrible to die of thirst at sea. Is it necessary that you should salt your truth that it will no longer quench thirst?

NIETZSCHE.

ALFRED NORTH WHITEHEAD

Indeed, history, down to the present day, is a melancholy record of the horrors which can attend religion: human sacrifice, and, in particular, the slaughter of children, cannibalism, sensual orgies, abject superstition, hatred as between races, the maintenance of degrading customs, hysteria, bigotry, can all be laid at its charge. Religion is the last refuge of human savagery.

ROBERT ANDREWS MILLIKAN

The anthropomorphic God of the ancient world—the God of human passions, frailties, caprices, and whims is gone, and with him the old duty to propiate him, so that he might be induced to treat you better than your neighbor. Can anyone question the advance that has been made in diminishing the prevalence of these medieval, essentially childish, and essentially selfish ideas? The new God is the God of law and order; the new duty, to know that order and to get into harmony with it, to learn how to make the world a better place for mankind to live in, not merely how to save your individual soul. However, once destroy our confidence in the principle of uniformity, our belief in the rule of law, and our effectiveness immediately disappears, our method ceases to be dependable, and our laboratories become deserted.

ALBERT C. DIEFFENBACH

The plain truth is, thousands upon thousands of men and women have gone out of the Church. They take no stock in its obsolete teachings to which they once subscribed in order to become members. After great tribulation, they have made their declaration of religious independence. They have taken the right turn for their own salvation. The churches as a whole do not know that today there is a violent intellectual revolution among all people who think. The so-called theism that is embalmed in the old theology and is still preached is utterly defunct for many persons of this generation. Like it or not, that is a fact.

DR. CHARLES W. ELIOT

The creeds of the churches contain conceptions of God's nature and of his action toward the human race which are intolerable to the ethical mind of the twentieth century. The conception of one being, human or divine, suffering, though innocent, for the sins of others, is revolting to the universal sense of justice and fair dealing. No school, no family, no court, would punish the innocent when the guilty were known. This Conception of God is hideous, cruel, insane, and no Christian church which tolerates it can be efficient in the promotion of human welfare and happiness.

CPSIA information can be obtained at www.ICGtesting.com
Printed in the USA
BVOW08s1845061015

421243BV00001B/15/P